THE LAST DRAGOMAN

THE SWEDISH ORIENTALIST JOHANNES KOLMODIN AS SCHOLAR, ACTIVIST AND DIPLOMAT

Johannes Kolmodin
1884-1933

Errata Slip

Elisabeth Özdalga ed.: *The Last Dragoman. The Swedish Orientalist Johannes Kolmodin as Scholar, Activist and Diplomat,* Stockholm: The Swedish Research Institution in Istanbul, Transactions Nr 16, 2006, distribution by I.B. Tauris, London.

Errata:

Page 9, line 7	Now: 'Ras Aulas' *should be* **Ras Alula**
Page 10, footnote 7	Now: '1975' *should be* **1977**
Page 24, line 18	Now: 'Professor Hedin' *should be* **Doctor Hedin**
Page 100, line 30	Now: 'h' *should be* **Lönnrot**
Page 123, lines 6, 8, 13	Now: 'Bennedict' *should be* **Bennedich**
Page 133, line 24	Now: 'its famous' *should be* **his famous**
Page 136, footnote 20	Now: 'to the cabinet minister Mia…' *should be* **to the cabinet minister's wife Mia…**
Page 136, footnote 20	Now: 'UD, HP 3C94,' *should be* **UD, HP 3694,**

THE LAST DRAGOMAN

THE SWEDISH ORIENTALIST JOHANNES KOLMODIN AS SCHOLAR, ACTIVIST AND DIPLOMAT

Editor: Elisabeth Özdalga

SWEDISH RESERCH INSTITUTE IN ISTANBUL
TRANSACTIONS VOL. 16

Front cover: Johannes Kolmodin 1884-1933.

Back cover: A translation into Swedish by Johannes Kolmodin of the Turkish national anthem - İstiklal Marşı - written by Mehmet Akif Ersoy. The Swedish translation was published in the Stockholm daily *Dagens Nyhcter*, 25 September, 1921.

© Swedish Research Institute in Istanbul and the authors.
Logotype: Bo Berndal

Prepared by
Kitap Yayınevi Ltd.

Printed in Turkey by
Mas Matbaacılık A.Ş.
Dereboyu Caddesi, Zagra İş Merkezi B Blok 1
Maslak-İstanbul

Istanbul 2006
Distributor: I. B. Tauris, London, England

ISBN: 9-86884-14-X
ISSN: 1100-0333

Acknowledgements

This publication would never have been possible had it not been for Carl Gustaf Kolmodin's biography, *Johannes Kolmodin i brev och skrifter* (Kungl. Vitterhets Historie och Antikvitets Akademien, *Filologiskt arkiv 41*, Stockholm: Almqvist and Wiksell International, 1999). To start with, Carl Gustaf Kolmodin's book about his older relative provided the inspiration for the conference, "Swedish Orientalism in Historical Perspective: Johannes Kolmodin as Scholar and Diplomat in Turkey of the 1920s," organised by the Swedish Research Institute in Istanbul on 24 and 25 May 2002. It was also a key reference for all those who, as participants to the conference, contributed to this volume. In addition to that Carl Gustaf Kolmodin has, at each stage of the work with this publication, generously contributed his knowledge both about Johannes Kolmodin as a person, and the epoch in Swedish history, when he was active.

Another major contributor is Sigrid Kahle, the daughter of H.S. Nyberg. Without her enthusiasm for and burning interest in the memory of her father's friend and colleague, this project would not have come to fruition. In the midst of innumerable other undertakings, she managed on a chilly day in October 2001, within a couple of hours of taking me by car to Johannelund in Uppsala to meet LarsOlov Eriksson, to introduce me to the archives at Uppsala University Library, show me the graveyard where Johannes Kolmodin was put to rest, and discuss alternative outlines for the planned conference.

I also owe the members of the board of the Swedish Research Institute in Istanbul many thanks for their willingness to back this project. Likewise, the financial as well as moral support of the Swedish Consulate General in Istanbul both during the conference and throughout the publication process has been invaluable. I am especially grateful to Consul General Ingmar Karlsson and Consul Annika Svahnström for their sensitivity to the various demands posed by the project.

I am also grateful to researcher Emma Jørum from Uppsala University, and Sidsel Braaten and Kari Çağatay at the Swedish Research Institute in Istanbul for their contributions in preparing for and bringing about the conference. Special thanks also go to the Swedish-English translator Jon van Leuven and language editor Peter Colenbrander.

The late Swedish ambassador and prominent Turkologist Gunnar Jarring (1907-2002) was familiar with and repeatedly expressed his admiration for Johannes Kolmodin and his work. Due to old age, he was not able to take part in the Istanbul conference. Sadly, only two days after the conference participants had sent their greetings, we received word of his death. This book is dedicated to his memory.

Elisabeth Özdalga

Ankara, January 2006

Abbreviations

Cpl	Constantinople	
KB	Kungliga Biblioteket	The Royal Library at Stockholm
KFÅ	Karolinska Förbundets årsbok	Year Book of the Carolinic Society
NSA	Nathan Söderbloms arkiv (UUB)	The Archive of Nathan Söderblom (UUB)
KUD	Kungl.Utrikesdepartementets arkiv	The Archive of the Swedish Foreign Office
RA	Riksarkivet	The National Archives of Sweden
SHA	Sven Hedins arkiv i RA	The archive of Sven Hedin at RA
UUB	Uppsala Universitetsbibliotek	The University Library at Uppsala

Contents

List of Participants

Docent LarsOlov Eriksson
EFS Teologiska Högskola Johannelund
Uppsala

Professor Ezra Gebremedhin
Department of Theology
Uppsala University

Dr. Sigrid Kahle
Uppsala

Med.lic. Carl Gustaf Kolmodin
Gothenburg

Docent Inga Sanner
Department of History of Ideas
Stockholm University

Professor Christopher Toll
Stockholm

Ambassador Torsten Örn
Lund

Professor Elisabeth Özdalga
Department of Sociology
Middle East Technical University
Ankara

Introduction

ELISABETH ÖZDALGA

Johannes Kolmodin (1884-1933) came to Istanbul in 1917. His purpose was to carry out historical archival studies into the Swedish king, Charles XII (r. 1697-1718), who had sought safe haven in the Ottoman Empire (Bender in southern Moldavia) after suffering serious military setbacks at the hands of the Russians at Poltava in 1709. The Swedish monarch was to remain on Ottoman soil until 1713, when he was forced to leave.

Although Kolmodin came to Istanbul to carry out scholarly work, because of economic difficulties (his Swedish scholarship was severely reduced by inflation) and his ambition to secure an institutional attachment, he joined the Swedish legation, where, over the years, he became an indispensable staff member, staying on for fourteen years until 1931. To begin with, Kolmodin worked as an honorary attaché, but within a couple of years he was appointed "dragoman." Since this was a position that was dying out and Kolmodin surely was one of its very last practitioners, he is remembered at "the last dragoman."

The profession of dragoman (Turkish: *tercüman*) had been part of the Ottoman imperial administration since the 14th century. Initially, dragomans had been used sporadically, but with time they became part of the permanent staff at the imperial court. As international relationships intensified during the 17th and 18th centuries, the dragomans increased even more in numbers and influence.

They were usually of non-Muslim origin. A commonly held notion was that Islamic law (*Şeriat*) prohibited the learning of a foreign Western language. At one time, the Orthodox community at Fener (in Constantinople) had the monopoly of the profession, while the Ottoman government controlled appointments. Eventually, however, Ottoman rulers became uneasy about the fact that too much power had passed into the hands of this professional group and, in order to break the influence of the Orthodox community, Mahmut II (r. 1808-39) gave permission for Muslims to become dragomans. A translation office (*Tercüme Odası*), attached to the chancery, was introduced in 1821. Towards the end the 19th century, foreign embassies started to recruit and organise their own dragomans (Great Britain in 1877).[1]

Dragomans were more than just interpreters. They assisted in different kinds of meetings, agreements, court cases, etc. This gave them insight into and, as a result, influence over the parties concerned, power that could also be turned into economic benefits and privileges.

Even though the influence of the traditional dragomans had vanished when Kolmodin arrived in Istanbul, his position was more than nominal. His knowledge of the Turkish language and history was such that he fell outside the definition of the normal embassy staff. So, in terms of his diplomatic services, he did

---

1 *AnaBritannica*, vol. 20, Istanbul: 1990; Lord Kinross: *The Ottoman Centuries.The Rise and Fall of the Turkish Empire*, New York: Morrow Quill, 1977; and Bernard Lewis: *The Emergence of Modern Turkey*, Oxford: Oxford University Press, 1968.*East,* Beacon Press, Boston, 2004.

not lack any of the qualifications applicable to a traditional dragoman: if anything, he was overqualified. However, regarding his ability to take personal
advantage of his skills, his scope of action was circumscribed by the ethics of the
modern "Weberian" state official. Kolmodin thus had a double identity, both as
dragoman and as modern embassy staff member. But Kolmodin experienced a
double identity in another respect as well, namely in having both diplomatic and
academic duties. He was torn between these two aspirations and never really succeeded in escaping from the ambiguity of serving two lords.

Johannes Kolmodin was 33 years old and well into his academic career when he
came to Istanbul. He had taken his doctor's degree in 1914 and had held the position as docent in Semitic languages at Uppsala University since then. His main disciplines were history and Semitic languages and his dissertation was based on the
philological fieldwork he had carried out in Ethiopia and Eritrea in 1908-10.

Thus, at the time of his arrival in Istanbul, Kolmodin was already an accom-
plished "Orientalist." However, he was a different kind of scholar in this field,
because, with his great sympathies for the Orient and contempt for the prevailing
"Occidental hubris," he was anything but a typical representative of the kind of
scholarship later criticised by Edward Said in *Orientalism* (1978). As a matter of
fact, he actively anticipated a criticism that would only engage wider circles of
intellectuals towards the last decades of the 20th century.

Equipped with his deep philological and historical knowledge, his great concern for Eastern cultures and peoples, and his enthusiasm for politics both on the
international and national levels, he became a keen observer of the developments
in Turkey during a dramatic and very important period of its history. Since he was
a diligent letter-writer, his observations both from Turkey and his earlier research
travels in Ethiopia and Eritrea are well documented. This correspondence (mainly to his mother and father) is what constitutes the main source material for the
chapters in this volume. But Kolmodin was also the leading author behind the
quarterly diplomatic reports and other official political analyses, even though
these were signed by the envoy (Gustaf Oscar Wallenberg 1920-31) when he was
present. Therefore, the reports also bear the stamp of Kolmodin and must be
regarded as important documentary material on his political ideas and opinions.

The purpose of the present volume is to call attention to Johannes Kolmodin's
life and work. Since he died at an early age (only 49 years old), before he was
able to publish more than a small part of the scientific materials he had collected
over the years, he soon fell into oblivion. This lack of attention also arose from
the darkening developments in Europe during the 1930s, followed by the Second
World War. Still another reason was Kolmodin's monarchical and anti-democratic conservatism, which were increasingly at odds with the direction of political developments after the end of the Second World War.

While his political ideas, especially his national concerns, belonged to the past,
his scholarly achievements were remarkably modern. Johannes Kolmodin had
studied history under Harald Hjärne and Semitic languages under Karl Vilhelm
Zetterstéen, both legendary professors at Uppsala University. These studies
endowed him with an unusual broadmindedness in his perceptions of world history, as well as a sound and deep knowledge of the different Semitic and other non-
Western cultures of the Middle East, especially Northeast Africa. These insights
had made him critical of the way Western scholars praised European achievements,
while looking down on the "backwardness" of the East, a criticism, which, as men-

tioned above, foreshadowed the Orientalism debate initiated in the late 1970s by scholars such as Edward Said. As part of this critique of an artificial and ethnocentric East-West divide, he was especially critical of the pro-Hellenistic tendency that had been prevalent in academic circles in Europe since the 19th century. Kolmodin was of the opinion that the cultural influence ascribed to Hellenistic traditions had been exaggerated, and that the influence of Semitic cultures had been undeservedly downplayed. In this way he had ideas, which later critical scholars such as Cyrus Gordon, Michael Astour, and Martin Bernal[2] articulated more programmatically, that set him apart from the wave of anti-Semitism these scholars have argued swept through Europe during the second half of the 19th century.

Johannes Kolmodin was also far-seeing about scientific methodology, at least in two respects. The first concerns the importance he ascribed to oral traditions in serious historical research. He was sceptical about the general positivistic attitude, in terms of which only written documents or material artefacts mattered. According to Kolmodin, oral traditions, combined with written documents, were indispensable for different kinds of historical research. The second concerned his way of looking at the relationship between different academic disciplines. During his philological research in Ethiopia and Eritrea, he simultaneously worked as a philologist *and* an historian. He adopted a multi-disciplinary approach (combining philology and history) not out of general interest, but out of scholarly necessity. Unfortunately, however, he did not live long enough to further develop his new methodological approaches. That task fell to his colleague and friend H.S. Nyberg, whose work has been documented in a recent volume edited by the Uppsala Iranologist, Bo Utas.[3]

Kolmodin was also a distinguished analyst of contemporary international politics, a skill that proved especially useful during and after the First World War. His criticism of the colonial powers' – especially Britain's – ambitions to rule in the Middle East was pointed and is not without resonance for the situation that has developed since the US-led invasions of Afghanistan and Iraq after the 11 September attacks in 2001. Kolmodin's analyses of the situation in Turkey and the Middle East can be read as pointed illustrations of the historian/political scientist Rashid Khalidi's observation that

[for] those with some knowledge of the modern history of the Middle East, it is hard to avoid feeling a sense of déjà vu, and deep misgivings, in watching the United States step into the boots of the former colonial rulers of this region as an occupying power, and as responsible for the creation of a new political order in a major Arab county. Nothing so ambitious, or so fraught with peril, has been tried in this part of the world since the years after World War I, when Britain and France engaged in their last burst of colonial expansion under the guise of League of Nations mandates in the Middle East.[4]

Kolmodin's analyses, reflected in his letters and diplomatic reports quoted in this volume, were, viewed in the rear view mirror, unusually perspicacious.

---

2 Martin Bernal: *Black Athena*, Rutger's University Press, New Brunswick, 1991.

3 H.S. Nyberg: *Muntlig tradition, skriftlig fixering och författarskap* (sammanställt enligt efterlämnade manuskript och kommenterat av Bo Utas), Skrifter utgivna av Kungliga Humanistiska Vetenskaps-samfundet i Uppsala, Nr 51, Uppsala, 2004.

4 Rashid Khalidi: *Resurrecting Empire. Western Footprints and America's Perilous Path in the Middle East*, Beacon Press, Boston, 2004, p. x.

They also bear witness to his strong sense of justice in regard to issues of world politics.

The present volume is a collection of biographical essays on Johannes Kolmodin. The intention has been to reflect different aspects of his life and work, from his youth as a child of a missionary family, over his years as an academically ambitious as well as politically committed student in Uppsala, to his years as researcher/diplomat in Istanbul, and finally as a special advisor to the Ethiopian emperor, Haile Selassie. The essays are of varying length, some of them based on extensive quotations from Kolmodin's letters and other written documents. The idea behind providing the abundant and lengthy quotations has been to convey to an English readership a sense of his style of writing, as well as his ideas. Several chapters should, therefore, be read as being a combination of documentary and biographical analysis.

Since Kolmodin's Turkish material quoted in this volume was written before the Turkish language reform of 1928 (from Arabic to Latin script), there was, in his time, no officially recognised transcription of Turkish words into the Latin alphabet. Instead of using the standard modern Turkish forms of place-names and proper names, Kolmodin's own transcriptions according to Swedish orthography (in its pre-1906 spelling reform guise – Kolmodin adhered to the old norm throughout his life) have been used, especially in quotations and paraphrased sections. This has been done in order to preserve the authenticity of his writings. In this way, contemporary pronunciations, as he perceived them, are best reproduced. The same principle has been followed in relation to his Ethiopian and Eritrean material. In all other sections, modern Swedish, Turkish, Amharic, Tigrinya conventions have been followed, while for internationally well-known place names like Istanbul, Izmir, and Addis Ababa, standard English spelling has been used.

Overview of the Book

The book opens with a long chapter by Sigrid Kahle. It is the most comprehensive of the chapters and gives a relatively extensive account of Kolmodin's life from his early youth until the end of his life. The chief focus of Kahle's portrayal is Kolmodin's linguistic genius and political thinking, which she embeds in his personal and professional life as it evolved in the shadow of dramatic world events.

The remaining chapters have been chronologically ordered. Consequently, the next chapter, by LarsOlov Eriksson, deals with the Johannes Kolmodin's family background and the Swedish Evangelical Mission, in which Johannes's father, Adolf Kolmodin, was active, both as principal at its educational centre in Johannelund (close to Uppsala) and as a leading missionary in Ethiopia, and later also as professor of theology at Uppsala University. This chapter portrays persons within this pious environment whom Johannes met and lived with during his adolescence. It offers important background information not only in relation to Johannes' idealism and conservative patriotism, but also to his early contacts with Ethiopia, which eventually led to the linguistic fieldwork on which his dissertation was based.

The next chapter concentrates on Kolmodin's dissertation: The Traditions of Tsazzega and Hazzega. The author, Ezra Gebremedhin, himself from Ethiopia, is also active in the Swedish Evangelical Mission. Here the reader is introduced to Kolmodin's contribution to the recording and analysis of very old oral traditions. The author discusses the traditions from the point of view of literary types and genres and other literary characteristics of special significance for this work. He also calls attention to Kolmodin's predilection for history, reflected in his dissertation, which was as much a work of history as of linguistics.

The fourth chapter, by Carl Gustaf Kolmodin, describes Johannes Kolmodin through his close friendships with three very different personalities. All three were well-known figures in Swedish cultural life in the early 20th century: Sven Hedin, explorer, especially of Central Asia, and outspoken opinion maker on the far right; Sven Lidman, the libertarian poet who surprised his friends by suddenly turning to religion and becoming a leading member of the Pentecostalists; and Nathan Söderblom, archbishop and member of the Swedish Academy. The fact that these three highly colourful personalities remained Johannes' friends for such a long time gives us an idea of his own broadmindedness and intellectual agility.

The fifth chapter, by Inga Sanner, is about the intellectual atmosphere in Sweden at the turn of the 20th century. Sanner builds her chapter on a vision of modernity that avoids simple and linear models and looks into the combination of contradictory elements. She focuses on well-known European thinkers such as Edmund Burke, renowned Swedish authors like August Strindberg, and early feminists such as Ellen Key. Relating these streams of thought to Kolmodin's mentor, the famous history professor Harald Hjärne, the author helps to paint a picture of an intellectual landscape in Kolmodin's time that possessed often divergent and non-harmonised colours.

The sixth chapter, written by Ambassador Torsten Örn, is about Swedish diplomacy during the 1920s, more exactly between 1917, when Kolmodin arrived in Istanbul, and 1931, when he left for a new position in Addis Ababa. This was a period when Sweden, through the League of Nations, directed its energy to the broader issues of peace and security. However, the rivalry between the Great Powers largely undermined these efforts. Instead, a new catastrophe was gathering momentum. Sweden's relations with Turkey were good, based, just as in the past, on the two countries' common interests in preventing Russia, now the Soviet Union, from further expansion. The Turkish reforms and efforts to draw the country closer to Europe were therefore looked upon with sympathy.

In chapter seven, Carl Gustaf Kolmodin analyses the relationship between Johannes Kolmodin and his superior, the envoy Gustaf Oscar Wallenberg (1863-1937). This chapter has a double purpose: historical and source critical. Historically, it presents an insight into the working conditions and interpersonal relationships existing at the Swedish Embassy during Kolmodin's stay; source critically, it offers an analysis of who composed the diplomatic reports, i.e., what kind of division of labour developed between the envoy and his dragoman. In order to do justice to Kolmodin's contributions, this chapter provides a necessary methodological or source-critical statement. However, one should by no means believe that compilation of the reports was totally delegated to Kolmodin, leaving only the signing of the documents to his superior. The relationship was more complicated than that and is aptly analysed and illustrated in this chapter.

Carl Gustaf Kolmodin's chapter is followed by a selection of excerpts from diplomatic reports, with short comments by Elisabeth Özdalga about the political context within which they were written.

The last chapter is by Professor Christopher Toll, one of Johannes Kolmodin's successors in the field of Semitic philology. To some extent inspired by the innovative scholarship of his predecessor (especially Johannes Kolmodin's dissertation on the Traditions of Tsazzega and Hazzega), the author presents his own view of what scholarship is, or ought to be. Professor Toll argues for a "creationist" rather than a simply descriptive form of scholarship. Scholarship should be understood as creative art. Without open-mindedness and a sense of innovation, any scholarship, be it within the sciences or the humanities, stagnates. This chapter, therefore, should be read as a tribute to a man who was politically a conservative, but who in terms of scholarly outlook and contribution was an innovator.

Since a large cast of characters appears throughout this work, personalities who may not be known to the modern, and especially the non-Swedish reader, a list of short biographies is added as an appendix. It goes without saying that the varying length of these entries does not reflect the characters' general fame or importance, but their relevance within the context of Johannes Kolmodin's life and work.

Johannes Kolmodin:
His Youth, Political Thinking, and Life with the Turks Reflected in His Letters to His Parents

SIGRID KAHLE

As Johannes Kolmodin lay dying in Addis Ababa, the emperor came to the sick room. Haile Selassie, The Lion of Judah, stood alone in the doorway, deep in thought. A few hours later, his irreplaceable counsellor and Swedish friend breathed his last at the age of 49. It was 9 October 1933, at 9.35 in the evening. Coincidentally, Johannes's wife Eva had visited the hospital together with their son, Olle, the same afternoon. On her way out from the hospital, it took her a while to understand that the car coming up the road was carrying her husband, paralysed and unable to speak.

Johannes had been increasingly aware of "a consuming fatigue" since the beginning of 1933. He had been feeling the lack of oxygen in the thin air of Addis, 2,500 metres above sea level. He did something rare for a man of his assiduous character: he granted himself a few days of rest, 600 metres downhill, at a hotel in the village of Bishofto. This did not help much and he felt just as exhausted upon his return. He began to worry about his research. Would he be able to finish his work? What would happen to his unfinished material on Ethiopian studies? Who would take care of his Turkish material and scholarly correspondence, contained in two wooden boxes and one tin trunk in Istanbul? He need not have worried about his papers. All the scholarly materials left in Istanbul, his previous domicile, were to be shipped by the Swedish Orient Line to Sweden and placed in Uppsala University Library, there to await scholarly attention.

Johannes Kolmodin's burial according to Lutheran church rites was arranged at 3 p.m. the next day by the Swedish colony. His coffin was draped with the Swedish flag. On the coffin, at the behest of the Emperor Haile Selassie, lay the Ethiopian Order of Trinity in gold. Abyssinian officers carried the body in state to the cemetery. As they withdrew, the palace honour guard saluted and the emperor's son-in-law, Ras Desda, relayed the emperor's condolences. The Ethiopian government, innumerable Ethiopians, the *corps diplomatique*, and many European expatriates attended.

At the wish of Mrs. Eva Kolmodin, Johannes's remains were later laid to rest in the old churchyard in Uppsala. Eva selected a tombstone in the form of a sun–wheel cross, and was buried alongside her husband in 1977, 44 years after her husband had died. Their son Olle also rests with them.

Who was this man of whom it was said at his hour of death that "his rich personality contained a unique combination of science and politics, humanism and diplomacy,"[1] and that "by his thorough knowledge, his clarity of view and human

---

1 Otto Järte: "Johannes Kolmodins död," *Svenska Dagbladet,* 12.10.1933.

love, his dignified but modest appearance he won the respect and trust, not only of the peoples of the East, but of everyone who came within his orbit";[2] of whose nature it was said that it was "equipped with the most rich intellectual gifts; a burning devotion, a self-forgetting passion in his routine work, a wide scope of thought and action, uplifted above all things puny and irrelevant";[3] and whose death was mourned as a loss of Swedish intellectual prestige in the outside world?

In the following narrative I try to give a personal portrait of this man whom I never knew but of whom I have heard since I was a child, for he was a friend of my father, Henrik Samuel Nyberg, professor of Semitic languages at the University of Uppsala from 1931 to 1954. They studied Oriental languages together in their youth and my father visited him in Constantinople. Throughout my childhood I heard my father talk in emotional and respectful terms about "my unforgettable friend Johannes Kolmodin." But alas, even the greatest scholar is soon forgotten. His early demise just after the outbreak of the great European barbarism in 1933 has resulted in his being neglected even by his own university. In our current collective effort to revive his memory, my contribution will be to evoke his personality and to assess his political thought on the basis of the letters he wrote to his parents between 1894 and 1933.[4]

Johannes Kolmodin's letters are both personally and politically important. First there is his handwriting, clear and flowing, the thin paper he used, the swiftness with which his hand moved across the paper. Then there is the language, with its careful grammatical periods, its subjunctives and many injunctions to express reservation and doubt, its sometimes long and winding sentences. They are written in the best Swedish style of the first part of the twentieth century, a style far easier to translate into German or French than into English, as unhappily I have had to do here.

The great virtue of these letters to my mind is their spontaneity, spirituality, family warmth, and political passion. They are written by a man deeply immersed in universal history, equally concerned with the past and future of Europe, Africa, and Asia as about his own Swedish nation in an era of nationalism, empire-building, and war.

Youth and Education

Children of missionaries have the advantage of growing up in international surroundings, whether at the mission station or in their parents' home, with its foreign guests. Such children have the chance to pick up unusual languages and often become linguists. They grow up with Africa and Asia as part of their world. Johannes Kolmodin had such a childhood.

Johannes's father, Adolf Kolmodin (1855-1928) was first teacher (starting in 1879), later director (1893-1903) and finally inspector (1903-09) of Johannelund Mission Institute at Ulvsunda Lake near Stockholm, run by Evangeliska

---

2 J. Iwarson: "Johannes Kolmodin in memoriam," *Svensk Missionstidning,* 21.10.1933.

3 H. S. Nyberg: "Johannes Kolmodin, orientalisten. Minnesord," *Svenska Dagbladet,* 12.10.1933.

4 Letters from Johannes Kolmodin to Adolf Kolmodin and Nelly Kolmodin in Uppsala University Library (UUB) T 3 1:18/19, containing 439 and 333 sheets (2 letter pages on each) respectively. References to these letters will be made with the date of the letter in parenthesis, e.g. (19.1.1918)

Fosterlandsstiftelsen (The Swedish Evangelical Mission, SEM), one of the "folk movements" typical of Swedish society in the early era of industrialisation. This school later moved to Uppsala and is today called the Johannelund Theological Seminary. The SEM educated missionaries for fieldwork in East Africa, Eritrea, and to a lesser extent India. The Kolmodin home, situated in its grounds, was open to Eritrean students, missionaries, and guests, who stirred Johannes' curiosity. "I became interested in Emperor Johannes, Ras Aulas, and other great Abyssinian personalities before I knew about politics in my own surroundings." He longed to go to "that mysterious Christian land in East Africa, that vital, half–barbarian world, where the genuine Middle Ages now encounter the modern age with violent confrontation."[5]

Johannes was sent to the Latin gymnasium in the diocese of Strängnäs, from which he matriculated with a brilliant record in 1901. He was, as could be expected, excellent in languages and also in history.[6] He wrote ambitious essays on religious and theological, historical and literary issues. He admired the exploits of Darius and Nero. Our flamboyant Swedish hero Charles XII (d. 1718) fired his imagination, especially his adventures at Bender in Ottoman Turkey (today in southern Moldavia). Above all, he was interested in Ethiopia. So what was more natural as he entered Uppsala University at the age of 17 than to start with Oriental languages?

His father was appointed professor of exegetics at the University of Uppsala in 1903 and was at the same time installed as vicar in the nearby parish of Uppsala Näs. The whole family moved to Uppsala, so that Johannes remained close to his parental home well into his student years. His letters give us a lively impression of his brothers Martin, Lennart, Gustaf, Rudolf (Lullu), Olle, Torsten, and his sister Anna (Lillan). The home was ruled with a determined but warm hand by Nelly von Post (1858-1944), daughter of a district judge, Axel von Post. She had grown up with the SEM movement, whose charismatic founder, Carl Olof Rosenius, was her father's close friend.

The Lutheran vicarage of the time was marked by piety and learning, by both a certain ritualism and a certain informality, generated by the many children. It had a democratic outlook, with all sorts of people coming in and going out. Adolf Kolmodin was the patriarch, perhaps a little dry as a character, but with a capacity for establishing warm relationships with his sons, especially Johannes, in spite of being nervously busy with his several academic and missionary tasks, such as editorship for the SEM magazine. So, the home where Johannes grew up was both missionary and academic, aristocratic and democratic, learned and emotional. The strict Lutheran discipline of work did not exclude a family sense of humour, so evident in the letters between family members.

Professor Adolf Kolmodin was a prominent, well-connected, and respected theologian at Uppsala University. A contemporary photo shows a slight man with thin lips, a stern face, and penetrating eyes. Add to this his extra large and complicated handwriting, his reputation for quick rejoinders and fast body movements (apparently inherited by Johannes), his conservatism and low–church

---

5 Johannes Kolmodin: "Meine Studienreise in Abessinien 1908-1910. Vorläufiger Bericht," *Le Monde Oriental*, No. 4, 1910, pp. 229-55.

6 For an explanation of Johannes Kolmodin's early interest in the Turkish language see Carl Gustaf Kolmodin's chapter "An Ill-matched Couple" in this volume.

in this way learnt to admire the brilliance, memory, and learning of the master, while he instilled the desire to self-activity. He stressed the duty of personal responsibility and encouraged the students never to hide under the pronoun *we*; behind every utterance there should be an *I* without falling into hubris. In his own scholarship he only used first hand sources and was the first to demand skill in the reading of old manuscripts. His description of the science of historiography emphasized the need for scientific criticism.[10]

Hjärne's authority with students in political matters was assured because he was a political practitioner, a member of parliament (*riksdag*), one who sometimes voted liberal, sometimes conservative (*höger*) and whose interpellations were eagerly listened to. Hjärne was born in the revolutionary year 1848 and educated while modern liberalism erupted in Sweden, H.S. Nyberg pointed out:

> Though often a conservative, he could never rid himself of the individualism, which was the A and O of liberalism. In his historical research he had the realistic approach, which characterised Sweden's intellectual climate in the 1880s, when he already pleaded for universal suffrage and one year's military conscription. In the 1890s, a new attitude to the national question had taken root. It was epitomised in the personality of Harald Hjärne, the Swedish patriot and nationalist.[11]

The Catastrophes of 1809 and 1905

Harald Hjärne was the first in Sweden to argue for the dismantling of the Norwegian fortifications in 1904, so as to create a neutral zone before the ending of the Swedish-Norwegian Union on 27 October 1905 – an important milestone in the history of Swedish nationalism. The union with Norway was the result of the war against Russia in 1809, when Finland was lost and the kingdom of Sweden was divided into two halves.

The "catastrophe of 1809" had threatened the existence of Sweden, until General Jean-Baptiste Bernadotte was elected crown prince and, as King Charles XIV John restored national prestige by creating the union with Norway. Those responsible for the defeat were called by students "the cowards of 1809," devoid of both loyalty and political judgment. The loss of Finland was explained away by lies, but it remained in the nation's sub-consciousness as *"unbewältigte Vergangenheit,"* even if the constitution of 1812 had restored the nation's self-respect.

The severance of the union in 1905, so hotly desired by the Norwegians and ratified by both *storting* and *riksdag,* was a trauma for Hjärne's nationalistic students, who flocked to his historical surveys. The union had long been nothing but a shell, it had been wrongly constructed from the start, and now it had ceased altogether to be a support for Sweden's foreign policy and a guarantee of its national security.

The break-up of the union with Norway was a national dilemma and the overwhelming foreign policy issue of the day for the young academic generation. The constitution of 1809, with its system of checks and balances, accentuated the decision-making power and leadership qualities of the monarch. In that form, the 1809 constitution, the political events of 1809 and 1905, together with Finland,

---

10 Ibid.

11 H.S. Nyberg: "Tal vid Föreningen Heimdals 75-årsjubileum den 24 April," *Heimdal,* 14 April 1966.

were central in the political thinking of the students who attended Harald Hjärne's lectures. The national question was their passion.[12]

Another event that aroused this student generation was the Russo-Japanese War, which ended on 1 May 1905, following Japan's overwhelming and surprising victory. Japan's first victorious engagement against a Western nation had tremendous significance in Europe, where East Asia had been considered an underdeveloped and isolated region to be conquered, exploited, and colonised. Johannes's mind had already turned towards East Africa. *Ex Oriente Lux,* the students of Zetterstéen were saying, looking towards Turkey, Russia's old enemy. The Turkey they admired could now experience certain relief from a Russian power that had always wanted to rule on the Bosphorus.

The Heimdal Radicals

For the generation of academics that so profoundly experienced the 1905 dilemma, the Heimdal students' club provided the debating forum they needed. Heimdal, Verdandi, and Laboremus were the important student debating associations at Uppsala University. Heimdal was the oldest. It was founded in 1895 as a cultural association, but with the worsening political climate it gradually changed into a debating club for the burning political issues of the day. It had no definite political colouring at the beginning, but was thought of as conservative. Verdandi was considered liberal, and Laboremus was social democratic.

> The founders of Heimdal were far from being a homogenous group. Some were outmoded idealists, others were champions of a new spirit seeking an outlet for their activism in radical groups. Some belonged to the conservative school of Oscar Alin. Others went their own way. All seem to have been aware of a new era awaiting their contribution. Party politics were not involved at the beginning. It was not until 1910, when differences of opinion separated them clearly on basic national questions from bourgeois liberalism, that Heimdal associated itself with a conservative political outlook, with *"högern."*[13]

Johannes Kolmodin was elected a member of Heimdal on 29 September 1905, and his close friend Erland Hjärne in 1906. Many Heimdalites were pupils of Harald Hjärne. They formed a circle of friends who were to make a mark on Sweden's intellectual history: Axel Boëthius, Bertil Boëthius, Arvid Uggla, and Hjalmar Haralds. University life was generally a male preserve in those days, but, surprisingly, there were a few female Heimdalites, even though there is no record of their taking part in the discussions.

In 1906, Johannes was elected secretary of Heimdal with Nils Herlitz as president, so from then on the huge ledgers are filled with his minutes, always signed by him. They are handwritten summaries of lectures, such as Harald Hjärne's magnificent speech on the 250th anniversary of the Roskilde Peace, to which students of all faculties were invited. When the Heimdal archives are opened we will be able to reconstruct these debates and feel the heat of the battles.

---

12 H.S. Nyberg (1889-1974): "Den svensk-nationella tanken. Tal vid Föreningen Heimdals 50-års-jubileum," *Svensk Tidskrift,* No. 28, 1941.

13 Ibid.

In 1907, Johannes was elected president of Heimdal and became an undisputed student leader. In spite of his versatile interests, he earned his Phil.Lic. degree in Ethiopian languages on 15 September 1908, just as a young student from Dalecarlia with whom Johannes would share many interests entered the university: Henrik Samuel Nyberg, who began his Arabic and Hebrew studies with K.V. Zetterstéen on 14 September 1908. The two Semitists could hardly have met at this point of time, however, for on 25 September, Johannes left Uppsala on an adventurous journey to a distant land.

A Young Linguist in Abyssinia

Adolf Kolmodin had to make an inspection tour of the Swedish mission stations in Eritrea. He needed an assistant who could speak Arabic and Ethiopian languages and made Johannes an offer to accompany him. What a unique chance to gather material for his doctoral thesis! He hoped to compare Tigré, Amharic, and Geez with Tigrinya, all Semitic languages, and if possible to investigate the other Eritrean Cushitic languages, Bilin and Kunnama. At least that is what he set out to do. He was to stay away for nearly two years.

After his return, Johannes published a scientific report in German, "Meine Studienreise in Abessinien, 1908-1910," in *Le Monde Oriental* (No. 4, 1910). The report starts on a personal note, but soon moves into the higher realms of philology. However, the fullest documentation from this period is his private letters, which make for wonderful reading and deserve to be published. We also have reports by the missionaries with whom he and his father stayed. I will use all these sources, plus Carl Gustaf Kolmodin's biography[14] and my own imagination to convey some fragmentary impressions of an Orientalist who knows the languages of the country through which he travels.

In October 1908, Adolf Kolmodin and son arrived at the port of Massawa on the Red Sea, and were struck by its hot humidity and drabness. Travelling through the Mediterranean Sea, Johannes had been seasick, but in the Suez he had recovered and begun to practise Arabic. Now he had arrived in his dream country. A winding road uphill revealed the stunning beauty of the countryside, though nothing is said about the beautiful Eritrean women who carried burdens on their heads up the road. After a mule trip to the oldest Swedish mission station at Moncallo, they felt enormous relief when they arrived in the cool Eritrean capital, Asmara, which was to remain their headquarters.

Johannes stayed for two months with the Swedish missionary J. Iwarson, who became a lifelong friend. The Swedish missions, their local Eritrean pastors and village school teachers always assisted him with board and lodging, logistics, their knowledge of local languages, customs, and personal contacts. The three African pastors, Twoldo Medhen, Marcus Ghermei, and Haile Micael Chidanu, who had been at Johannelund, became his assistants.

The Orthodox Ethiopian Church, with its ancient Jewish roots, monasticism, and Coptic affiliation, with its petrified rituals, and beautiful chanting and music, rarely used Bible or gospel texts or prayers.[15] Its lower priests and monks were

---

14 Carl Gustaf Kolmodin: *Johannes Kolmodin i brev och skrifter,* Kungliga Vitterhets Historie och Antikvitets Akademien, Filologiskt arkiv 41, Stockholm, 1999.

15 This alleged lack of Bible reading within the Orthodox Ethiopian Church may sound controversial today, but was a common conception among missionaries at that time.

unlearned and often superstitious. The mission distributed Bibles and New Testaments in Amharic and Tigrinya, founded schools and medical services, and worked for the evangelisation of the adherents of this church. Many Protestant missionaries had suffered persecution and reformed Eritreans were often accused of heresy and of hating the Virgin Mary. Nowadays, their educational work and devotion has made them respected.

Smaller expeditions north and west of Asmara took them to Carnescim, Dembesan, and Dec-Atescim, and at the beginning of December Johannes had his first experience of the discomforts of travelling in the wilderness while visiting Cheren and Gäläb. His first purpose was to listen to the way Tigrinya was spoken, investigate its sound system, learn its grammar, and master it in conversation. His sister Lillan was reported to have said that he would study "a language of the heathens." He retorted, via his mother: "Neither is this a pagan country, nor is Tigrinya a language of heathens: oh, if the Tigrinyans would hear such words they would become so terribly agitated that they would burst, or even worse!" (26.3.09)

The months passed quickly, with visits to other mission stations and rough expeditions. In January 1909, Johannes's father was to investigate the possibility of missionary work in Tigrai, a predominantly Muslim area in the northernmost province of Abyssinia. He asked his son to accompany him. An entry permit from Emperor Menelek was required, and this would also allow them entry into old churches and monasteries, where they hoped to uncover Bible manuscripts and books. The permit was obtained and was sanctioned by the Italian authorities.[16]

Pastor Iwarson organised the expedition and Twoldo Medhen was their companion and local expert. This was the most adventurous journey so far. They hired good riding mules and set off with six servants, camp beds, food, blankets, books, and gifts for the tribal chiefs. Iwarson has given a lively description in his memoirs of their mule ride through the wilderness, of their camping in tents, of their enjoyment of the hospitality of priests, of mission stations, and of a house belonging to the colonial authority. Adolf Kolmodin was always received with respect. Eventually, Italian carabineers escorted them to the Eritrean border at Gundet and they arrived in Menelek's classical Abyssinia.

It must have been an arduous journey. They had to ride in mountainous country without trodden paths, and with hardly any time to admire the magnificent beauty of the landscape, which is rarely mentioned in Johannes's letters. They took the same route the German Aksum expedition led by Enno Littmann had taken three years earlier. After two nights and a day, they reached Addi Abon, the residence of the Coptic Bishop Abuna Petrus, whose recommendation they needed in order to be able to enter churches and monasteries. A Bible in Amharic was presented and the ebullient Abuna Petrus was impressed with the learned professor from Sweden and his equally learned son. Religious disputes, hilarious episodes, offerings of honey-wine and coffee, and mountains of exquisite meat dishes offered relief from the exacting rides.

They entered Adua, the capital of Tigrai, where an historic bloody battle in 1896 had ended in Italy's defeat and the victory of Menelek II's troops. The party finally arrived in Aksum, the ancient capital of Ethiopia, where they found the population living under the influence of a thousand monks and priests. They were

---

16 Eritrea had been an Italian colony since 1860.

Northern Ethiopia and Eritrea today.

http://www.lib.utexas.edu/maps/africa/eritrea_ethiopia_rel99.jpg

allowed into the old Church of Mary, where all the Ethiopian emperors had been crowned and which, according to the traditions, contained the Ark of the Covenant from Jerusalem's temple – but this was not shown to them, in spite of the *laissez-passer* of the emperor.

The priests considered foreign scientific and archaeological expeditions a sacrilege. They hated the modern world and were furious with some modern improvements to the church's roof. They were even hostile. Johannes heard many stories about the German Aksum expedition. Drawn to a church by the chanting of priests, the sound of silver trumpets and big silver-plated drums, they were allowed to take part in a liturgical service according to the most ancient rites, with no readings from the Bible, no gospel, and no prayers.

Close to Adua was the famous Debre Damo monastery, situated high up on a cliff. With some persuasion, they were heaved up fifteen metres by ropes made from leather straps. The priests, some of whom were really nasty, revelled in hostile anecdotes about Littmann. The visitors took part in the service of Epiphany in a monastery containing 400 suspicious monks, served by 400 women living in the fields under the cliff. "A real robbers' nest." Owing to internal strife, they were not able to enter the mysterious monastery of Gundagunde. Extraordinary incidents, fascinating dialogues, and adventurous experiences nevertheless provided Johannes with opportunities to study the local speech and customs.

In fact, nowhere in Tigrai were they allowed to visit the libraries and treasuries of the monasteries or churches they entered. From that point of view, the expedition was a disappointment. They were admitted to the outer rooms, but no amount of pleading could persuade the priests to let them into the inner rooms, where the mortified Johannes could discern heaps of old parchment books within reach, yet unreachable. When they got to the reading room of the Church of Zion at Aksum, its over-anxious governor and treasurer, Gebre Selase, refused them access to the inventory of books, but Anania, at that time high priest in Adua, eventually handed Johannes a copy of the whole list of manuscripts both in his church and in certain other Aksum churches, after telling the other priests to go and sit behind a curtain!

> In that church library I found an old copy of Gadla Sädkän (The Life of Saints), an historical document of the greatest interest – which has put me in a position to determine the chronology for the most important events in Hamasén and Tigrai from 1350 to 1725! (19.4.1909)

Enno Littmann, the leader of the German expedition, had been no more successful. He had been able to publish just one list of old manuscripts, and that list was not complete. In the 1913 report of the German expedition,[17] Littmann has a photo of both Gabre Selase and Anania, which means that they must have been standing in the same reading room as Johannes. Littmann was the great authority on Ethiopics, but Johannes got the lists!

Littmann had been the guest of the Swedish mission for two months in 1905 and had praised its literary activities, such as its excellent translation of the New Testament into Tigré. The mission had introduced Tigré into the family of literary languages, and had thereby done a great service to the Eritrean people and to science and scholarship. He was convinced that Tigré was the most important and interesting of the living Abyssinian languages.[18]

Johannes started to organise and supplement the Tigré material from his Abyssinian journey by writing a grammar of Tigrinya. His intention was to map the expansion of Tigrinya speakers, Tigrinya's relationship to Tigré, and its position in relation to Amharic and Geez. He took notes of the local speech, studied where the accent lay, compared how differently the vowels were pronounced in various regions, and observed differences in vocabulary. After his father left Eritrea in March, he returned to his headquarters in Asmara and set out to gather more songs, anecdotes, and stories, and to attend local festivities, and made the following assessment:

---

17 a. E. Littmann und D. Krencher: *Vorbericht der deutschen Aksumexpedition*, mit 4 Tafeln, Abh. II, Akademie der Wissenschaftern, Berlin, 1906, pp. 1-37; b. Enno Littmann und Theodor von Lüpke: *Reisebericht der Expedition, Topographie und Geschichte Aksums*, mit 3 Tafeln und 44 Textabbildungen, Verlag von Theodor Reimer, Berlin, 1913, Bd. I.

18 Handwritten certificate dated 6.2.1906 contained in the correspondence between Enno Littmann and Johannes Kolmodin, in UUB Q 15:9.

There is no question of my being able to penetrate Tigré lexically and syntactically, but phonetically I am no doubt in a better position than Littmann was, and I probably will be able to correct him on important points. (27.7. 1909)

Very often it was his mother who received the long, humorous descriptions of occasions that few foreigners had experienced. Johannes always managed to make amusing or moving scenes alive. It could be an intermezzo during a wedding ceremony, interrupted by a heavy rain shower, or a funeral ceremony. A small book could be compiled using only these descriptions. Unwittingly, Johannes was acting both as an ethnologist, a social anthropologist, a dialectal linguist, and a pioneer in the research of oral traditions and genealogies.

Johannes had easy access to people, and made many lasting friends, not just among "the enemies of Mary" (as the monks called the Protestants) but among the local people. He approached singers, monks, beggars, women, groups of youngsters playing ball and noted down their rhymes, anecdotes, and conversations. He gained the women's confidence and they let him copy their intimate songs of childbirth, lamentation, and their hymns to the Virgin Mary.[19] Only the otherwise friendly guardians of monasteries and churches were unwilling to reveal their secrets.

For his cross-country rides, Johannes bought two riding mules, which he handled with tender care. He would not have got very far without them! Twoldo Medhen continued as his travel companion and advisor on local etiquette. He was an expert in Hebrew and the head translator of the Bible into Amharic in a project supervised by Johannes. The two of them visited Carnescim, Dembesan, Cheren, and Gäläb. Local mission-school teachers took him to ruined sites north and west of Asmara at Dec-Atescim, where there were rock inscriptions of an old Semitic type and stones with the sign of the cross and a wheel of a bronze-age type, all of which were different from known Southern inscriptions.

What a subject for a thesis! Johannes started working on it, but to this day no-one knows what happened to this rich material. During the course of his travels he became more and more entranced with the beauty and harshness of the mountains and the desert, the wilderness and the jungle, where leopards were close but never showed themselves and a famous lion never materialised.

Tsazzega and Hazzega

Inspired by his studies of Tigrinya, he began to travel to the highlands of Hamazen west of Asmara. Its ancient capital, Tsazzega, was the home of a noble clan, the Decatescim, who had played a leading role in this Eritrean province for 200 years. Pastor Svensson inspired him to write down the oral history of the Decatescim, "the children of Atescim," as told to him by the tribal people of Tigrinya.

During the months of April, May, and June 1909 he passed his days looking for the best Eritrean tradition bearers both in the noble family and in the villagers of Hazzega. Among the latter he found a young man of his own age, Tecle Michael Ughbagaber, called "Täklänke," who became a great help. Tecle accompanied

---

19 He collected 899 such items (of which only a few have been published). See *Tigrinische Wochenbettlieder*. Studier tillegnade Esaias Tegnér den 13 januari 1918, Lund 1918, pp. 65-101.

him everywhere and became a lasting friend. Johannes felt unsure whether to continue with grammatical questions or devote himself to Eritrean history.

> As for my thesis, I am not sure if I should take on my Tsazzega history, or rather as I first thought, something grammatical, such as "Studies on the Accent in Abyssinian"? That would give me the opportunity to correct errors regarding Tigrinya and Tigré, Amharic and Geez, while glancing at Bilin and Kunnama and possibly some other "Cushitic languages" such as Schaho. (11.8.1909)

Professor Zettertéen would have liked that – a proper philological thesis on Semitic languages, but it would mean much detailed and meticulous research.

> It might be more convenient to take my Tsazzega book. Apart from that I also have my big collection of songs in Tigrinya. Littmann has definitely not understood, or rather, he has *not at all* understood the Tigré accent, and in addition his ideas of vocalisation are very superficial. (13.8.1909)

Littmann had published his own strong ideas on this subject. Should he challenge them? Or, write the history of Eritrea? He shared his doubts with his father:

> I have reached conclusions that differ essentially from earlier European research, especially Littmann's. […] Papa must not think that this is a trifling matter. I have undoubtedly hit upon the solution of a problem that has never occurred to an Ethiopist before. (19.8.1909)

But his efforts to get permission from Addis Ababa to return to Aksum were in vain. In the end, it was not grammatical questions that were to be the subject of Johannes Kolmodin's doctoral thesis. He was to make an outstanding contribution to scholarship by registering the oral traditions that constitute the history of the province of Hamasén. That subject sat well with his temperament, interest in people, and passion for history.

> By a stroke of good luck, here in Tsazzega, I have found a superb storyteller, who apart from my old familiar *käntiba*, Mär'ed, is the best survivor in Hamasén of the old storyteller school; his name is Asgedom and he is old and leprous, so it is high time that his knowledge be used, or it will be lost to scholarship. (19.4.09)

In Hazzega, he also found a young man, Bahta, educated by Pastor Svensson. Bahta was taking part in the Bible translation project and was well versed in Tigrinya and knew people of every category. The two of them went out together to question people in the villages of Hamazen about what they remembered of their history. With that material, Johannes succeeded in compiling, in the words of Wittrock,

> … a list of Abyssinian tribal princes or village chiefs, comprising no less than 20 generations, going back to the middle of the 14th century, and all the names with the exception of three names can be verified. From the beginning of the 17th century he is able to add oral information about regency years, which at least in part harmonise with the past historical reality in view.[20]

The origin of Ethiopia's history was deeply hidden in myth and legend: Ethiopia was said to have been founded by Menelek, a son of King Solomon and the Queen of Sheba, who was supposed to have left Jerusalem and conquered

Ethiopia together with six Israelite tribes, who carried the Ark of the Covenant with them to East Africa, where they replaced the antique cults with Judaism. And now new light was being thrown on Eritrean history, based on the oral traditions and genealogies of the people of Hamazen, and this history could be brought all the way up to the beginning of the 20th century. Apart from being entertaining, Johannes wrote to his father, "my Zaasäga book will to a certain extent be a monument to Swedish mission work in Hamasén." The important questions of the value of oral traditions for all ancient history or the trustworthiness of genealogies were discussed at length by Johannes Kolmodin in the foreword to his thesis, and are still discussed among Bible researchers, scholars of Greek antiquity, and literary historians. For his own part, Kolmodin insisted that oral tradition is much more exact and trustworthy than historical science had been willing to admit, although it would of course be good if written sources could verify them.

But where to find such sources? Johannes luckily found some written sources in various village churches that confirmed what he had been told. To gain access to the libraries in the monasteries had been more difficult. The main monastery of Eritrea, Debre Bizen, had refused Johannes the opportunity to study its book treasures. He remembered his visit to the Zion Church in Aksum,

> ... when I held for a few moments a book in my hand, the value of which I did not know, but which I now fully appreciate. The title was *tarikä nägäst*, (the royal chronicle), and it seemed to contain genealogies of the various Abyssinian peoples. This is the book that those who know the traditions always point to when their own knowledge reaches its end. "In the *nägäst* at Aksum all is written," they say. If I could have had the chance to go through, relate, and partly copy this work, I would have done something that would surpass an enquiry into the monastery of Gundegunde. (19.8.1909)

In 1910, his time in Eritrea is approaching its end. He has to go home and use all his material and write a doctoral thesis.

> But there is one more important journey to make, to Ta'anke, in order to study the dying dialect of its inhabitants, the only branch of the great Tsazzega group that has preserved the non-Semitic language of their forefathers; all the others had adopted Tigrinya or Tigré. It is therefore imperative for me, who have made Tsazzega the centre of my studies here, to obtain some clarity regarding that language. High time, for this small language island is in the course of being washed away by Tigré. (19.8.10)

Sweden was already casting its shadow:

> Now I will soon leave here. What I wanted to gain by my journey is gained, on the whole. Some collections of poems and traditions I have not been able to put together, i.e., very little, but I have prepared myself for being able to work on them and giving them a scientific form. I have during these weeks worked through the grammar and got quite a bit further, beyond Rheinisch, and I have had the occasion to make some interesting phonetic observations as well. More I don't want to tackle just now. This will be enough.

This was written at Christmas, but in January, "Still in Asmara because of my mules. They were not quite well after the journey [...] and I cannot sell them until they have got a little better." (21.1.1910)

---

20 G.Wittrock: "Traditions de Tsazzega et Hazzega," *Historisk Tidskrift*, (review), 34, 1914, pp. 142-3.

He is restless and impatient. He plans his future personal and professional life. On his way home, he plans to take an English steamer from Massawa, go by railway from Suez to Alexandria, and then to Beirut by ship. He wants to place his assistant Tecle in a Syrian college in Lebanon and then sail to Constantinople. He has not forgotten his dream project – to study, from the Turkish point of view, the life of Charles XII when he was stuck at Bender. A Levantine Jew in Asmara has brushed up his Turkish. Letters about his first impressions of Constantinople are missing, but we may guess that the City of Bliss was love at first sight.

The Fruits of His Labour

Back in Uppsala, Johannes sent a copy of his field report "Meine Studienreise in Abessinien 1908-1910" to Littmann, who wrote that he was happy to win a collaborator in the field of dialect studies, but that he was on his way to a scientific mission in Asia Minor and could not read the report just now (16.11.1910). Four days later, however, he wrote from Cairo thanking Johannes "in the name of science for the new and interesting things you have taught me. You have as I see been working very thoroughly!" The letter continues:

> However, I must confess that discerning between the minutest vowel nuances in transcribed texts is unsympathetic to me. Besides, the pronunciation of vowels always differs from individual to individual; there we have to make compromises, as in Arabic. And it is methodologically wrong to draw conclusions from the Tigrinya of today and apply them to the ancient languages of 300-400 years ago. But you are perfectly right when, by registering the speech sounds, you try to bring life to the written language and to understand it phonetically. (20.10.1910)

Johannes had written in his report about the excursion to Adua (see above) and how open the suspicious monks had been in indicating how unwelcome they were, telling them malicious stories about the Germans who had been there before them. This upset Littmann:

> I was highly surprised and even indignant that you have *noted down* joking anecdotes about the German archaeologist and the ascent to Debra Damo. Thereby you have not only damaged the prestige of the Europeans and of the European learned community with the local people, but also hurt the integrity of the travel companions. Didn't the "noble priests" tell you that we gave them free medical care for three months, that we offered them rich presents, and that the high priest almost daily asked for backshish – and often received it, that they tried to attack us deceitfully at night? Didn't they tell you at Debra Damo how I was trying to grip the rope under severe pain with a purulent wound on my hand? (20.10.1910)

Johannes immediately wrote to mitigate the situation, whereupon Littmann answered that he was satisfied with Kolmodin's explanations.

> I am very happy that the misunderstanding has been clarified […] I have also here and there in Syria and Arabia heard jokes about my predecessors, but have taken great care not to write down such things heard from the mouths of the locals. After your clarification the whole matter is closed. (Cairo 13.1.1911)

Littmann returned from Cairo to his professor's chair in Strasbourg, which he "inherited" from his father-in-law, Professor Theodor Nöldeke. Johannes sent him his latest writings and when Littmann had studied Johannes's Tigrinya texts "Abessinische Glossen," the great Ethiopist came to the conclusion that Johannes was

> ... a skilful and very profoundly trained linguist. You have been able to do what I, because of lack of time, money, and opportunity have not been able to do in the field of Tigrinya! Learning that you have been working in other fields as well, I see that you have far-reaching, pertinent, and historical interests, through which alone linguistic study becomes really and truly valuable and alive.[21]

In 1912, Littmann thanked Kolmodin for "Les Traditions de Tsazzega et Hazzega. Textes Tigrinja," published in *Archives d'études orientales* (5:1, Uppsala 1912) with further praise: "The most important work ever written on Tigrinya." The next few years were filled with political and historical essays, while he prepared his doctoral thesis *Traditions de Tsazzega et Hazzega. Annales et documents,* which earned him the Ph.D. degree in 1914 and a three-year stipend in Semitic languages. Now, at last, he had earned the fruits of his labour, and could call himself Docent Kolmodin.

Littmann's high opinion of Kolmodin as a brilliant linguist (he did not say very much about his concept of oral history) was not shared by his professor, K.V. Zetterstéen, who had not been overly appreciative of Kolmodin's thesis. In his opinion

> ... it should rather have been judged from a historical than a philological point of view. Its object seems to have been to throw light on the importance of an oral tradition as a historical source; the purely philological side of the work has obviously interested the author less than the historical side, and the Ethiopian texts he has published here are very easy; the only difficulties being the Amharic words.[22]

This lack of generosity, not to say this animosity, may have been influenced by the effusive thanks Johannes gives in his introduction to his history teacher Harald Hjärne. In any case, Zetterstéen was a pure philologist with little understanding of the historical science. To be fair, Zetterstéen later acknowledged Kolmodin's mastery of Ottoman and modern Turkish, which by that time far exceeded his own, praising his Turkish archive studies and "his journeys in far countries which bear witness to an energy and a courage which remind us Swedes of the famous J.J. Björnståhl (d. 1779 in Saloniki)" and there was a friendly correspondence between them for many years.[23]

A Conservative Student Leader

Johannes Kolmodin had returned to a heated political situation in Sweden, and this was to consume his time and energy for years to come. He was full of

---

21 Letters between Enno Littmann and Johannes Kolmodin, correspondence in UUB Q 15:9.

22 Carl Gustaf Kolmodin: *Johannes Kolmodin,* p. 41. Charles Vilhelm Zetterstéen's views on Kolmodin's Ethiopian and Turkish scholarship have also been expressed in the following annuals: *Svenska Orientsällskapets årsbok,* 1924; *Karolinska förbundets årsbok,* 1937, and *Lychnos årsbok för idé- och lärdomshistoria* (Annual of the Swedish History of Ideas), 1941.

23 K.V. Zetterstéen: "De orientaliska studierna i Sverige," *Svenska Orientsällskapets årsbok,* 1924, pp. 28-9.

knowledge and experience of another world. He was eager to go home and do his best for his country in a situation that, to him and his friends, was already darkened by the threatening clouds of a great European war, as they saw it. He resumed his post as secretary of Heimdal in 1910 and became its vice-president in 1915. Nationalism was more or less the trend in all the students' associations.

After 1910, Heimdal changed its nature from a debating club aiming at popular education to a debating club on three burning political issues: the national question, the defence question, and the constitutional question. Twenty years earlier, Hjärne had coined the slogan, "defence and reforms." A new military organisation had been formed in 1901. Universal suffrage for men was introduced in 1909. The leftist parties wanted parliamentary government. The conservatives wanted strong power for the king. That was the constitutional question.

Heimdal had so far been politically neutral. Now, however, Fosterländska förbundet (The Patriotic Alliance), a nationalistic political club, wanted to merge with it. Should Heimdal allow that? Johannes Kolmodin stated that neutrality had been appropriate until Heimdal started talking of defence and reform, for thereby they had, in fact, already entered party politics. There was, therefore, no reason why national-minded liberals or conservative radicals should not feel at home in Heimdal.

Johannes's friend Arvid Uggla said that Heimdal honoured the national aspect above freedom of thought and speech, in contrast with Verdandi, for which freedom of thought and speech came before the national aspect. He was for the merger with Fosterländska förbundet. The student Hjalmar Haralds said that they could not call themselves "*höger*" (rightist), for the name was already associated with party issues of no concern to them. Finally, the merger was decided by general vote. Several students who voted against it left Heimdal, saying that the association was now a conservative political association and would be brought closer to Högerpartiet (the rightist party).

Now Heimdal was indeed a political association and Johannes Kolmodin had a leading role in this development. The ideas that held the conservative, nationalistic young men of Heimdal together in 1910 were anti-democratic and pro-monarchist. They were pro-Finland and anti-Norway. They wanted to recover Sweden's lost glory. They suffered from what they saw as the passivity, the cowardice, the defeatism, the lack of pride, and the unwillingness to defend themselves of contemporary Swedes. Were they fighting for lost causes?

Everything later generations learn at school about the modern parliamentary development of Sweden is stood on its head when you read about the conservative, anti-parliamentary ideals of these young men. According to them, Sweden's history was of its kings, and the Heimdalites forever referred to the greater or lesser kings of the past. A country's history is its living past, and its living past is alive in the present – that was the nucleus of what Harald Hjärne taught. A country's foreign policy grows out of its past experience. Historical patterns determine the present. Johannes was giving Eritrea its past history back so that it could live on consciously in the present.

Now it was Swedish history that mattered. Instead of missionaries, monks, priests, and young men in Eritrea, personalities like Sven Hedin, Olof Palme (uncle of the prime minister), Sven Lidman, and other rightist politicians entered Johannes's life as the principal actors. They shared Hjärne's adamant convictions about a strong state, with the duty of the individual to subordinate himself to it; but within the society, the individual would live a secure life, protected by state power. There he saw room for the free play of forces where the individual could stand upright and independent.

Hjärne could never understand the class struggle in modern society. His emancipation from the doctrines of political liberalism led to his assumption of the correctness of the sublime right of state power. An individual must be capable of entering the life of state and community without the intervening medium of class, corporation, or even commune. This historical rootedness in the cultural epoch of liberal individualism explains why he did not understand the forces that shaped the contemporary cultural epoch. We shall see how Johannes Kolmodin basically held fast to these ideas throughout his life.

A political chapter began with the constitutional crisis of 1911 and reached its climax in 1913-14, when the debate on national, constitutional, and defence questions divided Sweden politically and determined its future course. The Heimdalites saw the war clouds approaching, but the politicians behaved as if peace would be everlasting. When the liberal government of Karl Staaf prohibited the construction of an armoured warship, although this had been approved by parliament, there was an outcry among the rightists.

Professor Sven Hedin, author and explorer of inner Asia and a hero to many Swedes, had returned to Sweden in triumph in 1909. He agitated for the strong defence of Sweden in the pamphlet *Ett varningsord* (A Word of Warning), which was printed in a million copies and distributed to Swedish homes, and Heimdal started the journal *Vårdkasen* (The Beacon) to agitate on the defence question.

Johannes went into political action. On 13 November 1912, he organised a much-criticised meeting at Norrlands nation (a students college). Sven Hedin was the main speaker, but Johannes was the student star, not in the limelight but behind everything. "He was not only a representative leading figure, he was also to a great extent the worker who wrote brochures and handbooks, took part in debates, and organised expressions of opinion. I was charmed by his elegant, not infrequently sarcastic way of arguing, his clear presentation, quick understanding, and rapid powers of decision," wrote Gunnar Hesslén.[24]

On the occasion of the 50th anniversary of Heimdal in 1941, when nationalistic feelings ran high and the outcome of the Second World War was far from certain, the former Heimdalite H.S. Nyberg stated, not without triumphal feelings, "that the effort of Heimdal from 1911 to 1914 to propagate a stronger defence belongs to the great pages of its history. What we fought for then is now common knowledge and fully recognised even by our old adversaries."[25]

In February 1914, a constitutional crisis shook Sweden. Thousands of farmers marched to Stockholm. Thousands of Heimdalites and sympathisers demonstrated in front of King Gustaf V at Stockholm castle. A special train ran to Stockholm for 1,200 Uppsala students (of 2,000), who joined students from Stockholm, Lund, and Göteborg. A top-secret guideline and manifesto, nicknamed "Johannesevangeliet" (The Gospel of St John) was, of course, written by Kolmodin. A constitutional alliance was formed, committing itself to the constitution of 1809.

The rightist constitutional politics of Sven Hedin and the Heimdalites had won over the supporters of parliamentarianism and liberalism, and Johannes

25 H.S. Nyberg: "Den svensk-nationella tanken."

24 Gunnar Hesslén (1894-1958): "Några minnen från den 'politiska' våreterminen 1914. Bland professorer och studenter. Uppsalaminnen," i serien *Hågkomster och livsintryck av svenska män och kvinnor,* No. 19, 1938.

Kolmodin was now a brilliant nationalistic politician in Sweden, clearly stating his cause and honestly expounding his opinions.

When the World War that they had foreseen actually started, Sweden's policy of neutrality was the focus of general debate. Heimdal took an activist stand, though not in favour of siding with Germany, but pleading for "the Baltic solution" – the liberation of Finland and its attachment to Sweden. Sven Lidman started a journal *Svensk Lösen* (Swedish Watchword), to which Johannes Kolmodin contributed a profound historical background analysis *à la* Hjärne. Olof Palme and Johannes Kolmodin supported the Finnish activists and most Heimdalites did not support the German activists.

Another person of consequence was the greatest personality in Uppsala in this whole era, Nathan Söderblom, theologian and professor of the history of religions and later archbishop of Sweden. In that capacity, he was later to make good use of Johannes Kolmodin's Turkish affiliations for his ecumenical ideas and undertakings. This relationship developed into a friendship, treated elsewhere in this book[26] and therefore omitted here. It is necessary, however, to mention Nathan Söderblom's role in Kolmodin's life even at this early stage, as well as the close contact later on.

The political role of Johannes Kolmodin in the rightist student activist struggle of 1913 was crucial and his ideas met with aggressive criticism from his opponents. However, those who understood him never forgot him. "Let it be permitted to bind a garland of honour to my unforgettable friend Johannes Kolmodin, who during those years had to take the hardest and the most frequent blows," H.S. Nyberg said in his speech commemorating Heimdal's 50th anniversary in 1941.

> He, more than anyone, was a bearer of the living past. He knew our history and its problems, they lived in him, they sprung up like a geyser in the midst of the problems of the day. He possessed the theoretical training, clarity of thought, and spiritual energy, which made him one of the few political thinkers of class in our country. He was a living power station for all kinds of national ideas.
>
> He sacrificed everything for the national cause, even his political career at home, his scholarly career for which he possessed brilliant talents. His energy and capacity for work seemed unlimited, but in the course of years he acquired the light touch in the handling of the day-to-day issues. He radiated an idealism, which made the air clean and pure around him, on dusty and stuffy battlefields. Sweden became too narrow for him and he found a new field of action in international politics.[27]

Johannes Kolmodin and H.S. Nyberg

H.S.Nyberg was younger than Johannes Kolmodin by five years. He had started his Semitic studies in 1908 when Johannes had just obtained his Phil.Lic in Semitic philology and history. They must have met rather soon after Johannes returned from East Africa, while Johannes was working on his oral traditions of Eritrea from 1910 to 1914. Nyberg had similar ideas on folkloristic traditions and

---

26 See Carl Gustaf Kolmodin's chapter in this book "Friends and Compatriots: Sven Hedin, Sven Lidman and Nathan Söderblom."

27 H.S. Nyberg: "Högtidstal vid Föreningen Heimdals 50-årsfest," p. 257.

later applied the theory of history as oral tradition to his Old Testament studies and other research, and he remained convinced of the superiority of oral memory to written traditions in the ancient cultures of the Middle East. His six lectures in Copenhagen in 1948 on oral traditions in different cultures, published posthumously in 2004, still bear witness to his friendship with Johannes Kolmodin.[28]

They were both brilliant linguists and hardworking, each driven by the expectations of their respective fathers, but with different motive power. Nyberg came from a modest economic background with everything to win and nothing to lose, it was an "*ille-faciet*-syndrome," the son having to make up for the gifted father's quenched career, and he stood alone with the responsibility for seven younger orphaned brothers and sisters. Kolmodin started out from an established background in academic Uppsala, with an unbroken family life, protected by brothers and sisters, and with the ambition to excel above a prominent father and to fulfil the high academic ambitions of his background.

As active members of the Students' Semitist Club, they were interested in Egypt and the Arab-speaking world, but most of all in the reform movements and the modernisation of Islam. They studied Turkish, not a Semitic language, and observed with interest the revolutionary development of modern Turkey. They turned their eyes to Constantinople and said *"Ex Oriente Lux"* (The Light Comes from the East). Probably it was Johannes who set the tone, but they could also be less serious-minded. Self-discipline and hard reading were no obstacle to carousing and rollicking. Whoever could carry their liquor well could be sure of a place in the sun. Student life in those days was almost exclusively male. Witty and entertaining students were elected into secret orders, in which student pranks were developed into a higher form of witticism.

Admired for his formal artistry and exotic learning, Johannes was received into the legendary Juvenal Order in 1911, rose to be grand master from 1913 to1916, and was addressed as Johannes the Felicitous. The Juvenal Order was a parody of the system of orders prevalent in the Swedish monarchy at the time and its mock constitution paraphrased the constitution of 1809, with its absolute monarchy. The grand master was an autocratic ruler, a role that must have well suited Kolmodin. In this witty hierarchy, jest and mockery were highly prized. "H.S.," whose repartee and *esprit* were not insignificant, was also a Juvenal brother, though devoting less time to it. This mocking jargon coloured the correspondence of Nyberg and Kolmodin long after they ceased to be students.

Another similarity was that they took time for administrative tasks. Kolmodin was first curator of Gotlands nation, and it did not take long before the freshman Nyberg was elected first curator of Västmanland-Dala nation. These student "nations" fulfilled a social function, and to be elected to administer them was a sign of merit. They shared historical and political interests. Nyberg followed Johannes and was drawn into the defence debate of 1911 and into the agitation during the constitutional crisis, and they sympathised with the Finland activists. Like all nationalistic students, they admired Charles XII as a political genius. Was it Johannes who inspired H.S. Nyberg to take Harald Hjärne's history course in 1912? Was it Johannes who persuaded him to become a member of Heimdal in 1914? Kolmodin was president of Heimdal in

---

28 H.S. Nyberg: *Muntlig tradition, skriftlig fixering och författarskap* (sammanställt enligt efterlämnade manuskript av Bo Utas), Acta Societatis Litterarum Humaniorum Regiae Upsaliensis 51, Uppsala 2004.

1915 and Nyberg was his successor from 1916 to1918. Other Heimdalites included Ivar Andersson, Nils Ahnlund, Erland Hjärne, and Erik Leijonhufvud.

It is hard to know how close the friendship between Johannes and my father was. Certainly, it was not as close as that with Erland Hjärne or Sven Lidman, with whom Johannes could be very personal. "H.S.," however, was the only Orientalist among his friends. In 1925, he visited Johannes in Constantinople. One has the impression that here were two giants of erudition exchanging views over a glass of whisky (*grogg*) with a lot of laughter and many anecdotes, academic malice, a passion for politics, and sympathy for everything Oriental. On the other hand, my father might have represented to Johannes, at certain bitter moments later in life, the dream of an academic career and a path that he did not choose in life but could well have chosen.

"Will you take over my Abyssinian material if I do not return from the war? There is a lot lying there waiting to be worked upon. I have decided in my testament that it shall be offered to you," Enno Littmann writes to Johannes Kolmodin in 1915.[29] Kolmodin had sent him a patriotic speech by himself and a copy of Sven Lidman's magazine *Svensk Lösen* (Swedish Watchword). Littmann is glad that Sweden remembers its great past and does not placidly submit itself into Britain's hands. "We Germans have such few friends in the world that we are doubly grateful to those who affirm their friendship." In 1916, Littmann is called to do military service, but not yet in arms, and in March 1917 he sounds desperate about the future of Ethiopics: "Except for you and Conti-Rossini, nobody is as close to Northern Abyssinia, so important for our *Spezialwissenschaft*, as you are."

But Johannes seems to neglect his Abyssinian material more and more. From the scientific material he had brought with him from Ethiopia, he published only three major articles in *Le Monde Oriental* during the years 1914 to 1916, and one cannot avoid the impression that the outbreak of the World War made him neglect the Ethiopian material in favour of Turkish, as he became more and more involved in wartime events. After "Abessinische Bücherverzeichnisse" in *Le Monde Oriental* in 1916,[30] he devoted most of his time to writing political and nationalistic articles and to agitating for Finland. If he did his military service, there is no trace of it to be found in the documents. "There was a touch of an original about him as he hurried through the streets of Uppsala with his somewhat careless walk, day and night, in restless activity," my father remembers.

The restless activity continued more than ever during the war years 1914 to 1917 and eventually he left for Turkey. Why? Probably from a combination of interests: his fascination with Charles XII; his interest in the Turkish language; his involvement in the history and the future of Europe; his strong emotions about the war's events; and his new friendship with Sven Hedin, who admired Charles XII and encouraged him to do research on him in Turkish archives and who even got the permission of the Grand Vizier for this purpose, as well as helping him to finance it, with the aid of the Caroline Society. Or was it the cold indifference of Zetterstéen to his Ethiopian work? Or, yet again, was it that he wanted to get away from the stifling atmosphere of a small university town, turn his back on his many political opponents, and breathe some international and Oriental air again? "The thought about the country at home weighs on me with

29 UUB Manuscript collection, Q 15:9.

30 Johannes Kolmodin: "Abessinische Bücherverzeichnisse," *Le Monde Oriental,* 10, 1916, pp. 241-55.

tremendous pressure, but I also feel clearly that I could be of no use there," he was later to write in one of his first letters from Constantinople. (17.1.1918)

Berlin: Summer 1917

In June 1917, in the middle of the World War, Johannes Kolmodin went to Berlin to study Turkish at the Oriental Seminar. Now, after eleven years of correspondence (!) he was to know Enno Littmann personally – the scholar in whose footsteps he had been walking at Aksum. Littmann immediately invited Johannes to tea at a famous club and introduced him to "important political personalities," and he wrote to his father that he found Littmann "a broad and very entertaining person, not without a certain family likeness with Professor Harald Hjärne!"

Another person who happened to be in Berlin that summer was H.S. Nyberg, who was doing research on Ibn al-'Arabi in the Prussian library. Johannes took him to a café to meet Littmann, who was pleased to know two "such patriotic young Swedes" and introduced them to the famous Semitists Eugen Mittwoch and Eduard Meyer, who with Littmann became lifelong colleagues of H.S. Nyberg. In Berlin, food was scarce and one Sunday all three of them went on an excursion into the countryside to obtain some food not to be had in starving Berlin. This was, apparently, a merry occasion, to judge from both oral and written tradition![31]

H.S. Nyberg was received by Littmann at the headquarters of the general staff, where his military task was to lecture to German soldiers on Islam! He found in Littmann a staunch nationalist and an admirer of King Gustavus Adolphus of Sweden. Littmann survived the war and succeeded Julius Wellhausen as professor in Tübingen in 1919.

Preparing for Turkey

Johannes Kolmodin finally went to Turkey in November 1917. Little did he know that he was never to return, except on holidays. Our principal source for the Turkish period is his letters to his father (and sometimes to both parents or to his mother). Below, I shall let him speak mainly through these letters, without necessarily referring to every line in a scientific way. My aim remains to piece together a tentative personal portrait and a summary of his non-official political views. I wanted to study the development of his political ideas in an international context and point out their consistency. My contention is that he never really changed the structure of his political thought and his basic values, and that he remained forever a pupil of Harald Hjärne. Let us see if the proofs hold.

I was also interested in his moral values. How did he look upon anti-Semitism and racism? He was a declared anti-racist. The issue of race was on the agenda in Sweden as early as 1911, when the professor of political science Rudolf Kjellén introduced it in his book, *The Great Orient*. Kjellén was an ultra-conservative pro-German activist during the First World War. In his review of the book, Kolmodin lashes out against "Chamberlain, Drews, Lidfors and others," who believed in the superiority of the whites. "As for our 'Aryan' forefathers, they were wandering about in their northern forests at a time when the ancient central

---

31 Correspondence Littmann to Kolmodin (19) in UUB Manuscript collection, Q 15:9, and Littmann to Nyberg (41) in UUB.

lands of the west were ruled by peoples whose ethnological rootlets point partly to yellow Asia but predominantly to black Africa."[32]

There is something much more essential in history than the racial context, and that is the cultural context, he continues. Race is a creation of culture and not the other way round.

> When you find the same totemic clan systems (slightly modified) among the Nubians of the Black Nile, the Papuas of North Australia and the Comanches and the Apaches of North America, and when you find the strange inheritance laws of the Central Asian Tatars among the Negroes of Egyptian Sudan, or when you recognise the concept of justice in the old Swedish landscape laws in the Cushitic tribal laws of modern Abyssinia, then you feel rather less inclined to defend the opinion that views the spiritual life of man from the biological point of view.[33]

One central political opinion of Kolmodin that has struck me is his belief in the authority of the state and the necessity of an autocratic leader. Charles XII was his great autocratic model in Swedish history, and it is interesting to see how he looks at another autocratic model, one of Napoleon's generals, who succeeded to the Swedish throne. The great achievement from 1812 to 1815 of Jean Baptiste Bernadotte, later Charles XIV John (1763-1844), was Sweden's political survival in its most difficult crisis in modern times by integrating Norway, but Johannes discards the "Charles XIV John tradition" and "Scandinavianism" in favour of another central idea, "the maintenance of our ancient Baltic unity with Finland and Åland," he writes in 1913.

I have tried to be faithful to Kolmodin's circumstantial style in my English translation of his letters. Kolmodin's more easygoing letters to his parents concern private matters, but also provide a running commentary on the foreign policy of Sweden and the Great Powers during the war, and contain his critical analyses of the policies of Britain, France, Germany, and Russia, starting with the European balance of power in the 19th century, to which Charles XIV John contributed through his friendly policy towards Russia.

Johannes's letters to friends will only be quoted in passing. They deal with a variety of specialised subjects elaborated in other parts of this book. Johannes corresponded with Sven Hedin, who partly financed his research on Charles XII, with Archbishop Nathan Söderblom, who asked him to approach the Greek Orthodox patriarchy, and with the charismatic author Sven Lidman, about very personal things. All of them became his lifelong friends. For my purposes, it is enough to take note of Johannes Kolmodin's wide-ranging interests, his insider's knowledge of theological and missionary work, his understanding of the problems of church organisation, and his capacity for personal relations – qualities that could be useful at home, in addition to the value of his official diplomatic reports and general usefulness. It was an advantage for many interested parties to have "ein Mädchen für alles" in Istanbul, especially one who was gratuitous, since he was also "Our Man in Constantinople"!

---

32 Johannes Kolmodin: "Rasproblemet. Rudolf Kjelléns 'Den stora Orienten,'" *Det Nya Sverige,* No. 6, 1912, pp. 84-8.

33 Ibid.

Panoramic view of Tophane and the Bosphorus in the 1920's.

Cengiz Kahraman archive

Turkey and the World War

When Johannes arrived in Constantinople in November 1917, the World War had lasted for three years. Turkey had more or less slipped into the war on the side of Germany, and found itself at war with the Allies on several fronts: the Suez Canal, in Mesopotamia, the Caucasus, and the Dardanelles. In March 1917, General Maude captured Baghdad. In the same year, Palestine was conquered and on 9 December Jerusalem was evacuated and General Allenby entered the city in triumph. Germany was fighting against Turkey's arch-enemy Russia. The Finnish parliament passed a formal declaration of independence on 6 December.

Johannes installs himself in his first lodgings with a pleasant Armenian family. He plunges himself into the practice of Turkish and his French is improving. He immediately becomes acquainted with Djemal Pasha and wins a friend in the Turkish diplomat Tewfik Bey. He writes enthusiastically about conversations with Turkish beys and tea parties with Armenian ladies. He discusses Luther and Muhammed, Sweden, and Turkestan with a sheikh. During the next months he acquires more and more Turkish friends. He is looking forward to starting to delve into the Turkish archives for information on Charles XII at Bender. This is made difficult by the Turkish bureaucracy, but with the help of the history professor Ahmad Refik, he can get all the manuscripts he needs. Another Turkish friend forever!

In January 1918, he starts his work as an honorary attaché at the Swedish legation, an arrangement made by Sweden's prime minister, Arvid Lindman. Diplomatic status is a help, and in time he hopes to get a small salary. His first task is to bring order to the chaotic archives. He is invited to the Palais de Suède by the envoy, Anckarsvärd. The military attaché, Major af Wirsén, offers him his house while he is away in Bulgaria. The new attaché, Paul Mohn, is quite young. Colonel Ahlgren handles the American interests. He wonders how he will be able to cope with the envoy, on the one hand, and the Americans, a Belgian, an Armenian dragoman, some typing girls, and a few Serbian and Albanian "kavass-

The "Dragoman House," annexe to the Swedish Embassy in Constantinople; today used by the Swedish Research Institute in Istanbul.

Einar af Wirsén: *Minnan från krig och fred*, Stockholm, 1942

es," on the other. It is his first experience of the diplomatic profession. "Here you have to try to interpret even the very worst for the best, especially when you pretend to be a diplomat [...] you have to watch your steps," he writes home.

What occupies him most is the political situation at home. Finland is fighting for its independence and Sweden refuses to intervene! In April, a newspaper cutting informs Johannes that his friend Olof Palme has fallen as a volunteer in Finland.

> Strange that he is gone. May his last hope [...] that his sacrifice might be a seed for the future be fulfilled soon! If I were to send Olle Palme a wreath I would inscribe it with a verse from Tegnér's poem, Svea: "Thou unborn avenger, come without delay!" (6.5.1918)

Now there will be nothing left in Sweden but cowards. The old idea of political cowardice always haunts Johannes.

> The libs and the sossies [liberals and socialists] are the ones who most fear a revolutionary explosion. They feel in their bones that if it would succeed they would soon be outdone, and if beaten, they would disappear in the reaction. The "*Höger*" [the Right] ought not to have the same fear. The nonsensical ideal of the libs, the practice of temporised cowardice, is a boil on society's body. The various democratic constitutional ideals are buried rather quietly. The Government of Edén – the Government of Cowardice. (11.5.1918)

That was his final verdict on Sweden. From now on, his focus will be on Turkey. Docent Johannes Komodin will in due time write most of the political reports from the Swedish legation in Constantinople to the foreign ministry in Stockholm, even though they will be signed by the minister, first envoy Cosswa Anckarswärd and, after 1920, envoy Gustaf Oscar Wallenberg.[34] Compared to

---

34 See Carl Gustaf Kolmodin's chapter "An Ill-matched Couple" in this volume.

The Topkapı Palace (background) and the entrance to the Golden Horn in the early 20th century.
Cengiz Kahraman archive

the reports, which are long-winded and sometimes hard to read, his letters are natural and easy. Therefore I shall quote Kolmodin's letters extensively, as a matter for future analysis, and as an insight into Turkish life at a critical period in its history.

The Great Powers at War

It is the last year of the German Empire. Russia has collapsed. After the Communist revolution in Russia, Turkey and its allies concluded a peace treaty with Russia at Brest-Litovsk on 3 March 1918, by which Turkey regained Kars, Ardahan, and Batum, territories ceded to Russia in 1878. The World War is entering its final phase, but Johannes thinks that it will go on for a long time yet.

> Not only in the case that the British, relying on the Americans, continue the war even after their probable expulsion from the continent, [...] they will prolong the European war as long as they can. Not even a separate Austrian peace could lead to a real victory for the Entente, now that the connection with the Orient can be maintained via Odessa and Sevastopol. (11.5.1918)
>
> Jerusalem – which the British occupy at present with the aid of Hindus (so they have taken it from the Mohammedans in order to give it over to the heathens!) will no doubt be taken in the autumn. Should the campaign in France succeed, and the British want to continue the war all the same, I suppose that Egypt's turn will come in earnest. (Ibid.)

The Entente is bombarding Constantinople but the bombs are small and weak and Johannes sleeps well. On 8 August, "the black day for the German army," the British broke through the German lines. Johannes is bitter, even sarcastic about Germany. This nation from which he expected heroism, idealism, and contempt for death has thoroughly disappointed him. He does not mind the Pan-Germans, "die All-Deutsche," for whom he has quite a lot of sympathy, he tells his father, continuing:

A view from Tophane (by the Bosphorus, close to Galata Bridge) with the Nusretiye Mosque partially hidden by a street-car driven by horses.

Cengiz Kahraman archive

... the danger is the small-minded German capitalism with its exploitative tendencies [...] and that danger will in my opinion grow, if the Entente will show that they are able to keep the Germans away from the world ocean. If we were ever capable of living with the Germans, it could only be in their capacity as victors; otherwise they can be unpleasant, as their present petty Russian policy shows. [...] By this policy they have hurt themselves in the East to such an extent that one almost worries more about their final fate than about their defeats in the West – their effort to galvanise Russia is strictly a betrayal of their historical destiny. Truly, they are busy doing the same thing, from a Swedish point of view, as our gracious government has done in Finland. As you might conclude, Father, from what I have said, there is probably no great difference between Hjärne's idea about this and mine. (7.9. 1918)

In Constantinople, the Turks enjoy their summer holiday, he had written in an earlier letter:

Not much happens right now, except that my dear old friend the Pan-Islamist and Timurid heir, Sheikh Abdurrashid Ibrahim Kan (who had got lost after the great fire in Stambul, when everything he owned went up in smoke) has turned up again and we had a very nice chat about Sweden and Turkestan and Luther and Muhammed. As far as my experience goes, I am very fond of the higher Muslim priesthood – they are pleasantly intelligent and enlightened people [...] Today the Sultan [Mehmet VI] "takes the sabre" – the Turkish coronation. The solemn cortège through Stambul will be a sight. The air raids are likely to stop for some time when the moonshine is gone – last Wednesday night the Turks managed to shoot an Englishman. (31.8.1918)

In September, General Ludendorff lost his nerve and declared that an immediate armistice was necessary. In the east, the situation for Turkey in the Arab provinces had become disastrous. Thousands of Turkish soldiers had perished in the Caucasus and a whole army had been put out of action. The Russians had forced the Turks to evacuate the fort at Erzurum. The Turkish armies retreated to

Syria and eventually to Anatolia under Mustafa Kemal, who managed to stop the Russian advance at Lake Van. In September, the name of the future hero Mustafa Kemal is mentioned for the first time in the Kolmodin letters.

Turkey, Germany, and Russia, 1918

"Today it is Khurban Bairam, the second biggest celebration of the Mohammedans," Johannes writes in September. The general mood has brightened considerably, which is due to the news of the fall of Baku.

It was a victory for the Turks, which in the mind of most Turks probably outweighs the loss of Jerusalem, and even that of Baghdad – and will not be less appreciated because they have won, at least halfway, over their German allies, who in the supplement to the treaty of Brest-Litovsk wanted to hand the city back to Russia. I doubt whether Berlin can fulfil that promise. There would have to be some kind of agreement between the Moscow Government and the Turkish Republic Azerbaijan, where Germany would have to act the godfather. The Jewish finance in *Berliner Tageblatt* will naturally curse, but the real Germans in *Berliner Tageszeitung* will probably adjust. (17.9.1918)

The Turkish mood has improved slightly after the successful occupation of Baku, but – after the vulgar flirtation with the Bolsheviks last summer – it places the Germans in a serious dilemma. The great historical problem in world politics today happens to be whether the Germans will be tough enough to keep the steam up – not at the front but at home. There seems to be a strong mood among the general public in Germany that, be it as it will with the war, it is peace they want. But if they manage to pull themselves together, it is probably much too early for the Entente to triumph. (21.9. 1918)

Summa summarum: Europe is to be pitied and so are we, to the extent that we have interests in common. Europe may, however, find comfort in the thought that if the worst were to befall Central Europe, the central power idea (as I would like to call it) will not die, but will soon be revived in new forms rather like those of the 17th century, and we ourselves may find comfort in the thought of Russia's unholy demise. (Ibid.)

The war is developing into the greatest tragedy in world history – Europe's tragedy: it will from now on be something like Greece in the area of the Achean and Cetolian alliances, with America in the role of Rome. It is true that Rome was not a particularly nice gentleman in its behaviour towards the Hellenistic world – but America! *Diese verfluchten Amerikaner!* (24.9.1918)

Damascus might fall any day now, but the Turks comfort themselves with Baku. The Turks are not sorry about the dissolution of Bulgaria, which as long as their neighbour had the reputation of being strong, they feared almost more than England, but now a stone has fallen from their breasts. (1.10.1918)

Which countries would be most prone to fall to the Bolsheviks? The Bulgarians, a suspect source of infection? On the Entente side, Italy may be most exposed, and on the side of the Central Powers, Austria may, next to Bulgaria, be the dangerous points. In Germany there's probably no great risk of infection, though it is not as immune as America. In excellent old Turkey, robbers in the true old traditional style may arise from time to time, but never Bolsheviks! (Ibid.)

Events developed fast during October and November. Ludendorff declared the war as lost. Germany was ordered to be a constitutional monarchy. The liberal conciliator, Prince Max of Baden, became chancellor. Ludendorff retired and

Hindenburg became head of the general staff. Kolmodin, writing just after the event, does not hide his bitter scorn:

> The Germans had the Trojan horse *intra muros* – it becomes more obvious every day – in the form of libs and sossies who never wanted the Reich to win the war, because they were afraid in such a case of not getting their parliamentarianism and are quite pleased with things as they are [...] Thank God they were at least able to crush Russia, before they lost their drive. [...] Well, it is not yet out of the question that it might still come to a *guerre d'outrance*, something which would of course have its hazardous sides, not only for the warring parties. (12.10.1918)
>
> The defeat of Germany (Wilson!) leaves the Turks rather indifferent, inasmuch as Germany was preparing to take up its old position in the Great Power concert [...] and in the future it will want to play a role in the Last Judgment on Turkey. [...] It is not certain that Izzet Pasha's Government, moved by the old Turkish moral code, will be able to arrange a free exit for the Germans in the armistice negotiations. Germany is now ready to give up the game. Austria is cracking up. Poor island! The only thing left might be that we go Bolshevik all of us together! The alternative is to place ourselves under Wilson's rule. Sacrifices would be needed in both cases. (31.10.1918)
>
> I am beginning to believe in the general peace now. Germany seems willing to give up. Three causes have worked together: 1) the Bulgarian crisis 2) the internal crisis 3) the mass production of tanks by the Americans. The last is the main cause, if it does come to giving up. We glide into the Anglo-Saxon World Empire and must adjust ourselves to that fact. (8.10.1918)
>
> The German people were growing impatient. Mutiny broke out in Kiel and on 9 November 1918, Liebknecht, the Spartacist leader, prepared to proclaim a soviet republic. Prince Max's cabinet tried to counter by proclaiming the abdication of the emperor. Scheidemann, the social democrat, proclaimed the republic to forestall Liebknecht, much to the fury of the other social democrat Friedrich Ebert, to whom Prince Max handed over his office. The emperor fled to the Netherlands and the same day the workers' and soldiers' councils of Berlin gave a revolutionary blessing to Friedrich Ebert's democratic regime. "Now there is revolution in Germany!" (10.11.1918)

On 9 November, a German provisional government was formed, which, in the words of the British historian John Wheeler-Bennett, was "a pact concluded between a defeated army and a tottering semi-revolutionary régime; a pact destined to save both parties from the extreme elements of revolution but, as a result of which, the Weimar Republic was doomed at birth."[35] The armistice was signed two days later, on 11 November 1918.

It is one year since Johannes came to Constantinople. He has no permanent lodgings. Just now he is the caretaker of the Zafirid Palace (Zarifi Köşkü). The new attaché Paul Mohn, is staying with a German pastor. A bit later Johannes moves to a German *Geheimrat*. There he meets a German officer, Joachim von Ribbentrop. One cannot help wondering what the future foreign minister of Nazi Germany and Johannes Kolmodin discussed while playing bridge (which Johannes did passionately) at this terrible moment in German history. The letter of thanks carries Ribbentrop's enormous signature. In spite of everything, Johannes seems to like the upheavals. At the end of the year, he writes home: "Am exceedingly well and provided for. The servant in the Zafirid Palace looks after me in every way. I work more regularly than in the transition period."

---

35 John Wheeler-Bennett: *The Nemesis of Power*, Macmillan, New York, 1954.

Turkey's Defeat

After Germany's defeat, the hour had also struck for Turkey. Turkey paid a high price for siding with Germany. Russian troops had evacuated East Anatolia after the October revolution and an armistice was signed with Russia, but Turkish resistance was exhausted. On 30 October 1918, the sultan was forced to sign an armistice at Mudros. The victorious Allied powers divided up Turkey into spheres of interest and stipulated that Constantinople was to be occupied by the Allies. Johannes wrote:

> The streets of Constantinople are full of soldiers, German prisoners-of-war in civil clothing, British prisoners from Kut al-Amarna, divisions of French and English soldiers. Jubilant demonstrators greet the arrival of the fleet of the Entente and Izzet Pasha's cabinet is falling. (23.11.1918)

The Turkish capitulations caused a great deal of extra work at the legation, which was looking after German and Bulgarian interests as well as the refugees from Bolshevik Russia who started coming in. In the middle of the Bulgarian crisis, Johannes had to give a formal dinner for "Söderblom's Metropolitan," and Johannes's benefactor Ahmad Refik was awarded the Vasa order by the Swedish king. Everybody at the office was overworked and Kolmodin probably most of all. There was no news from Europe or Sweden for ages and the legation felt cut off from the world. The last Balkan train through Europe had left. "If I go back home now it may not be possible to come back here again," Johannes complained.

At last the long awaited letter from his father arrived. Food had been scarce at home, too, and many people did not have enough to eat, although Sweden was living in peace. The Spanish flu had claimed many lives and to his horror he read that H.S. Nyberg had caught the disease, and, with an added gall bladder complication, had nearly died. "Thank you for the news from Uppsala – I was especially glad that H.S. Nyberg has recovered. Greet him and Zetterstéen!" Then he jumps to his favourite subject: the world situation as seen from Turkey. "The war has gone on too long. It calls for an historical analysis."

> Russia will not be reconstituted. America might perhaps want to grab it, in order to have a counterweight to Japan. Germany was necessary to us (and the Turks) as long as Russia existed; Russia was necessary to France (and England) as long as Germany existed; just like France, we (Swedes) could well do without them both. The important question now is whether we will in time get used to thinking in a, let me say, 17th century fashion. (16.11.1918)

He goes on speculating about Russia's future in a marathon sentence typical of Kolmodin, but worth considering particularly from the perspective of the 21st century. It is a long-winded letter and its universalistic perspective makes it indubitable that its author is a former disciple of Harald Hjärne:

> Regarding Russia, I do not want to relinquish the hope that the decision-makers of the Western powers would gradually arrive at the insight that if you want the *centrifugal* forces to get the upper hand in Central Europe (which is what Western Europe and particularly France must be wanting), you must take care not to let the *centripetal* forces take the upper hand in Eastern

Europe – and realise that the precondition for such a divided and weak Central Europe is a divided and weak Eastern Europe. For us, such a solution to the problem would be quite satisfactory – not least because our national ambitions in this situation might connect us with our traditional position in the 17th and 18th century as a Nordic cornerstone in what was then called the French System. (30.11.1918)

Charles XII and the War

On 30 November 1918, his political friends in Sweden will be commemorating the 200th anniversary of the death of Charles XII. H.S. Nyberg gives a big speech in Uppsala. In several letters, Johannes cogitates on the universal role of the Swedish monarch in a long letter.

More than ever, one is bothered by this: what would not the world have been spared if Charles XII had succeeded in fulfilling his accepted task! But Poland and Turkey did not recognise the hour of their visitation and the German powers stabbed us in the back – well, the poor Germans may now lie on their bed as they have made it! (30.11.1918)

One friend we did have, who really understood what it was all about: Louis XIV, but he was held in check by the gentlemen Marlborough & Co, who might have understood that the victories of Charles XII would have meant increased chances for France in the naval and colonial struggle for competition. And when at last he became free of them in Utrecht, he laid himself down and died. Thus happened what must happen: we were sacrificed, and Europe was presented with Russia and Germany as a gift. Both of them important as counterweights to each other, but the one almost as useless as the other, if they both were to vanish! (Ibid.)

The Germans have sickened me (*ils m'ont dégoutés!!*) with their capitulation policy: a nation which respects itself does not have the right, however much they themselves are to be blamed for it, to lay themselves down for a thrashing. Note the contrast with Napoleon, who rejected all peace offers and continued all the way to Paris! (6.12.1918)

If Charles XII and Sweden had not been left in the lurch by Europe 200 years ago, our continent might have been spared going through the troublesome Russian-Prussian period. Prussian Germany was in reality nothing but the defence organ that Europe had to afford to itself, after it had permitted Tsar Peter to intrude on its territory – therein lay its historic justification. If only Russia had been blocked in time, Central Europe could easily have continued to develop itself in the direction of particularism. (10.12.1918)

In my opinion, it would have been the duty of the Germans to carry on all the way to Berlin, I would then have been more confident about their future. Since they did not have the strength to "*mourir debout*" one cannot be surprised when the French, who on many occasions have shown themselves masters in this most difficult art of a real *Herrenvolk,* to despise them as "*lâches.*" Among the Entente peoples, the English are the ones whose code of honour is most like ours. (Ibid.)

If this is applied to modern conditions, the moral will be that if the New World Order is not so keen to be forced to deal with a consolidated Central Europe again, it should be careful not to restore Russia. There indubitably exists some sort of mystical link here. Europe might, if need be, do without both Russia and Germany, but it could never get along with just one of them and might best of all be rid of them both. (Ibid.)

A lot of what was best in the political development in the 19th century seems to have got lost in the tremendous crisis of the past few years – but maybe it only seems so. *Allah taala bilir* – God only knows. Not so little depends on ourselves from the moral point of view. We must take with us into the New World Era the faith in the spiritual quality of sovereignty which Gustavus Adolphus once vindicated against the Habsburg efforts to establish "an unlawful *monarchia,*" and in the name of that faith, maintain our right to form our judgment as *Swedes*, not as *-ists* or *-ates* of the one or the other kind. (20.12.1918)

He writes from his temporary residence, a palace in "Syra Selvi." "I am very well looked after by a servant and the view over the Bosphorus is fantastic."

In his new year's letter of 1919, Johannes expresses the hope that the new year will mean the great turning point for "us Swedes," on condition that there is a minimum of faith and will in the nation.

> If only those responsible at home would take the necessary measures for the future security of our nation! How can anybody be interested in election laws and such things in great times like these? We have been sleeping ourselves into the position as the gravitation point for Protestantism in our continent – will we never wake up and face it? (13.1.1919)

He feels that Sweden has been sufficiently punished for its surrender and defeat against Russia at Poltava in 1709, which was like the present German defeat. He despises the Germans.

> Can you imagine anything more devoid of style, anything more tasteless and flat than this German revolution? (3.1.1919)
>
> The devastating effects of the dishonourable capitulation are more manifest than ever. Now it is time to return to the order of the day for both Germany and Russia. I hope that the good-natured "Germanophiles" of the ordinary unpolitical rightist kind have now ceased to lie like faithful dogs on Germany's grave and howl, *à la* that misfortune Kjellén. For that there is no cause whatsoever. (10.1.1919)
>
> The more engrossed I have become in its history, the clearer do I see that there is a higher justice of world history in the circumstance of Germany herself not getting to enjoy the fruits of her victory over Russia. Farewell to them both! May they rest in peace! The devotion to our own inalienable tasks in the East can begin to express itself more actively. Even the socialists seem to have acquiesced in this today. I cannot help hoping that the time has come for the fulfilment of those expectations for which Olof Palme went to his death. (Ibid.)

Just at that moment he hears rumours that his twin brothers, both officers, might be facing the same fate as Olof Palme. They are reported as having volunteered to fight the Bolsheviks in Finland and to help the Estonians "get Narva back." Johannes is in a moral quandary and an emotional conflict, as this sequence of letters shows:

> It is difficult to live down here and not know if perhaps Lullu or Gustaf or both are already out to fight the Bolsheviks in Estonia. Imagine, taking part in occupying Narva! I feel as if the curse that has rested upon us for two centuries will at last recede! But I must keep calm. If they have gone, they have done right. I will sit here writing and translating for another couple of weeks. The work on the resurrection of Charles XII has in the course of events turned out to be a more urgent and worthy work than ever. It belongs to the task of upholding Sweden and Swedish thought in the world by also maintaining their history. (10.1.1919)
>
> Today is Gustaf's and Lullu's birthday. But where are they? What are they doing? I was misled by a telegram, the miserable system of communications is utterly trying. Will mail from Sweden ever find its way here again? (17.1.1919)

The rumours cannot be confirmed, neither those about the fall of Narva nor those about a Swedish battalion to take part in the conquest of Narva. In fact, his brothers never even got permission to leave by their superior officers, but for weeks Johannes lives with the uncertainty until,

> … only yesterday I saw in a French paper that our government has declared that they have no reason to help the Estonians, and now there is the news that *the Estonians have already taken Narva themselves* – with Finnish aid! No news whatsoever about a Swedish battalion! I get more and more jealous of Mannerheim's Finland. (24.1.1919)
>
> More than ever I feel that my research on Charles XII's literary resurrection is a burning and worthy task. The task of upholding Sweden and Swedish thought in the world also involves the upholding of Sweden's history. (19.2.1919)
>
> The French consul general has shown a great deal of interest in my research on Charles XII; on the whole, I have found it to be a valuable point of contact. It cannot be disputed that the only one in Western Europe who understood what Charles XII's great struggle was about was Louis XIV – a king whom I have long been inclined to appreciate more than our history books usually do. They are, as in so many other places, full of Jewish liberal prejudices. (4.3.1919)

Johannes congratulates himself on having a circle of friends "on the whole far more interesting than what the *Corps Diplomatique* in general has to make do with." He is planning "a theological tea for the metropolitans and other such folks," and he had given a Turkish tea the previous Saturday for "prophets and poets" ("siare och skalder").

The military attaché, Major af Wirsén, is expected back from one of his journeys. "Wirsén is to be *chargé d'affaires*, while the envoy Anckarsvärd has got smallpox. Strange how he could get infected, since he does not come into contact with any but the upper class and always travels by car!" Johannes remarks, not without malice. "And utterly inconvenient at the present time, when we have half the world on our doorstep, taking care of their interests!"

Johannes feels "mouldy" and tired and during March, April, and May he plans to go to Europe on holiday. But will he be able to go or not? With Wirsén at the helm and Balkan trains moving regularly again, he eventually manages to make travel arrangements to go to Rome, Berlin, and Bern, whence he sends fully scribbled postcards to his mother (Germany in ruins, Switzerland smug and self-satisfied, Rome wonderful). His suitcase is stolen, but happily he gets his new dinner jacket back! And when he returns to Constantinople on 3 June, he finds that the whole of Anatolia is like a volcano.

Beginning of the Turkish War of Liberation

For a historian such as Johannes Kolmodin, with his passionate interest in international relations, it must have been *gefundenes Fressen* to find himself in the middle of an historical situation in which an empire breathed its last and a modern country was created before his very eyes, and his nationalistic ideas of a strong state, a constitution, and a gifted autocratic leader with great powers and individual freedom were put into practice. And this country was Turkey, whose language he spoke and whose people he loved more and more, as he assures those at home.

After the first relief from the suffering at the end of the war, the Turkish people experienced the humiliation of defeat. Soon, however, both in Istanbul and the provinces, officers of the disbanded army and members of the intellectual

The invasion of Izmir by Greek forces led to a series of protest meetings in Istanbul between 23 May 1919 and 13 January 1920 in the Hippodrome. The second meeting took place on 30 May 1919, the one which Kolmodin mentioned. The picture above shows the meeting of 23 May 1919, in which the famous Turkish writer Halide Edip (Adıvar) addressed the people.

Cengiz Kahraman archive

middle class met in secret and began to discuss how to secure tolerable peace conditions. Gradually, a nationalistic movement developed to replace the old and now defunct loyalty to the Ottoman Empire.

The humiliations increased when the Allies handed parts of Anatolia over to Italy, and Britain helped the Greeks to land at Smyrna (Izmir) and march into the interior in 1919. A puppet sultan ruled in Istanbul as Mehmet VI, who appointed as ministers persons who had opposed the Young Turks and were prepared to carry out the Allies' terms. Mustafa Kemal had left Istanbul commanded to act as inspector-general of the eastern Turkish forces, and arrived at Samsun on 19 May.

In fact, the sultan had made this appointment to get him out of the way, as he was making trouble by opposing the Allies in Istanbul. From Samsun, Mustafa Kemal moved inland to Amasya, where a declaration for an independent Turkish state was signed by Rauf Bey, Ali Fuad Pasha, General Kazim Kara Bekir, and several local leaders.

Johannes wrote that the future of Turkey looked much brighter now than before, because the Turks had at last shown themselves capable of unanimity. There had been gigantic mass meetings in Stambul in his absence. On 30 May, hundreds of thousands of men and women had marched in total silence with black flags of mourning from the great mosques to the Hippodrome, and suddenly the old Turkish battle cry *Allah akbar! Allah akbar!* had erupted. Flaming speeches were delivered, along with the appeal by Hamdullah Subhi, "Do not touch our Anatolia!," followed by a prayer for the sultan and the realm, then again *Allah akbar!* The flags decorating the dais carried the slogan, "Turkey cannot perish!"

40   *Sigrid Kahle*

Terapia (Tarabya) in the early 20th century.
Cengiz Kahraman archive

In July, a congress was held at Erzurum made up of delegates from the eastern parts of Turkey free of foreign occupation. The delegation confirmed the protocol and elected Mustafa Kemal as their president. The Grand Vizier had been allowed to go to Paris and had taken his friend, the minister of finance, with him, and in August there was a full cabinet crisis in Constantinople/Istanbul.

> We have a ministerial crisis here, according to what I hear, due to the fact that Enver (Pasha's) father-in-law [should be half-uncle Halil Pasha (Kut)] has managed to get out of prison. The main thing is disagreement about which attitude to adopt towards the national movement in Anatolia. (14.8.1919)

Envoy Anckarsvärd had also returned from Europe and had settled down in the legation's summer residence in Terapia (Tarabya), having first asked Johannes to stay at the legation while he was away, confident that the Turks would not in the meantime try to regain power in Palestine. This possibility, "I for my part would not find so upsetting," Johannes admits to his father in a long letter on 14 August, in which for the first time he touches upon "the Armenian question."

Professor Adolf Kolmodin had asked his son's opinion about the Armenian request for an independent state in eastern Turkey, which was to be sponsored by the Allies. This idea was highly favoured in Europe, where the Armenian massacres of 1915 had filled all informed citizens with horror and pity. In theological and missionary circles, there were deep feelings of sympathy for the Armenian victims. Johannes, in his cold political thinking, separated these wartime events dating back before his arrival from the political issue. He explained to his father why he considered an Armenian state in eastern Anatolia a political disaster.

> Regarding the Armenian question, the heart of the matter is that, even before the so-called massacres, in no part of so-called Turkish Armenia did the Armenians amount to more than one-third of the Turks (one-fourth of the whole population); to separate the province in question from Turkey and call it Armenia would only lead to a situation where the Turkish majority population would rise

in despair and kill the rest of the Armenians. Don't forget that Erzurum is now the seat of the revolutionary Turkish anti-government in Anatolia, from where the national (people's) war against the Greeks is waged and where a Turkish national congress has recently been convened. (14.8.1919)

It seems at present much more likely that the Greeks will soon be pushed out of Smyrna, than that an Armenian government will possess Erzurum. Some small expansion at the cost of Turkey will and perhaps ought to be handed to the former Russian Armenia, Republika Yerevan, where an Armenian majority in reality does exist – but to give the Armenians even half of what they demanded would be to substitute one injustice with a worse injustice and would probably be most dangerous for the Armenians themselves. (Ibid.)

In the same letter, Johannes tells his father about his application for employment at the legation. He is still an honorary attaché. "I would be willing to accept a diplomatic or consular appointment here in Constantinople, in the Caucasus or Persia (possibly Syria, Egypt)," he writes, conscious of the fact that this would imply resigning from his position as docent at Uppsala. He complains about lack of time for his scholarly work because the military attaché af Wirsén is frequently away on official tours. Now the major has returned, and Johannes, who has been caretaker at the major's hired palace, has moved to "more modest lodgings with a narrow iron bed."

In September 1919, a new nationalist conference met at Sivas. "The provinces have united in a general federation with its seat in Sivas and have cancelled all treaties of the central government." (19.9.1919) The conference signed a national pact for an independent Turkey and the liberation of all Turkish territory from foreign rule. Plans were made for the creation of an armed force under the control of the signatories of the national pact. In Istanbul, the parliament, which showed sympathy with the national movement, was shut down and the Allies arrested its national leaders. The internal crisis was coming to a head.

The internal crisis apparently has reached the decisive point. Ferid Pasha's government has fallen, after the English realised that there is neither a point to keeping it up, nor to negotiating with a government that no longer has anybody behind it in the country. We should now be getting a nationalistic government, which at least stands a chance to even out its relationship to the movement in Anatolia. Mustafa Pasha – the Turkish Engelbrekt[36] – stands close to his goal. (2.10.1919)

There is something really grand and uplifting that has occurred: a vanquished nation, believed to be sentenced to death, has risen to defend its right to live – against overwhelming pressure – and has chosen – to quote one of the publishers of the national movement – "rather to risk being crushed than submit to the ignominious fate which seems reserved for it – *indeed, let itself be crushed in order to rise again so much stronger.*" That indeed is something other than the German, Austrian, and Bulgarian tail wagging. Thank God for at least one example of a people that did not surrender! (Ibid.)

How would the Sultan Mehmet VI react in this situation and how would he manage his relations with the Entente powers? Who would he appoint to his new cabinet? Was there still a danger that Turkey might be partitioned?

The Sultan has not yet managed to overcome himself by turning to the men who in the first place deserve his confidence, but he has at least dismissed the perverse national elements in the old cabinet. (3.10.1919)

---

36 Engelbrekt Engelbrektsson (d. 1436), a mine owner from the petty nobility who led a popular rebellion in 1434, when King Erich of Pommerania strove to weld the Scandinavian kingdoms into a centralised absolute monarchy.

As a consequence of the change in government, the unity between the capital and the provinces has been restored. The Turkish Entente-ists have been found useless even by the Entente itself and will now creep back into their rat-holes, applauded by the Entente itself. After this it can hardly be a question of partitioning Turkey – and for those strongly Bolshevik-minded Armenian minorities in the eastern provinces, nobody cares any more, except possibly some Americans. One may sooner expect the well-deserved expulsion of the Greeks from Smyrna. (10.10. 1919)

The old Hjärne disciple Johannes found a historical parallel between the situation in Sweden in the 15th century and his Turkey.

A total agreement about national demands naturally does not exist here [in Turkey] either; a kind of Jöns Bengtsson[37] has popped up in Sivas, a certain Sheikh Rajîb, (a dervish leader), who together with other "notables" has done what he can to spoil the picture. In certain districts, the farmers might perhaps also be persuaded to revolt by other forces than the national ones. A certain Galeb Bej, a kind of Erik Karlsson, who operates in Kurdestan. It is difficult to have an opinion about how it will end. I am beginning to think that on the nationalist side a kind of understanding will have to be reached with the Russians in order to wrest the Western powers back from the Greeks (or at least make them less interesting for them). (30.10.1919)

In October and November, he is preoccupied with ecumenical business for Nathan Söderblom and other Swedish issues, but events at home begin to pale compared to the grand drama of Turkey.

The national movement – the Sivas Committee – is the obvious, undisputed lord in the whole of Anatolia, where the general security does not leave anything to be desired at present. The efforts to lure the Turkish farmers into dubious enterprises are a failure (in spite of the lure of gold). Brigandage exists only in the areas that are practically under occupation of the Entente – as in the surroundings of the capital. (29.12.1919)

Mustafa Kemal, on the other hand, keeps everything in order on his side; the life and property of Christians are placed under the combined guarantee of the confederation – with exception of those convicted of treacherous plots. The prospects are of course not bright, since the Allies are motivated mainly by vengeful feelings. Otherwise, the weakening position of the "Whites" in Southern Russia ought to be a warning to help Turkey to stand on its own legs as soon as possible, and not mess everything up by granting uncalled-for concessions to the Levantine rabble. (Ibid.)

President Wilson, never mentioned favourably by Kolmodin (who did not believe in the League of Nations either), had been uttering strong warning words about "massacres in Cilicia" (Çukurova). Johannes writes:

Such tales are totally fabricated. Wilson, poor devil, is talking through his hat. If security in this city is threatened, it is not so from the side of the Turks. The Levantines are fooling themselves if they imagine that they have anything to gain by these tales. (27.1.1920)

And on top of it these irresponsible Levantine tales about "massacres of Armenians" organised by Mustafa Kemal!! and the Turkish National Federation! Lies, all of it, of course! The French are responsible! With the Poles you can at least argue reasonably! (4.3. 1920)

---

37 Jons Bengtsson, Erik Karlsson – minority leaders who did not follow Engelbrekt – are compared to the Dervish leader Sheikh Rajib of Sivas and the Kurdish rebel Ghalib Bey of Kurdistan, who did not follow Mustafa Kemal.

Another cabinet crisis is brewing. Izzet Pasha is returning. And again those untruthful rumours about Armenian massacres. The consequence: an eternal guerrilla war in Anatolia like the war of the Spaniards against Napoleon 1807-08. (10.3. 1920)

"The events in the Orient roll along just as I have foreseen," Johannes boasts: The Soviet republic of Baku was declared on 27 April 1920. In Ukraine, the Caspian provinces, Azerbaijan, and Armenia the Turks were fighting against the Soviet army. Johannes heard reports that the rightist party *Ittihad-i-Islam* (Unity of Islam) had collaborated with the Bolsheviks, while the attention of the latter was directed at the Armenians

> … who during the last critical weeks, with the hopeless infatuation characteristic of that impossi-
> ble ethnicity, have tried to get armed possession of certain controversial borderlands. It looks as
> if the main forces of Mustafa Kemal are now standing at Erzurum, ready to take the enemy from
> behind […] I suspect that the ephemeral saga of the Armenian republic is now over. (3.5.1920)

This republic would turn out to be far from ephemeral. The Allies recognised the Armenian republic *de jure* in the Treaty of Sèvres, 10 August 1920. The Turks attacked this short-lived republic at the end of September 1920, while the Russians simultaneously advanced on it from Azerbaijan, and the provisions of the Treaty of Sèvres relating to Armenia were annulled. The Armenian signatories had to recognise that there were no Armenian majorities anywhere in Turkey. That was the end of the Armenian republic – but not the end of the stories of new Turkish atrocities against the Armenians. They circulated even at the Conference of Lausanne in 1922-23, as we shall see.

Johannes Kolmodin was a staunch believer in Mustafa Kemal's political aims, a friend of the Muslims and Islamic culture, and an eternal friend of Turkey. What would a man with such loyalties have said about successive modern Turkish governments' refusal to take responsibility for the Armenian massacres of 1895 and 1915? If he could have looked into the future, he would have seen the birth of the first sovereign Armenian republic, the former Soviet state of Armenia, in 1991 – a lonely roost for 3 million inhabitants, cut off from the Russian cultural context, vainly looking towards the EU, while millions of Armenians are doing well in exile in the rest of the world, though no longer in their ancient homeland of Turkey.

Private and Public Affairs, 1920-21

Docent Kolmodin had come to Turkey to do research, but his job at the legation was consuming all his time. What bothered him was his position and low salary.

> My prospects at home seem blocked, too. The best will probably be that I hold out here for some
> time until I have achieved such a position as a Turkologist that they have to give me a profes-
> sor's chair, with the aid of Söderblom. The fact that I have left the main road to the extent that
> I have is taking its revenge. (18.2.1920)

He has, nevertheless, enjoyed one long, intensive research period, delving into Charles XII's Turkish times, adoring "his" viziers, chamberlains, and eunuchs, and making a register of all the Turks who played a role in Charles XII's history, at the same time bringing the chaotic archives of the legation into order.

Grand Rue de Pera in the late 1920s.
Cengiz Kahraman archive

"People at home have no idea what a mess it is to work with Turkish material!" (31.3.1920). He decided to see more of the high Ottoman dynasty still exercising its court life, who knew for how much longer.

> Yesterday, I was invited to an especially private and discreet masked ball, arranged so that the poor little Turkish princesses would have some amusement. I danced the Boston with a little princess in red and sat for a while in a corner with the daughter of the Sultan, princess Karanfil ("carnation"), and quoted Turkish poetry to her. Her husband Daoud Ismail Hakki Bey – the son of the former Grand Vizier Tewfik Pasha – was also there; I have known him for a long time. I have planned to devote myself more than hitherto to the high Ottoman dynasty. The younger princes are very nice people, almost like Prussian lieutenants of the good old days, and the princesses are, as far as can be judged from their eyes and stature, outstandingly sweet. (18.3.1920)
>
> This afternoon I had tea with Prince Osman Fuad, the representative of the Sultan in Tripolis during the war; he has recently married quite a delightful little Egyptian princess – I have never seen such a charming feminine creature. The prince himself has the merit of mixing superb *cocktails* – (these are as we know forbidden in the Koran). (31.3.1920)

Johannes Kolmodin had become indispensable. His inside information and efficiency were unmatched. His Turkish was perfect. However, he had neither the position nor the salary of a diplomat. Was he to aim at employment or pursue a scholarly career? His Tigrinya grammar had never appeared, although it had been lying ready in 1915! His friend Axel Boëthius suggested that he should teach history and political science for a year at Stockholm University. But what would then happen to his position at the embassy and his position as docent at Uppsala University? What to do, really?

Envoy Anckarsvärd was to be posted to Warsaw and the controversial envoy Gustaf Wallenberg would come from Stockholm (his previous position had been Tokyo, 1906-18) to take his place during the spring of 1920.

Panoramic view of the Golden Horn in the early 20th century.

I will not be able to say anything about my diplomatic position for certain until I have met the new minister. (27.2.1920)

Anckarswärds left last Sunday. Wallenberg's arrival is postponed until the end of the month. It will be interesting to know this man. I hope he will be more rewarding than his predecessor. (10.3.1920)

At last envoy Wallenberg arrived and a new era started at the Swedish legation, an era that would last as long as Kolmodin stayed in Istanbul. His expectations were high.

Envoy Wallenberg seems to be an unusually energetic person, of quite different metal from his predecessor. (8.4.1920) The new minister is busy as a bee and has a need to be informed about everything, which his predecessor lacked. He interests me as a phenomenon. (12.4.1920) Last Monday the minister handed over his credentials and I had the honour to be introduced to his Majesty the Padishah – this time in the Yildiz kiosk. Such pageants are always amusing. (28.4.1920)

I could not write to Papa today, because I had to run errands for the new minister this morning. He has taken up my time night and day during the past week. (7.6.1920)

Johannes expected the new envoy to bring him news about his future.

The issue about my future has got into a tangle. The Foreign Ministry has written to him that they want to employ me (in which capacity I do not know), but then the counsellor, Major Lind af Hageby, would become redundant. I only earn half the salary of Lind but they think that I am a greater acquisition than he. I think they are right, if I may say so myself [...] I think that we could do without Lind. He was employed mainly to take care of the German interests (the Germans paid half his salary). The minister is happy to have us both, but seems a bit scared of Lind. (11.6.1920)

Saint Sophia (Aya Sofya) and the Fountain of Wilhelm II in Sultanahmet Square.
Cengiz Kahraman archive

> Wallenberg has asked the ministry for a new military attaché or a lawyer. Hope they won't
> send another officer but instead increase mine and Broman's salaries. What we need is a typist.
> Quiet, hardworking people, to whom I really belong, don't amount to much in this world! One
> might wish to be a Bolshevik! (Ibid.)

Wallenberg went on European leave and Johannes was hurt when the envoy
did not make him *chargé d'affaires* but chose instead Lind af Hageby, a man who
was a real problem for Johannes. He confesses to his mother:

> Lind is now better so that he can resume at least part of his work – but instead there has been
> extra work at the legation. Wallenberg is ill in Stockholm. (31.10.20)
> Lind af Hageby is ill again. This time it is typhoid. It would be a sheer scandal if a man like
> him would be able to wheedle himself into the Foreign Ministry. He just doesn't do any work
> […] Now Lind af Hageby is beginning to turn up at the legation, but sporadically; he is almost
> more of a bother than when he was lying ill at home. It is without parallel that a deputy chief of
> mission has been ill for a month without informing the people at home. (21.12.20)

In the autumn 1920, docent Johannes Kolmodin was granted prolonged leave
from Uppsala University and envoy Wallenberg had finally negotiated a position
for him as "extraordinary dragoman of the legation" (the title used for the official translators to the Sublime Porte) with a better salary for him. "Happy news!
He managed to get me more than 7,000, yes 10,000. Things are beginning to
shape up. I hope to be able to send some home!" Johannes writes to his mother.
(24.9.1920)

His life changed for the better in September 1920 when he moved into the
upper floor of a modest but charming house in the old Turkish quarters of
Stambul with a view over the Marmara Sea, "far away from Pera and the diplomatic tea parties." In Pera, such an apartment would cost four times as much.
"Don't worry, Mother! Stambul has more sun and air than Pera; it reminds me of

Strängnäs!" Here it would be easier to live frugally and to devote himself to his own work.

Stambul was an excellent address for someone who wanted to absorb and observe Turkish life from the inside, but many a career diplomat raised an eyebrow. An important member of the Swedish colony, Fröken Ullin, helps him to move in. He tells his mother about the furniture he is buying, about the size of the rooms, about the garden plants. He employs a Turkish housekeeper, Aisja Kadyn, who becomes a dear character in his letters home.

Whoever visits this neighbourhood today can still feel what its peace and harmony must have meant to the overworked diplomat. The balcony overlooked a small courtyard with a tiny mosque (Keçecipaşazade) from whose minaret the muezzin called followers to prayer five times a day. The quarters all around were and still are inhabited by ordinary Turks whose daily rhythms of life were determined by their religious habits and feasts. He happened to arrive just in time for the celebration of "*Bairam*," the end of Ramadan, and from now on his letters are full of descriptions of Muslim customs, ceremonies, and festivities, whose dignity he admires.

He has the additional role of cultural attaché, both in a public and a private capacity. He moves with intellectuals, he goes to a Turkish operetta with the action set in the Tulip epoch, "but a poetic evening with Turkish poets was not so well attended." He gives literary teas at which Ottoman poets recite poetry. He is interested in folklore, as he was in Eritrea, and translates the simple songs of the people. Nationalistic poets come to him. He translates difficult Turkish poetry, including the Independence March (later the national anthem), and asks Nathan Söderblom to get them into a Swedish newspaper along with an article on "Ottoman Poets in Sorrow" (*Dagens Nyheter*, 25 September 1921). He comments that "my translations are quite successful *if I may say so myself.*" He gives talks about Swedish literature and writes to Selma Lagerlöf and asks her if he may use a recently published story of hers. She refuses rather coldly, but suggests that he may find an old story in a magazine called *The Ghost Tracks*. He writes in another context that he wished that she had never won the Nobel Prize.[38]

A treatise on Caroline Grand Viziers is in preparation. He has found new facts about Turkish-Russian relations just before the Swedish king Charles XII arrived in Turkey. He asks his father to send off-prints of a minor Turcological work, *Tschakydschy der Blitz,* to Nyberg, Hjärne, Littmann, Haralds, Zetterstéen, etc. – proof that he still does academic work! He is working on a treatise on Tjörlulu (Çorlulu) Pasha.

His social life seems to be very far from being boring!

Last Sunday, all the poets of Stambul of the "new school" came to my house for *aksjandjylik,* "evening meeting." They recited their latest poems and had even composed a ghazel for me. I offered them anchovy sandwiches (I had recently been given a tin by a captain of the Orient Line), which was much appreciated. A newly arrived poet from Angora joined us. (16.10.1921)

German professors, that is nowadays they are properly speaking from Bohemia, are beginning to surface here. Yesterday (Sunday) I had a visit from 2 of them. It was quite pleasant to have some academic company again, Orientalists at that, the one an Arabist, the other one a Turcologist, with abstruse and Kufic special interests, such as preparations for a thesis on the rites of circumcision! (28.11. 1921)

---

38 Selma Lagerlöf was awarded the Noble Prize in 1909.

The Greco-Turkish War

Now let us turn to the macro events of the day and Kolmodin's reactions to the ongoing drama. We left the main forces of Mustafa Kemal at Erzurum in 1920, ready to take the confederate forces from behind. "The effort to strike down the Turkish confederate forces by internal forces is now over," he stated at the end of May.

> The Turkish nationalists now seem to have taken steps to join the Bolsheviks. France is beginning to withdraw from this hazardous game. They have left Cilicia except for the harbour of Marina. We must reckon with the English keeping the Dardanelles over the summer. (7.6.1920)
>
> Here in Constantinople we are now, on the other hand, over the last few days within sound of Mustafa Kemal's cannons; there is fighting on the other side of Skutari [Üsküdar], and it appears so far as if the nationalists are doing well and had a good deal more artillery – even big artillery – than one could have imagined. The English have blown up the forts on the Bosphorus in order to stop them from digging in there. Difficult, however, to believe that this is already the main attack; I suspect that it will take place in the Caucasus and Baghdad – in order to drop the curtain which, after the fall of Baku, is being pulled down between the Mediterranean and Indian spheres of interest of the British. (19.6. 1920)

It turned out that the main attack would be directed against Greece. The Greek army had been authorised by the Allied supreme council to land at Smyrna in May the year before. In June 1920, the Greeks proceeded to occupy western Anatolia and eastern Thrace. Shortly afterwards, hostilities broke out between Greeks and Turks. On 3 July, the Greek offensive was stopped. Johannes heard rumours of a successful Turkish counter-offensive:

> … but it is not very likely that Mustafa Kemal can really think about a general counter-offensive now; for his main armed force is no doubt the guerrilla, which can only be mobilised further into the country –where the 'Hellenes' of course will avoid to go. (3.7.1920)

Shortly afterwards, Johannes set out on a diplomatic mission to Smyrna via Piraeus, from where he sailed to Cairo by boat and from there to Jaffa, Bethlehem, and Jerusalem. It had taken long to get the *laisser-passer*. One wonders what this exact mission was. An effort to convince the Allied authorities of the just Turkish cause? To sound out the political situation in the Near East? ("All is quiet in Palestine.") Well, it was financed by SEM, so it was perhaps just a holiday, but it gave him an opportunity to see Smyrna and to make official calls everywhere. We can be sure that he made full use of his personal experiences.

On 10 August 1920, the Treaty of Sèvres was signed by Sultan Mohammed VI's envoys as dictated by the Allied powers. Under the terms of the treaty, Greece was awarded eastern Thrace up to the Çatalca Line, including Gallipoli, together with the district of Smyrna (Izmir). The Treaty of Sèvres meant that Turkey would lose all its former empire and it deliberately aimed at completely destroying the independence of Turkey. The sultan was allowed to remain at Istanbul but under Allied protection. A tripartite agreement between Britain, France, and Italy laid out French and Italian spheres of influence in Anatolia. The six eastern *vilayets* (provinces) were to be handed over to the Armenian Republic, the exact boundaries to be confirmed through the arbitration of President Woodrow Wilson.

The news that the sultan had signed led to a wave of indignation in the National Assembly in Ankara and in all the parts of Anatolia that were not under Allied occupation. Kolmodin noted that the great national surge he had witnessed at the meetings to protest the occupation of Smyrna in 1919 visibly changed into a mood of sorrow and dejection among nationalistic Turks. The Sublime Porte did not have the power to refuse to sign what was popularly known as "the nation's death sentence." Any hope built on the improvised national contingency plan of Mustafa Kemal had been thwarted. "The mood in Constantinople is dark."

Turkey eventually refused to ratify the Treaty of Sèvres, and from this opposition emerged the great national revival under Mustafa Kemal Pasha. The situation was complicated by events in Greece. In the elections of 14 November 1920, Venizelos was defeated and a royalist majority was returned. King Constantine was restored to the throne, although the Allies had formerly dethroned him. The fall of Venizelos alienated the Allies, especially France. Owing also to the dismissal of Venizelist officers, some of whom were executed, the Greek army was seriously weakened.

In January 1921, a poorly equipped and underpaid Greek army prepared an offensive into Anatolia, with the connivance of British Prime Minister Lloyd George, in order to extend Greek territory beyond what was permitted by the Treaty of Sèvres and to seize control of a large part of western Anatolia and so break the Turkish national movement. "It has been an agonising time ever since the Greek offensive started on 22 March," Johannes wrote.

> The war seems, however, to work out better than expected, I don't think the Greeks stand much of a chance to get out of this foolish war of plunder, which started by their getting a thorough beating. Their "morale" should be somewhat low after this. (12.4.1921)

The Greeks advanced in January, February, and March, but were forced to withdraw in April 1921 as a result of a Turkish victory under Ismet Pasha at İnönü. The sacrifice of so much indisputably Turkish territory aroused great feeling at Ankara. The Grand National Assembly appointed Mustafa Kemal generalissimo with almost dictatorial powers. He dug in on the Sakarya River and forbade any soldier on pain of death to retire from his position. The siege was to last for almost a year.

All of this was with the connivance Lloyd George. Kolmodin, who follows the events step by step in his letters, was grieved at Britain's anti-Turkish attitude:

> While the All India Party believes that Turkey is the root and origin of all troubles in the colonial world and, therefore, wishes to crush it in cold blood, which no doubt has helped to push the Greeks forward, there exist on the other hand in Angora agents of a different policy, who all the time have desired an understanding with the Turks and keep inciting them not to reduce their claims under any circumstances. (12.4.21)

"England is incapable of conducting a land war just now," he speculates.

> But it has nothing against Greece wearing itself out, for it is hoping that the Turks as victors will also be quite worn out afterwards, which perhaps is not so certain, when a people have gone through such a holy experience as the Anatolian national revolt, and have such

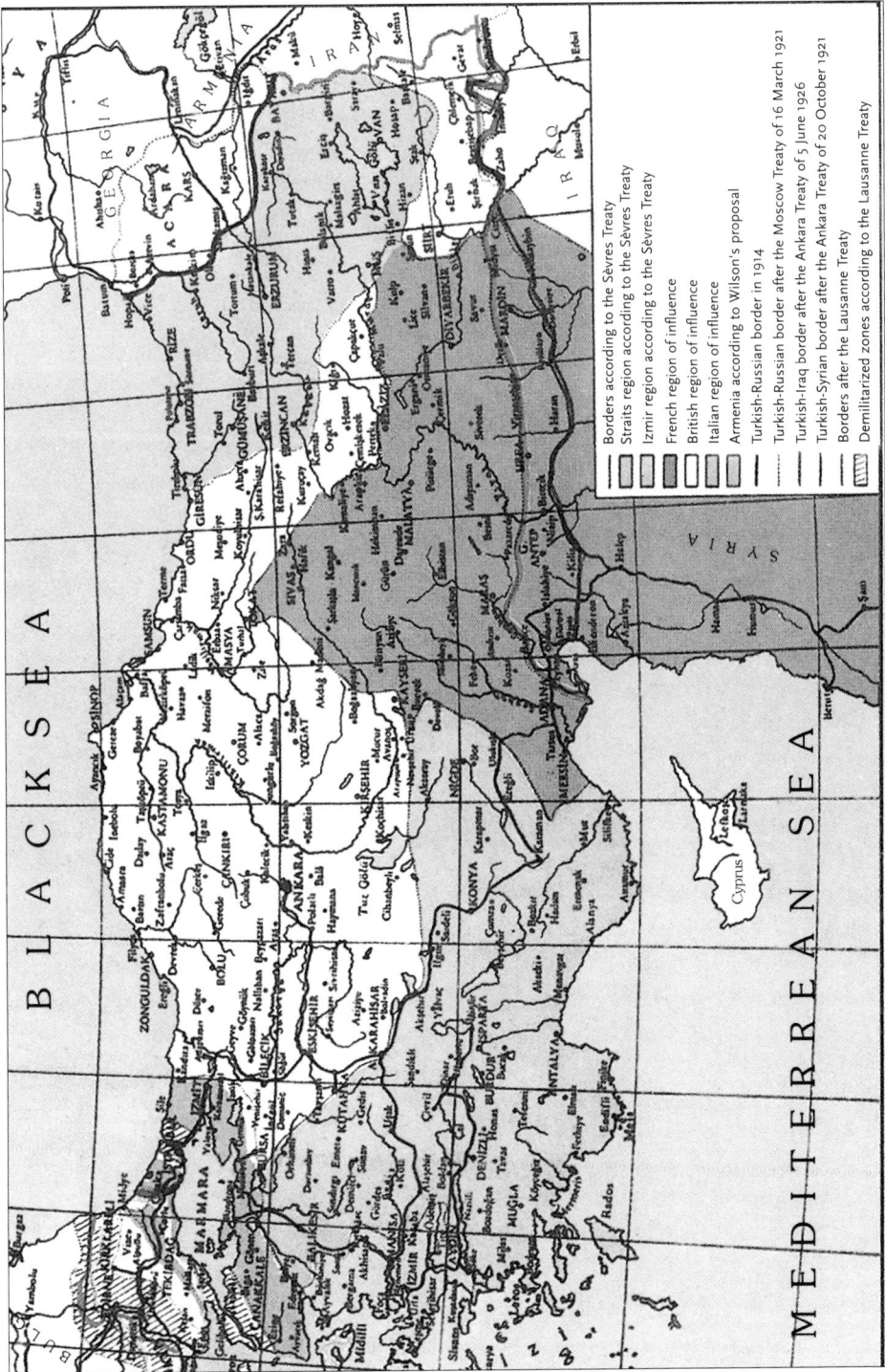

Turkey after the Treaty of Sèvres.

Atatürk, *Nutuk*, (Edited by: Kemal Bek), Bordo Siyah Yayınları, Istanbul, 2005

a leader by God's grace as Mustafa Kemal. The latter does not want a full-scale war if he can help it, I think. The behaviour of the Greeks towards the poor Muhammedan population in the occupied territory cries out to the heavens. Mustafa Kemal rules in an ideal way in the interior of the country, where no uncalled-for interventions can bring disorder and anarchy. (Ibid.)

During the spring (March 1921) , a Turkish delegation signed a friendship treaty in Moscow with Russia after the commander at Erzurum had driven the Armenians out of the Caucasus and made contacts with Russia in Georgia. The Russians agreed to send arms and munitions to the new Turkish national army. By this treaty, the USSR was the first country to recognise the national government of Turkey. The Menshevik government of Georgia was overthrown and a Bolshevik government was set up and recognised the Turkish claim to territories that had earlier belonged to Turkey.

Johannes had been overloaded with work at the legation due to a shortage of staff and feels too tired at night to write private letters. The summer unfolds at Terapia (Tarabya) and is rather calm. But in July 1921, the Greeks resumed their offensive in order to forestall a Turkish attack. Kolmodin speculates:

It is their first offensive but I think that it might be the last, because if they are beaten again – as it now looks likely – they probably will not manage another. I suspect that Ismet Pasha has all sorts of surprises ready for the army of invasion. The decisive moment has not yet come. The outcome will not be decided on the battlefield only but [...] also in Moscow. I ask myself if England may be trying to separate the Bolsheviks from the Turks by offering Lenin and Trotsky the ownership of Constantinople? Since these gentlemen have rather clever heads, I fear that no more would come out of it for English politics than half a year ago, when they sacrificed Georgia to the Russians. (11.7.1921)

His mother Nelly seems particularly interested in the outcome of the war, for his letters are now often to "dear little Mama." She feels for Greece. In July he tells her:

Greek successes will probably prove more dangerous for the Greeks themselves, not to speak of how dangerous for England. The Turkish army is intact although it has lost ground because of some unhappy coincidence. And Rusiloff is in Angora. The Turks have good nerves – you see it here also, and in Angora they seem not to have the slightest doubt of the final victory. (31.7.1921)

The Greeks managed to take back Eskişehir and Kütahya and pressed forward in the direction of Ankara. Nelly Kolmodin thought that they had won. But he assures her:

No, the Greeks have *not* won the war yet! The Turkish army has been out-manoeuvred from Eskisehir, but it is intact and the Greek losses are much greater than the Turkish losses, their booty is next to none, and their prisoners few. The Greeks stand far inside the country without communications and with insufficient ammunition. The disappointment in the Greek press is so great [...] that there have been speculations about treason in the general staff. Even more than at the beginning of the offensive, I think one may cast the horoscope such that Greece, unless unforeseen circumstances occur, simply *cannot* win this war. They have at the most succeeded in postponing the catastrophe. (7.8.1921)

On 16 August 1921, Johannes is going to a soirée at the Greek high commissioner's summer palace. "One has to keep up with that side also," as he writes to his Mama.

There I was told that the Greek offensive was resumed yesterday morning. Since I have reason to believe that the Turks are not willing to fight in earnest for another couple of weeks, I am inclined to think that they will retreat slightly. The sack into which they will tie the Themistocleans will afterwards be so much deeper and easier to close. Mustafa Kemal in his 6 August proclamation, when he was taking over the highest command, at any rate promised the *annihilation* of the enemy. I think that will be the way it goes.

I just had a greeting today from Angora, from one of my friends there. They seem not to have the slightest doubt of the final victory. And probably they are right. For they really need a reminder of the power of *faith* and *justice* on this corrupted planet. That does not mean that one cannot communicate with the Greeks also, since they after all do exist, and apart from that fact constitute quite an interesting phenomenon. The High Commissioner himself is undoubtedly a man of honour. And so probably is King Constantine, in spite of having the unthankful task of trying to create order in the complicated heritage left by that swindler Venizelos. (16.8.1921)

"The war is in the balance," he has to admit to Mama a week later, however.

Mustafa Kemal has not yet brought forth his Caucasian army to the Western front; but the Greeks on the other side were not willing to wait until then – they have attacked before their preparations were finished. The battle apparently is fought around the ruins of the old Phrygian capital Gordium; let us see if any of the parties may untie the Gordian knot. The information is contradictory, but that much seems evident, that the Greeks are encountering much greater difficulties in their continued forward movement than they thought earlier. (24.8.1921)

Meanwhile, the Turkish army had been organised and trained. Ammunition was obtained from old German stocks and new Russian sources.

My predictions about the Greek-Turkish war are beginning to prove right. The Greeks have not arrived at Angora and in the streets of Stambul people are singing, "To Angora Constantine's way will never sway." But on the other hand the Greeks do have certain chances of getting out of the dangerous blind alley in which they find themselves, because Mustafa Kemal does not have enough ammunition to be able to exploit the situation effectively (which reminds me of Tsar Peter's situation at Prut). But, will the British take Smyrna from the Greeks before the Turks have the time to get there? (10.9.1921)

The Greeks were severely checked by Kemal on 13 September 1921 on the Sakarya River, and were obliged to withdraw. On 20 September, Johannes writes a very long letter to "My own little Mama:"

The past week has been very rich in events. Since the 13th it is now clear that I will in any case be proved right in my estimation of the future of the Turks and the Greeks. That was the day when the Greeks were driven back over the Sakarya River with losses which the most sanguine friends of the Greeks estimated at 30,000 and enthusiastic friends of the Turks at 60,000. Seeing that Mustafa Kemal conducted his defensive war with a minimum of people, and brought forth fresh troops from the border of Caucasus only at the moment of victory, the chances for the Greeks to succeed in saving a functioning army by retreating to the coast are not particularly bright.

Like the signal of a hunter to his companions when the exhausted game can finally be hunted to its death is the resounding call in the Regent's proclamation to the general popular uprising in the whole of Anatolia – the enemies who run away will obviously be declared scot-free
for all. I strongly suspect that the Greeks' flight will be as worthy of the inventor of the
Marathon run as their famous flight from Larissa in 1896 – under Crown Prince Contantine's
more or less nominal higher command. Poor king, all right – but why on earth should he tackle
the shining and terrible hero, who God "in his mercy upon the world" has resuscitated here,
comforting those who had begun to despair about universal reason? (20.9.1921)

This rhetorical "masterpiece," referring to the Greco-Turkish war of 1896-97,
was further developed in a greeting to his brother Torsten, whose sentimentality
about King Constantine's kingdom Johannes found "rather exaggerated," since
His Very Royal Majesty, more or less against his free will, in any event half
against his better knowledge, had made himself a tool of Britain.

King Constantine will have the alibi that he probably has acted against better knowledge, if
any. It will be amusing to see if the Greeks will put the crown on their stupidities by driving
him away now after having taken him back once. That would probably be the end to the Greek
ditty. Constantine has made himself the instrument of England. Good-natured people in Europe
see this as decency towards the vanquished – and do not see the ugly things happening on the
larger scene in the East. As though it were for the sake of "right and righteousness" that Lloyd
George took his stand in the question of Upper Cilicia! It is good to have something to put
pressure on France when it is a question of continuation with the violation of Islam!
(10.9.1921)

It is interesting that Johannes considers violation of Turkey equal to violation
of Islam. Already, the Heimdal students at Uppsala considered Turkey and Islam
as identical twins in the process of the awakening of the East. Also, one cannot
help sensing a tone of *schadenfreude* as soon as things go wrong between
England and France, things that divide the Great Power camp.

In October, the retreating Greeks had reached Yenişehir and Inegöl east of
Bursa. "For Greece it goes backward steadily," Johannes wrote to his father.

After months of negotiations, an agreement between France and Turkey was
signed on 20 October 1921 at Ankara. France gave up its claim to Cilicia, retaining only the *sanjak* of Alexandretta (Iskenderun), and undertook to supply
Turkey with arms. Whatever sympathy France had for Greece was diminished
when Aristide Briand's government fell in January 1922 and was succeeded by
that of Raymond Poincaré.

Regarding the misdeeds of the Greeks *à propos* an article in *Nya Dagligt Allehanda* (by Miss
Ellen von Platen) for which she got the material partly from me, partly from the International
Red Cross in Geneva, an Allied, not pro-Turkish investigation commission, which, upon the
demand of the Sublime Porte visited the occupied areas south of the Marmara Sea (and was
accompanied by a delegate from the International Red Cross, Mr. Maurice Gebri) has reached
the conclusion that the Greek military authorities systematically and deliberately aimed for the
extinction of the Turkish population.

It appears to me, if one wants to be fair, that this must be seen as something rather more
important than what the Turks can be blamed for in Armenia. The Turks defended their country against the Russians and in the course of that did perhaps exercise more violence than the

situation demanded, against an unpatriotic population element suspected of lack of patriotism and collusion with the enemy behind the army's back. The Greeks have come as conquerors to a foreign land and have permitted themselves to massacre to a great extent the foreign population they have encountered there.

Anything as awful as that only medieval Byzantine history can match. If ever a people has placed itself outside civilisation, I might say it is the Greeks now. (23.10.1921)

And here we leave the Greco-Turkish war for the time being to consider Johannes Kolmodin, the private person, for a while.

Kolmodin in Stambul 1922

On New Year's Day 1922, he receives the tins of Swedish herring, long underpants, and a novel by Gjellerup that the Kolmodin family has sent him. In his new year letter, Johannes complains of an unpleasant bout of malaria, to be cured with castor oil. Johannes hates the harsh winters in Istanbul. He sends greetings to Mama, Martin and Gerda, Lennart and Ulla, Lillan, Gustaf, Lullu, Olle, Torsten, and old aunt Edla, wanting details about their lives. He always writes for their birthdays. He is in frequent contact with his father. Most of all he is longing for his mother. He loves her handwriting: "It is as open, sweet, and peaceful as your face; yes, I can see your face in your handwriting."

He is 36 years old and homesick and always has a Swedish flag on his table: "I always have Mother's and Father's portraits in front of me. I am *longing* for you but don't see any chance of visiting home Mama dear! If I could only hold my arms around Mama properly just now just once this evening! And Papa, too!" he wrote on New Year's Day 1922.

On 31 January, Adolf Kolmodin writes to him from Sweden that Harald Hjärne has died. Johannes only comment: "Strange that he is gone." What an understatement! On 22 February "mine and George Washington's birthday was celebrated." In March: "It has fallen to my lot to negotiate with Russians of the Red kind and I manage quite well with them. Moreover I cannot deny the fact that as an old enemy of democracy I have a certain sympathy for the Russian oligarchy." (10.3.1922)

On another day, Johannes visits his old friend Hamdullah Subhi Bey and, on that occasion, meets Mustafa Kemal's commissioner for foreign affairs. He gives two teas in the afternoon, one for Hasan Tahsin Bey, a former minister of finance, and one for Mme Grégoire Apikian and her friend Joachim von Ribbentrop, later Hitler's foreign minister, together with Captain von Holstein. Aisja Kadyn does her best to serve elegant teas. On 24 March 1922, the Paris inter-allied conference recommends an armistice between the Greek and Turkish armies, but the Turks under Kemal demand the total evacuation of Anatolia.

In April, there is a lot of coming and going at the legation. Lind af Hageby leaves the legation, "probably for good this time." What a relief! Einar af Wirsén passes through on his way to Athens.

He is now Envoy af Wirsén. But what an unfortunate moment to hand over diplomatic letters of credit to King Constantine! I have not yet heard from Axel Boëthius. Has he left Uppsala? We are expecting Professor Fredrik Böök from Lund, who travels for *Svenska Dagbladet*. Then there has been a little sossie, Phil.Cand. from Lund. Cple's relations with the homeland are getting quite animated. (2.4.1922)

In April, there is a flurry of Swedish visitors. Count and Countess Wrangel *en route* from Egypt, archaeologists, insist on being taken to the famous Dr. Kolmodin in Stambul and to be taken by him to the Topkapi Serai and the Sultan Ahmed (Blue) Mosque. "There are so many visitors that I have no time to write letters," he complains, "[but] a guest from Uppsala is always welcome." (12.4.1922)

During this spring, every intellectual Swede of any stature coming to Turkey seems eager to visit the legendary Kolmodin in his charming Stambul home. Some are old friends. Axel Boëthius wants to rent a house in Constantinople for the Swedish Orient Society. Johannes finds that hospitality costs money. The rise in his salary was a chimera. He has almost paid his debt to Sven Hedin, and if he just sits still he may be able to return to Sweden next year, he hopes. The recent visit of Levi Petrus has made him think of Sven Lidman, whom he has not heard from for a very long time. The isolation of the war years has been broken, and he is not forgotten although he is neglected. He rather enjoys his guests from home after all. "They will see who is running the legation," he writes to his mother.

> It is rather amusing that quiet workers – to whom I myself probably belong – do not have so much to reckon with in this world. Wallenberg, for instance, who cannot manage anything without me, could not imagine me as his *chargé d'affaires* [...] Today, Fredrik Böök is coming, en route from Konstanza. I have already started preparations with the Turks for his visit – a kind of impresario service. I am Böök's *Effendi*. It will result in a lecture in French at the Turkish university about modern Swedish literature. We are of course going to push for him wherever we can. (28.4.1922)

Fredrik Böök writes in his book, *Journey to Constantinople*,[39] about the wonderful evenings on Dr. Kolmodin's balcony in the moonlight, with Swedish herring and schnapps and fabulous conversations. Johannes introduces him to the witty figure and legendary humorous character Nasreddin Hodja and inspires in him a passion for Mustafa Kemal, whom they both compare to Engelbrekt and Gustav Vasa. No doubt the views Böök expresses in the book on Mustafa Kemal's heroic struggle and the Greco-Turkish War reflect the views on the subject of his host. Böök gives Johannes an acute feeling that he ought to have some scientific baggage with him on his return to Sweden. Then, another visitor arrives.

> Böök left yesterday – and I thought that for a while I would be left in peace by travelling Swedes (which does not mean to say that I did not enjoy both Kjellberg and Böök), but today, there was the sudden appearance of a sossie, Phil.Cand. Allan Vougt, a collaborator of Artur Engberg, with whom I shall probably have a lot of trouble. He had forgotten to get an Allied visa and was nearly not allowed to go ashore. Otherwise, he has some kind of a student scholarship. (6.5.1922)

A week later, Johannes has somewhat changed his mind about the young socialist.

> The boy turned out to be quite refreshing and had the whole "wisdom" of academic leftists, for whom all problems are truly solved. He wants a Swedish republic and such nonsense. But he has been sitting in Malmö, where he has acquired certain views on the Oriental problems, which are not too different from mine. Yes, this sossie turned out to be quite o.k. (18.5.1922)

---

39 Fredrik Böök: *Resa till Konstantinopel genom Mellanmeuropa våren 1922*, Stockholm, 1922.

In May, the tide is out in his letters to his parents. He feels worn out. There has been a week of tropical heat and he has been bathing in the Black Sea. "Here it is Ramadan now," he writes in a long pencilled letter,

> ... this wonderful popular feast, when life is upside down for a whole month, when people sleep in the daytime and are out at night, when the light crowns of the minarets burn every night over the festive Stambul, when the drums go at 1/2 3 every night to wake up the faithful, who may have gone to sleep, so that they should put something into their stomachs before the new day of fast arises. Aisja Kadyn is not to be counted on – she is in the mosque almost the whole night (at the Nur-i-Osmanli, a delightful baroque mosque, the mosque of the ladies this year), and when she returns and has eaten her early morning meal she is too sleepy to [prepare] breakfast […] At night, she excels in giving us sweets. (8.5.1922)

We students of Kolmodin's life who have visited the street where he lived in old Stambul can almost feel what the atmosphere was like when the little mosque in his courtyard was lit up on Almighty Night, as K.V. Zettersten has it in the Swedish version of the Koran, but which Johannes calls The Night of Fate.

> We approach the Night of Fate, *kádyr gédje-si* between 26 and 27 Ramazan, when the Angel Gabriel appeared to the Prophet for the first time, *leilat ul-qádir*, the greatest feast of Islam. The Night of Fate is better than a thousand days. When the angels and the Spirit come down on the table of their Lord for the sake of their Lord. Let us see what sources of strength the united prayers or nights of millions can open for the East, which is fighting for its freedom. (16.5. 1922)

The young socialist Alan Vougt is still around. Now he has Johannes to introduce him to a Turkish socialist, not a species to be seen at Johannes Kolmodin's tea parties.

> It was hard to find someone, but after some time I got hold of a chap who was the head of some kind of *isjgi derneji* (workers' union) and was supposed to be a sossie. Vogt went there but returned somewhat disappointed when it turned out that the man was a communist. The organisation apparently does not have a large following, its organ *Zia* (The Light) is printed in Bulgaria. Communism in Bulgaria doesn't seem to be as harmful as it appeared from a distance. (2.6.1922)

Johannes Kolmodin felt genuinely sorry when, on the very day of "zoctsibairam" (Şeker Bayramı) when the fast is broken, "that nice young socialist Allan Vougt left Constantinople." At about the same time, his letters home show increased concern about the rumours of renewed Armenian massacres, at a time when world opinion seemed to disregard reports of Greek misdeeds.

Turks, Armenians, Greeks

In May and June 1922, the "old stories of Turkish atrocities towards the Armenians" were circulating again. Johannes thought he knew where they came from.

> An American idiot, sent out by the American Relief of the Middle East, has worked to sow the seeds of mistrust between Turks and Armenians, so that the authorities thought it safest to expel him, to avoid clashes with local elements. [He] invented a lot of cock-and-bull stories and when he was expelled by the local authorities, who were informed about the true circumstance

through Jowell's own superiors, he turned to the British, in whose policy we hear the old hack-
neyed song against the Turks. (18.5.1922)

The result is a big commotion caused by a vengeful adventurer's unproved and rejected propositions, while the outrageous evil deeds of the Greeks in West Asia, certified by an international
commission, are hardly mentioned in the world press! World opinion is a nice humbug indeed!
Most unpleasantly, one cannot help remembering that the same kinds of gossiping chatterboxes
were in action during the weeks just before the occupation of Constantinople in 1920. The head of
the local Standard Oil, a distinguished American, told me today as we happened to meet in the
street: *"This looks bad. May the English be wise enough not to make a mess of it again. It is a bad
sign that the English censorship here does not allow the press to counter these lies."* (Ibid)

Johannes was conscious of Swedish missionary feelings of solidarity and compassion with the Christian Armenians after what had happened in 1915. He was
afraid that the missionaries might be ready to believe the rumours that such atrocities were happening again and on the command of his "shining hero," Mustafa
Kemal.

Regarding Mr. Jowell's black picture of Anatolia, the truth is now coming out. The Anatolian
orthodox congress of Kayseri have protested against the slander, expressing regrets that the government had thought it sufficient to expel Jowell, who deserved death for his intrigues. The
Congress altogether denies that there are minorities in Anatolia. There are only Turks there,
(Muhammedans and Christians), who are all determined to continue the struggle for their freedom and independence. Both among Muhammedans and Christians there have unfortunately
been some traitors, against whom the Government has acted, as was its right and duty, without
considering their religion. The Congress, on behalf of the Anatolian Christians, declines every
foreign intervention as neither necessary nor useful and expresses its full confidence in the government of National Defence. (2.6.1922)

The rumours eventually reached generalissimo Mustafa Kemal himself. In a
speech on 18 June, in Izmid (Nicodemia) at the reception for the French writer
Claude Farrère, the generalissimo denied the rumours in rather strong terms:

Our enemies insist, basing themselves upon the dirty pamphlet of the liar Jowell, that Turkey is
persecuting Christians, but there is nothing to support it, except their wish to bring confusion in
the civilised world, and to scare away those people who are beginning to recognise Turkey's
rights and the sanctity of the cause for which it struggles. All their propositions are nothing but
heinous slander. (From the type-written speech of Mustafa Kemal, June 1922.)

Johannes translated the speech and sent it to his father on 28 June asking him
to give it to the newspapers in order to help in quashing the rumour about
Turkish persecutions of the Christians. "Please show it to the Archbishop when
you see him!" His father answered by sending a cutting from *Svenska
Morgonbladet.*

The cutting that Papa sent me about alleged Turkish atrocities was not from different sources,
but from just one ill-willed and coloured one. I believe I can state with even greater certainty
than in May that this cruelty campaign against the Turks is forged from beginning to end, in the
interests of big power politics, the victim of which public opinion in Sweden and other minor
countries has become. (28.6.1922)

This was the letter in which Johannes also mentioned that he has had an interesting guest lately, Levi Petrus, the leader of the Swedish Pentecost movement. "I invited him and the two of us spent an interesting evening together." It seems unlikely that Johannes did not try to convince his influential guest not to believe the "horror stories." In his next letter, Johannes had second thoughts about having asked his father to give publicity to Mustafa Kemal's speech.

Regarding Mustafa Kemal's speech, it was good that Papa did *not* send it to the press. It would have gone to U.D. [the foreign ministry] and I don't think they would like an official report to be published in the press without their co-operation. However, I wish to emphasize once more that I have informed myself thoroughly of the origin and credibility of the cock-and-bull-stories that have been spread around; I would bet on anything that *no Christian within Mustafa Kemal's orbit has been persecuted for the sake of his Christian faith.* (28.7.1922)

Regarding negotiations between Ankara and Athens, which should have led to better relations between Turks and Greeks than the failed mediation by the Allied powers, they did not inspire much hope, he felt. And regarding Pontus, once an antique kingdom on the Black Sea, where a terrible uprising had taken place, Johannes states that

… it was intentionally planned to have erupted at the same moment as the Greek offensive last summer, making use of the absence of the Turkish men who were called up to the front. The remaining women and children were to be massacred and a "Pontic Republic" declared ... "Christian martyrs" is hardly an apt description for these adventurers, some of whom were hanged. As for the Armenians of Kharpont, there is *not a word of truth* in what has been said about their persecution. Is it not typical that alarmist reports should have come out of this nonsense, while the world press has kept silent about the fact of Greek misbehaviour 1919 & 1920 in the zone of occupation, although it was confirmed by two international committees. (28.7.1922)

No matter how Johannes argued, he could not influence opinion at home either about the purity of Mustafa Kemal or about the evil actions of the Greeks. In his letter of 14 August he sounds extremely irritated after reading in *Svenska Morgonbladet* a full-page interview with the following headline: "Armenians in thousands are still hunted to death by the Turks. Kemal Pasha's 'peaceful' Government exposed to light by a returning missionary."

He immediately wrote a letter to the editor of *Svenska Morgonbladet*, asking his father to have it published. "Papa must of course not present me as the first dragoman of the Royal Legation but rather stress that I have been here for five years for studies and have had the occasion to get absorbed into the milieu here." He did not mince his words:

With utter amazement have I read the interview with a traumatised missionary in *Svenska Morgonbladet*. I have met this missionary, Miss Alma Johansson, several times and I do not doubt that she has lived through terrible things in the world war, when she was stationed far east in Musch, which makes it psychologically understandable that she still thinks the worst of Turks. Such a predisposed person, who for natural reasons has kept very limited company, could easily have fallen for the Armenian propaganda.

Apparently, he is trying to be sharp without hurting the feelings of the missionary, and, diplomatically, he places the question in a wider context:

Certainly, the poor refugees are to be pitied. We have many kinds of them here in Constantinople – Russians, Georgians, and Tartars who have escaped from the Bolsheviks, Turks who have escaped from the Greeks, Greeks who have fled from the Turks, and also a great number of Armenians (whose total number of 150 to 200 thousand must also include the settled Armenian population). A great part of the latter would, however, consist of persons who, frightened by meddlesome agitators, have emigrated from Cilicia, before the French gave this province back to the Turks, and they accordingly have themselves to blame when they now find themselves, here or elsewhere, separated from their homes.

Others have, like most of the Greek refugees from Asia Minor, preferred to follow the Greek army when they evacuated a temporarily occupied spot, because they didn't have a clean conscience vis-à-vis the Turks. Indubitably they often, more than often, find themselves in great distress – though no worse than the poor Turkish refugees – and when they presented themselves to the aid organisations here they naturally repeated horror stories – though not more horrible than many others – in order to prove their claim to compassion. Whoever hears these one-sided stories will get a distorted picture. The Swedish missionary woman has composed a story in which most traits, unknown to herself, have come from her own reminiscences. She has behind her certain rather shattering experiences in 1915, and one can see how her imagination has worked on this material. (Pencil draft, to his father, 14.8.1922)

In the accompanying private letter to his father Johannes is more outspoken, even blunt, as he describes the agitation as an expression of Christian Islamophobia and anti-Turkish racism and strongly attacks the missionaries in general.

I hope I have said enough to make it clear that her mission society ought to think twice before they send her out again. She certainly has not served the cause of Christianity, in which Christians have long since ceased to be anything but transmitters of shady conspiracies! Has she not on the contrary given the Turks the right to say: *"All right, we can understand the missionaries. Their hate for the Muhammedans is so deep that their religion tells them to hate anything that is Islamic. They mean it from the depths of their heart when they speak of 'the damned Turkish dog' ['den förbannade hundturken']. Whoever wants to, can examine it and find out that this is how it is. Otherwise he will only demonstrate that he does not know the missionaries."* (Ibid.)

He is horrified that Miss Alma Johansson is planning to start a school for Armenian children in Anatolia and asks his father to use his influence to prevent it.

We simply cannot sneak in such an education for the children of the Turkish Armenians [...] Try to prevent this Swedish woman from being sent out again as she will only compromise both the Turkish and the Swedish name here. The interview bears witness to a *fanatical* credulity bordering on *crime!* I will not help her into Anatolia as she wishes, if she comes here, after having discredited herself totally. (Ibid.)

A Contemporary Evaluation of Kolmodin's Political Thought

At this point, one is tempted to quote what Kolmodin's best colleague and friend Einar af Wirsén has said about him in his memoirs.[40] "I have never met a person so

---

40 Einar af Wirsén: *Minnen från fred och krig* (Memories from Peace and War), Bonnier, Stockholm 1942, pp 256-9.

completely free of political sentimentality as Kolmodin." Since we are dealing with Kolmodin's own version of things, and since some of his opinions may seem cold-hearted or even harsh to us, it might be interesting to glean a few more observations from Wirsén's book, for he was the only colleague who could match Kolmodin's political passion and connections and who was respected by Kolmodin.

Kolmodin's political thinking was speculative to a degree and also constructive. Perhaps he started out too much from the assumption that the leading statesmen in different countries had a more profound view of things than they actually had [...] For Mustafa Kemal's goals he had a sharp and clear eye, and he pointed out the similarity between the Turkish leader's constitution and the Swedish constitution, similarities which were striking although hidden by the great authority of Mustafa Kemal and his overwhelming influence. Kolmodin was of the opinion that the Turks had deliberately taken up the principles of our "Era of Freedom." [...]

In his relations to the Bolsheviks, who took power in Russia in the autumn of 1917, he was equally free of sentimental traits. He did not judge them exclusively as wild animals but also [saw them] as human beings, whose leaders acted according to certain principles and a designed plan. He did not think much of the Greeks. He always thought that their capability was overrated, and he loved to call them "waiter souls," an allusion to the character development that the Turkish pressure had evoked in the Greek citizens of Turkey [...]

Latterly, Kolmodin wrote most of the political reports of the legation. They always had the nature of wanting to find out definite motivations for the actions of the leading statesmen. The reports were rather long and formulated in long sentences, interspersed with parentheses and were not always easy to read, but always to the highest degree worth reading. The services he rendered to the legation by contributing to its political orientation were enormous. The qualities that characterised him in his youth already were developed in full and he would have deserved quicker advancement. The officials at the Foreign Ministry, however, thought that his reports were tiresome to read [...]

Kolmodin was both witty, original, and highly absent-minded. His conversation sparkled with brilliant ideas marked by genius, which he enjoyed developing. His habits were those of an Uppsala student. He was determined to have dinner at four as he was used to in Uppsala, and after a lot of difficulties he found a small innkeeper in Galata who was prepared to serve him dinner at this – for people with continental habits – very unusual hour.

Wirsén has many anecdotes about Kolmodin's astonishing absent-minded-ness and what it could lead to, such as how he once put his head through the glass of a closed window or simply forgot to put on his socks and shoes on a cold day in March. He never noticed whether it was warm or cold outside because he always walked about deeply plunged in thought. (In his letters, however, he is very conscious of the weather!) This does not sound like the description of a career diplomat, such as Kolmodin now wished to be (or not to be!) but —

Kolmodin was not only an original by nature, he was also one of the most gifted and learned human beings I have ever met, and I hardly know anyone who by his conversation has given me such rich profit as he. His talent for analysing the most intricate problems was unbelievable.[41]

So let us now see what his predictions for and analysis of the Greco-Turkish war were leading to, how he dealt with the Greeks and the Armenian tragedy (as

41 Ibid. All quotations in this section are from the mentioned source.

we now must call it) as an issue in the coming peace negotiations, and what the aims of the national struggle that Mustafa Kemal was heading were during the year 1922.

The Climax of the Greco-Turkish War

The Greco-Turkish War had been going on at a low level during the whole winter of 1922. The efforts of the Allies to mediate between Turkey and Greece in March had come to nought because the Turks had refused to negotiate as long as there were Greek soldiers on Turkish soil. The Allies then gave up and declared their neutrality. During the summer, the Turkish army was organised and trained, thanks to the ammunition obtained from old German stocks and new Russian sources. The generalissimo was digging in at Sakarya River with his troops, preparing for an offensive. When would the decisive battle happen? "The 'event' here at the moment is the Turkish offensive. [...] The other side of the story is that the Turkish pound is rising with dizzying speed." (26.8.1922)

The tension rose, but the calm tone of Johannes's letters in August and September 1922 indicates that he never for a moment doubted the final Turkish victory.

> The Greek débacle unfolds itself and it looks as if their southern army will be *annihilated* before it reaches the coast. The Turkish offensive and the total collapse of the Greek front – if success-ful – will mean the end of the Greek adventure. It will be "the hour of punishment" for the Greeks, and "divine justice" when the Greek murderers and arsonists are revenged and the Southern Greek Army annihilated. (4.9.1922)

The Turkish army entered Izmir on 9 September and a great number of Greeks left the town in disorder. That was the final triumph of the Turkish national army and "the great and shining hero" Mustafa Kemal.

> The great miracle has occurred – within two weeks Mustafa Kemal has virtually swept the Greeks out of Asia Minor! I cannot judge the victory from a military point of view, but even the British Chief of Staff has expressed his admiration for this military feat. (10.9. 1922)

On 13 September the news came that the central parts of Izmir were burnt to the ground – by whom? By the Turks or the Greeks? Many news media spread the report that when the Turkish army recaptured Smyrna they massacred a large part of the Greek population. Johannes did not for a moment doubt that the Greeks were responsible, yet

> ... the most important thing to do in the present situation would be to prevent the same misery here in Constantinople. The best would be if the Allies could agree on handing the city over to Kemal as soon as possible. England's ambition to stay on as long as possible is a crime against humanity, with incalculable risks. There are too many potential arsonists running loose here. The central task just now can only be the orderly occupation by the Turks of their capital. (14.9.1922)

The Kemalist army was free to march to the Bosphorus. The French authori-ties allowed them to enter Constantinople and the British authorities were forced to follow their example. Istanbul was Turkish again! The Allied concessions might, however, have serious consequences for international politics.

> The Turkish victory has, on account of its surprising and overwhelming character, disturbed all international circles to the extent that we may be on the threshold of a new world war. The snag is Lloyd George. His speech on 3 August, which tied England to a brittle and temporary situation, is now turned upside down. This turnabout appears to the entire world as the collapse of the British Oriental policy. The English nervousness may have wholly incalculable consequences. And this nervousness has led to a very critical point, as the latest telegrams show. (20.9.1922)

"What do they say nowadays at home about the Greeks?" Johannes asks in the middle of this letter:

> Yes, what do you say about the Greek retreat, during which approximately 250 villages and towns were burnt by the beaten army of invasion, and of the great fire of Smyrna, for which they did not dare take responsibility openly but which was – as it now seems clearly proven – arranged before the evacuation? Lousy poodles, aren't they? (20.9.1922)

Adolf Kolmodin found it difficult to believe in such statements. While admiring the Turks for their victory, both he and the family and others at home found it hard to rejoice in the humiliating Greek defeat. "It is probably hopeless to make certain circles see reason in the case of Turks and Greeks," Johannes writes sarcastically.

> As for the case of Smyrna, I only wish to clarify three things, namely
>
> 1. The former Greek commanding general Papoulos declared last spring *in public* that if the Greeks would be forced to evacuate Anatolia, they would know how to devastate the country so thoroughly that the Turks would not be able to rebuild it in 250 years. Everybody shrugged their shoulders and said it was exaggerated. But events during the military catastrophe in August now show that it was serious. The Greek army soon lost its fighting capability but their arsonist trait stuck unto the last. During their retreat the Greeks have burned, wholly or partly, 250 Turkish villages and towns. Where they could they gathered the inhabitants in the mosque and burned it.
>
> 2. Where Smyrna is concerned they obviously did not dare take responsibility for the fire. But everything indicates that it was prepared beforehand in order to break out immediately after their retreat. The Turks, upon entering, found the water pipes *systematically* destroyed [...] I have personally heard, through *Armenian* merchants interested in the petroleum trade, that their Greek opposites had imported great masses of burning oil to Smyrna during the weeks before the evacuation. Nobody here doubts that Smyrna was deliberately set on fire. (P.S. possibly in part by Armenians.)
>
> 3. It is quite illogical to think that the Turks could have been interested in setting Smyrna on fire. For Kemal it was precisely the European and Levantine character of Smyrna, with its stocks and supplies, its trade houses and established connections, that gave it the role of a window on the world, which he naturally had no wish to smash. The fire has deprived him of all that – even if his soldiers, here as in other places where the Greek arsonists have wreaked havoc – have made superhuman efforts to save what could be saved. (26.9.1922)

After Victory

The annihilation of the Greek army had created a dangerous situation. The neutral zone established by the Treaty of Sèvres around Istanbul and the straits was occupied by British, French, and Italian troops. The so-called Chanak[42] incident, caused by the defiance of Lloyd George, could have resulted in armed conflict, but the situation was resolved through the wisdom of Mustafa Kemal and the Allied generals. Eventually, a military convention confirming the armistice was signed at Mudanya on 11 October.

The New Turkey was born.

> Just now there is of course great Turkish delight in the streets and a general display of flags! I have 2 Swedish flags and 1 Turkish flag outside the window of my office. The Pera Street is wholly covered in red. Wallenberg is back – annoyed because Angora is to remain the capital, although Constantinople has been reconquered. One cannot deny that the history of the past three years speaks for this transfer – it is obvious that the Russians are grateful to Lenin for the brilliant stroke of moving the capital back to Moscow. What about transferring Stockholm to Örebro? (14.10.1922)

Johannes himself was not exactly jubilant. On the contrary, he was quite unmoved. "Don't think that I am in the least worried. I might on the contrary be amused about the situation – which in everything corresponds to my expectations over three years," he had told his parents in his September letter. He had foreseen it all in detail! He only regretted being so busy at the office that there was little time for private political analysis.

> *J'ai été accablé* to such a degree that I have had no time before to write a private letter. I have got lots of extra work, uninteresting and time-consuming, like legislation, visa matters. I even had to sit down at the typewriter myself at times. I have never seen the situation here as especially critical, although the British have done what they could to make people nervous. (14.10.1922)

At last he writes a long letter to his parents on 14 October about all the official and unofficial visitors who flocked to Constantinople in the hour of victory:

> I have met Frithiof Nansen, who is here for the League of Nations to look after different kinds of refugees. He will also travel to Anatolia to see the Greek ravages. A journalist from *Dagens Nyheter*, Carlholm, is like a working machine. He is getting an interview with Mustafa Kemal, probably in Bursa where the Marshal is just now. I also met Evtynios [Papa Eftim] of Koskin [Keskin] of the new Turkish Orthodox Church. The ecumenical patriarchy is probably finished.
>
> Constantinople will be a more characteristically Turkish city after the peace than it has ever been. There will hardly be room for a privileged separate organisation of non-Turkish-speaking nationality – the Ottoman Christians will have to bring themselves to learning Turkish.
>
> If this may seem harsh – well, it will have to be admitted that they have deserved their fate. I would have respected the Constantinople Greeks more if they had gone with the Greek army and fought for their "ideal," but they have always pointed to their being Turkish subjects, as soon as the Greek High Commissioner wanted to mobilise them, and reduced their action to slander and intrigues. (14.10.1922)

Again and again, Johannes comes back to "the mendacious stories about massacres of the Greek population in Smyrna" and rumours that the Turks had

---

42 Chanak (Çanakkale) was the southern frontier of the neutral zone held by the Allies around Constantinople. On Johannes Kolmodin's apprehensions that Britain was trying to build another "Gibraltar" at the entrance to the Dardanelles, see Carl Gustaf Kolmodin's chapter "An Ill-matched Couple" in this volume.

caused the great conflagration. Why, for instance, were the Turkish quarters spared?

> The Turkish part of Smyrna was spared because the wind was in the opposite direction. The European and Levantine quarters were burnt down in spite of the superhuman efforts of Turkish soldiers to save what could be saved. Petroleum containers were seen to be handed out to the believers by priests. The Greek consul had to leave his burning home. The Metropolitan Chrysostomos was, by the way, shot by *Greeks* as a traitor to his country. (14.10.1922)

In the face of all the publicity at home about "Christian martyrs," Johannes wanted to make it perfectly clear to the missionary organisations at home that religion was not the issue here.

> There is one point, which, according to my firm conviction, must be kept strictly in mind, and that is that never during the tragic events that have occurred between Turks and the minorities, now and ever since 1896, has there ever been a question of religion, but only one of *nationality*. Where the Turks are concerned, their alleged "hatred of Christianity" is altogether non-existent, but it is their firm decision not to tolerate any disloyal citizens, or turn a blind eye to their traitorous plots. (24.10,1922)

And it would be much better if outside powers stopped meddling in Turkish affairs altogether, he finds.

> The day the Christian minorities in Turkey will learn, like the Jews, only to trust themselves and not to look across the borders for foreign intervention – and the day Europe and America will learn that it is not their business to interfere in the internal affairs of an independent state, all harassment from the side of the Turks will belong to history. Sad to say, one finds the kind of persons who will not understand this truth, and therefore cause much trouble, more frequently among the Protestant missionaries than among more educated Catholic persons. All those stupid propositions about "a national home" for the Armenians etc. have nothing to do with the Turks but with those occidental powers who have seduced the minorities to revolt. (24.10.1922)

The political convulsions, the new establishment, and changes in the administration affected everybody in the "City of Light."

> We in Constantinople have come under "The Government of the Great National Congress of Turkey." While the previous Turkish government, "The Sublime Porte," was an authority tolerated by powerful strangers, the Allies are now the tolerated guests of a powerful indigenous government. It is very important to call the system "republic" because the caliphate, which is to remain, is on no account a papistry, but a secular general representation of Islam for which the Turkish people's state will be the foundation. Which will not mean that the Caliph, though deprived of an insider's power, cannot keep considerable influence on the general orientation of Turkish policies, something like a monarch. (19.11.22)

At the Swedish legation, the changes were also felt.

> Sweden's relationship with the new establishment shapes up well. I personally drove in the peace delegation, headed by Ismet Pasha, the Moltke of Turkey, who had heard of me and was superbly

gracious [...] The British were in a ludicrous situation, 200 Armenians had taken refuge in the British Embassy. I have sent a diplomatic report in which I had to consider Wallenberg's opinion but I am quite pleased with it anyway and have sent a copy to Söderblom. (Ibid.)

Lausanne

The peace conference agreed upon at Mudanya convened at Lausanne on 20 November 1922. The Turkish delegation arrived as victors and on an equal footing with the principal Allied powers. Johannes Kolmodin was sent by the Swedish foreign ministry as an expert assistant to Sweden's representative, Envoy Adlercreutz, with whom he celebrated Christmas at Caux.

Johannes wrote many letters and dispatches from Lausanne, but he was not a conference man and would have preferred stay in Constantinople, where he saw his real task, as a letter to Torvald Höjer reveals:

Ever since the establishment in Constantinople of the government of the Great National Congregation it has been clear to me that there is a task for me in this field for which I have very special qualifications – and it cannot be helped that I therefore hesitated to leave Constantinople just now, where I was perhaps more needed than here. Since through my friend Hamid Bey I had a grasp of the situation twenty-four hours before it had reached the newspapers, I could luckily give the envoy and the other neutral delegates all the information beforehand. (22.12.1922)

"Thanks to personal connections, I am already useful here," he wrote to his father.

We have a full crisis already, because of the mountain oil in Mosul [...] Lord Curzon's completely unreasonable attitude on the Mosul question has spoilt the whole thing and the session had to be adjourned. Lord Curzon fears a return of the Turks to Northern Mesopotamia as the beginning of a Turkish attack on the Persian Gulf, with incalculable consequences. But England does not consider Mosul worth a war. Not only the Greeks but England have been defeated by the Turks and will have to take the consequences. (19.1. 1923)

The question of the minorities was on the conference agenda.

Lord Curzon's main interest in Lausanne is not the minorities, but Mosul and the petroleum wells. The Turks insist on their "national pact" and have turned down all stupid propositions of "a national home for the Armenians"... The more the solution would be in the direction of reducing Europe's interest in this question, the happier the outcome would be for all the minorities. The Armenians will remain suspect as long as they are "protected," but if that unfortunate protection were to be withdrawn, there might be a chance that they will succeed in finding means and ways to live in concord with the authorities. (27.1.1922)

The rumours of Turkish atrocities against the Armenians during Mustafa Kemal's War of Liberation had reached Lausanne. He found the Americans the most reasonable, and one of them confirmed his views, as he insisted to his father,

... that the so-called "atrocities" are an invention by the Near Eastern Relief Fund, whose alarm telegram about atrocities is, if not frankly untrue, made in order to collect funds. Unless these people serve up, week after week, a menu of suitable "atrocities" they will not get funds for their useful charitable work, whereby they assume a terrible responsibility, but they do not understand this, they just want their accounts full. In my view we can leave all American missionary information aside. (31.1.1923)

In Swedish newspaper cuttings people sent to him he saw the same stories about "Turkish atrocities" repeated. He furiously dismissed them as "malevolent and coloured." He became more and more convinced that "this cruelty campaign against the Turks is forged and pieced together from beginning to end in the interests of the Great Powers, to whom public opinion in Sweden and other smaller countries has become servile." (31.1. 1923)

The Lausanne Peace Treaty was signed on 24 July 1923. The Turks secured practically everything they demanded in their "national pact" adopted at Erzurum. In Constantinople, 101 cannon shots were fired, the steam whistles of all the Turkish and Allied vessels hooted, and from the minarets the muezzins called out the great event: peace in the East. Johannes Kolmodin asked Aisja Kadyn to go out and buy a sheep. It was ritually slaughtered and distributed to the poor.

Postscript

I have come to the end of my study of Johannes Kolmodin's political thought and life in Sweden, Eritrea, and Turkey. What has interested me most in undertaking this study is his personality, his linguistic genius, and his political thinking: his attitude to Britain, France, Russia, and Germany, the great powers of the time; his reaction to the First World War; his thoughts on Europe and particularly Northern Europe; his descriptions of life in Constantinople; and his life as a diplomat.

It seems that he never changed his most profound views and structures of thought. When the conservatives of his generation lost their battle against parliamentary democracy, when their conservative, constitutional, and anti-democratic goals failed to materialise, he fled Sweden, I believe. His autocratic ideals, his belief in a strong state, and his conservative values were a product of the political events of his time and of the teaching of Harald Hjärne, and when he could not see his ideals being fulfilled in the homeland, he transferred them to other ages and other lands.

He was lucky to find two living political figures who matched his autocratic ideal of a strong sovereign in a strong state – Mustafa Kemal of Turkey and later Haile Selassie of Ethiopia –and to watch them from up close. In Turkey, he could develop in practice all his brilliant qualities and gifts of personality, his interest in people, and his distracted charm, but they were also exploited, while his instinct for learning was dissipated by his passion for current political realities and dramas. The conflict between life as an oriental philologist and historian and being a lifelong diplomat was never resolved.

It might have been resolved if a long life had been granted him. For when, by the mediation of Nathan Söderblom, he was offered the high post as advisor to Ras Tafari, later Emperor Haile Selassie of Ethiopia, he could return to his first field of interest, linguistics, while organising the foreign service of the Ethiopian government. His plan was to return to Sweden afterwards in a worthy position at the Swedish foreign office and to be able to work on all the scientific material he had gathered in Ethiopia and Turkey and deposited at Uppsala University.

Eva Forsslöf and Johannes
Kolmodin during their wedding
ceremony in January 1925.

Carl Gustaf Kolmodin: *Johannes Kolmodin i brev
och skrifter*, Stockholm 1999

About a year after our story ends, Johannes married Eva Forslöf, whom he had known since childhood. This changed his personal life in every way. His correspondence with his parents became rare and he became a man of the world. The wedding portrait shows a stately and upright gentleman, far from the original described by his Uppsala friends.

He then acquired the highest diplomatic office imaginable in the Kingdom of Ethiopia. We know very little about that part of his life. His early death in 1933 makes it impossible to know whether the dictatorships of the 1930s and the Second World War would have changed his ideas about government and state. His nationalism had made him insensitive to the problem of the minorities in Turkey. What would he have thought of the German dictator's merciless treatment of German Jews?

Hypothetical questions. I like to believe that Johannes Kolmodin, like so many others, would have changed his views and even "the basic structures of his thought" dramatically if he had lived to see the consequences of Hitler's extreme and murderous nationalism and anti-Semitism. The fact that he was an enemy of every tendency to explain human differences in terms of race, believing only in cultural differences and possessing a genius for penetrating cultures other than his own, is clear from all his actions and writings.

When he died suddenly in Addis Ababa in 1933 – just in time not to have to see the political consequences of Germany's "dishonourable defeat" in the First World War – his wife Eva took his body to Uppsala to be buried there. But before

Johannes Kolmodin and his son Olle in Addis Ababa in 1932.

Carl Gustaf Kolmodin: *Johannes Kolmodin i brev och skrifter*, Stockholm 1999

long, Johannes Kolmodin was forgotten, both by the foreign office and Uppsala University, to which he had donated his scholarly legacy.

One day in 2001, I was shocked to discover that the Kolmodin tombstone had been removed and that the family grave was about to be emptied (the latter eventuality was fortunately prevented at the last moment). For me, the discovery of this scandalous neglect and ignorance of the memory of Johannes Kolmodin was the prompting I needed to remind Sweden of the outstanding contribution of Johannes Kolmodin to Swedish diplomacy and to the international community of Oriental scholarship.

Note: All descriptions of political events that are not quotations are taken from Encyclopaedia Britannica 1970, or from memory. In translating Kolmodin's old-fashioned Swedish, with its many periods and conversational turns (really, no doubt, at any rate, on the whole, probably, at all events) subjunctives, auxiliary verbs, love of parentheses and somewhat strange syntax, I have sometimes had to alter and simplify the original in the interests of comprehension. The result is that in attempting the difficult task of making his involved syntax sound like English, I may have made his style appear more modern than it was. He was in essence a very conservative writer and person, a fact that does not diminish his boldness and genius.

Ida Flärdah

Überreicht vom Verfasser.

MEINE STUDIENREISE IN
ABESSINIEN 1908—1910

VORLÄUFIGER BERICHT

VON

J. KOLMODIN
Liz. Phil.

(SONDERABDRUCK AUS »LE MONDE ORIENTAL» IV, 1910)

UPPSALA 1910
ALMQVIST & WIKSELLS BOKTRYCKERI-A.-B.

Front cover of Johannes Kolmodin's *My Study Tour to Abyssinia 1908-1910*.

The Swedish Evangelical Mission as a Background to Johannes Kolmodin's Life and Work

LARSOLOV ERIKSSON

There is evidence from Johannes Kolmodin's own writings that his background in the Swedish Evangelical Mission (SEM)[1] had a decisive influence on his life and work. In his article, "My Study Tour to Abyssinia 1908-1910,"[2] he starts – after a note on the transcription of Ethiopian[3] words and names – his presentation of his journey in the following way:

> It had long been my dream to make a journey through the secret Christian world of East Africa. From childhood I have time and again heard about the Swedish mission in the Red Sea area. My father, professor and doctor of theology A. Kolmodin, was for 30 years employed first as teacher at the Mission Institute Johannelund (close to Stockholm), then as principal of the institute and inspector of the mission for the Swedish Evangelical Mission. I myself spent my childhood at Johannelund, where there were three young Abyssinians at that time among the students at the institute. My first memories have to do with letters from missionaries, who tell of the affliction and the chaotic events during the time of the dervishes and the earliest years of the Italian occupation. The names and deeds of Emperor Yohannes, Ras Alula, and other Abyssinian dignitaries were known to me and of interest to me before I ever inquired into political events in my own vicinity. In this way, a living interest was awakened in me for this vital, half-barbarian world, a world where the genuine Middle Ages now meet with modern times in a violent confrontation.[4]

---

1 The Swedish missionary organization *Evangeliska Fosterlands-Stiftelsen* (EFS) is internationally known as the Swedish Evangelical Mission (SEM).

2 Published in German as "Meine Studienreise in Abessinien 1908-1910," *Le Monde Oriental,* No 4, 1910, pp. 229–55.

3 At least partly aware of the problems of terminology, I here use the more modern word "Ethiopian" for the older "Abyssinian."

4 Kolmodin, Johannes, "Meine studienreise," p. 230. The translation is my own. Also Carl Gustaf Kolmodin cites part of this passage in his insightful and interesting book *Johannes Kolmodin i brev och skrifter* (Kungl. Vitterhets Historie och Antikvitets Akademien. *Filologiskt arkiv 41*, Stockholm: Almqvist and Wiksell International 1999) as part of the short biographical sketch of Johannes Kolmodin's background, childhood and youth, p. 12. Johannes Kolmodin's own words in German are: "Schon längst war es mein traum gewesen, eine reise in dem geheimnisvollen christenlande Ostafrikas zu machen. Von kindheit an habe ich immer und immer von der schwedischen mission im Rotenmeer-gebiete reden hören. Mein Vater, Professor Dr. Theol. A. KOLMODIN, war 30 jahre lang zuerst als lehrer am missionsinstitut zu Johannelund (unweit Stockholm), dann als direktor dieser anstalt und inspektor der mission, an der s. g. 'Evangelischen Vaterlandsstiftung' angestellt. Ich habe selbst in Johannelund meine kinderjahre zugebracht, wo damals unter den schülern der anstalt auch drei junge abessinier waren. Meine ersten erinnerungen beziehen sich auf die briefe der missionäre, die von der trübsal und den wüsten ereignissen der derwischzeit und der ersten italienischen occupationsjahre erzählten. Die namen und taten Kaiser Johannes', Ras Alulas und anderer abessinischen grossen waren mir bekannt und inter-

I will touch upon Johannes Kolmodin's African journey later, but for now I use this short passage as a point of departure for structuring my paper.

First, I give a brief outline of the early history of the Swedish Evangelical Mission, the revival and mission movement in which the father of Johannes Kolmodin, Adolf Kolmodin, was a prominent and influential leader for many years, as noted above by his son. Second, I try to give an idea of what the young Johannes Kolmodin might have heard and learnt at his home at Johannelund about the mission work in Eritrea and other areas, since he explicitly mentions this as a source of inspiration. Third, I try to provide some brief details of the life of the Kolmodin family as it appears in the weekly chronicles of Johannelund – these chronicles being the diaries kept by the students as part of their practical duties at the institute.

The Swedish Evangelical Mission

The Swedish Evangelical Mission was founded in 1856 as a society for evangelistic work within Sweden. From the beginning, the aim of the society was to produce and distribute good Christian (Lutheran) tracts and writings and to provide opportunities for people to support this work with gifts and contributions of other types.[5] In the beginning, there was no intention of taking up foreign mission: that came later – actually only a very few years later (1861) – as a result of the desires and requests of the donors to the society and on the direct suggestion of one of the founders of the SEM, Hans Jacob Lundborg.

The SEM was part of a larger Christian revival movement in Sweden during the early and mid-19th century, which arose mainly as a result of influences from Germany but also in part from Great Britain and the United States of America.[6] There had been earlier pietistic and Moravian revivals, but they had not had a very deep or lasting influence on Swedish society. In this instance, however, the situation was somewhat different. Two dominant currents can be detected, one Lutheran and one Baptist. Initially, the currents remained together, but in 1848 the first split occurred when a free Baptist congregation was formed in Varberg on the west coast of Sweden. The leader of the Baptist branch of the revival was a former Lutheran minister, Anders Wiberg.

The SEM was firmly part of the Lutheran current, and its leadership stressed the bonds with the Swedish Lutheran Church. It was never the intention of the SEM to become a free church, and many of its leading men were Lutheran ministers – if they were not members of the Swedish nobility. However, even if the intention was to remain within the Swedish church, this was not always easy,

---

essierten mich, ehe ich noch nach den politischen ereignissen in nächster nähe je gefragt hatte. So wurde in mir ein lebhaftes interesse für diese rührige, halbbarbarische welt erweckt, wo das genuine mittelalter jetzt der modernen neuzeit in heftiger krise begegnet." Adolf Kolmodin gave his account of the journey in the book *Några minnen från min resa till Ost-Afrika 1908-1909*, Stockholm: Evang. Fosterlands-Stiftelsens Förlags-expedition 1909.

5 For a short and selective introduction to the history of the SEM, see Hofgren, Allan, *EFS rötter: De trodde och vågade*, Uppsala: EFS-förlaget 1988.

6 For a broad presentation of this period in Swedish church life, see e.g., Kjellberg, Knut, *Folkväckelse i Sverige under 1800-talet: uppkomst och genombrott*, Stockholm: Carlssons 1994 and Jarlert, Anders, *Sveriges kyrkohistoria 6: Romantikens och liberalismens tid*, Stockholm: Verbum 2001. See also the forthcoming volume 7 in the same series as Jarlert's book.

since there were strong theological and organisational tensions. In 1878, the revival experienced its second split, when the Swedish Covenant Church was formed under the leadership of Paul Petter Waldenström, who was at the time of the schism an ordained minister in the Swedish church.

The theological background or roots of the SEM can be described through four concepts or designations.

First of all, the SEM was – and is – a Lutheran movement. From Lutheranism it borrowed its teaching of law and gospel and its Christocentric emphasis: Jesus Christ is the centre of Christian faith and he is the redeemer of mankind and the example for every Christian to follow. The Bible is the Holy Scripture and the sole guiding source for faith and life. Also part of the Lutheran heritage is the interest in caring for the world as God's creation: it is a Christian duty to help all in need and especially to serve one's brothers and sisters in faith.

Second, the SEM was a pietistic movement. From German Lutheran pietism came a strong interest in stressing the *life* of the Christian in contrast to focusing most attention on the *doctrine* of the Christian faith. Pietism is a reaction against dull orthodoxy and focuses more on personal belief than on correct doctrine. It also affords lay people a prominent place in the work of the church. There is, furthermore, in pietistic movements a strongly critical tendency regarding the organisation and hierarchy of the church. Mysticism is a further trait connected to the pietistic idea, because of the interest in the development of the individual's personal faith. Pietism is in many ways a reform movement, which focuses on the believers within the church and preaches the need for everyone to be converted.

Third, the SEM was a Moravian movement. From the Moravians the founding fathers[7] of the SEM adopted an emphasis on fellowship rather than on dogmatics, thereby strengthening the avoidance of dogmatics derived from their pietistic background. This opened the way for what we today call ecumenism. From Moravianism also came the interest in foreign mission, an interest that was, only a few years after the founding of the SEM, to become one of the pillars of the movement. From the beginning, the Moravian heritage was most prominent in the very personal way the relationship between Christ and the Christian was described and understood. As far as doctrine is concerned, both pietistic and Moravian movements were basically Lutheran. Neither had any initial intention of forming their own church bodies. In this respect also, the SEM shared the basic ideas and ideals of the two older movements.

Fourth, the SEM was a movement influenced by Methodism. However, the extent to which Methodism actually had an effect on the theology of the SEM is much disputed . Probably its influence in this regard is very limited, even if there were early and close contacts between, for example, Carl Olof Rosenius – the most influential theologian among the founders of the SEM – and the Methodist pastor George Scott.[8] Rather, the influence of Methodism can be detected in the way the young movement chose to work as a free organisation in close affiliation with the state church.

---

7 I call them fathers, even if most of them were quite young (about 25-30 years old). They were, I any event, all men.

8 The standard biography of Carl Olof Rosenius is still Lodin, Sven, *C.O. Rosenius, hans liv och gärning,* Stockholm: Evangeliska Fosterlands-Stiftelsens Bokförlag 1956. For the contacts between Rosenius and Scott, see especially pp. 77-121.

This, then, in short is the background to the SEM's theology: a free Lutheran movement open to influences from other branches of the Christian church. The piety within the movement was firmly low church, and he focus was on evangelism in Sweden and, after a few years, on missionary work in Africa and India.

This was also the ideological background of Johannes Kolmodin, since his father and mother can be described as fairly typical representatives of the SEM movement. Johannes Kolmodin's mother, Nelly Kolmodin, née von Post, was the daughter of Axel von Post, district judge in the city of Gävle and one of the main lay leaders of the SEM in that part of the country at the end of the 19th century. He was also a personal friend of Rosenius. And Johannes Kolmodin's father was, of course, employed by the SEM in leading positions for more than 20 years.[9] Adolf Kolmodin was born in 1855, one year before the SEM was founded. When he was 24 years old, in 1879, he was appointed a teacher at Johannelund, the institute where missionaries and later also pastors for the SEM were trained. From the very beginning, Adolf Kolmodin was a highly influential person within the SEM. He was too young to be one of the founders, but he came to be one of the leading theologians and ideologues in the SEM around the turn of the century. This position was further strengthened when he was elected mission director in 1893, an appointment which made him the highest official in the SEM movement and at the same time the principal of the Johannelund Mission Institute.

In parallel with holding these positions, Adolf Kolmodin also had close contacts with the University of Uppsala, where he was an acting professor for several semesters before being appointed professor of exegetics in 1903. He continued as director of the foreign mission work of the SEM but left Johannelund and moved with his family to Uppsala. As a matter of interest, it can be mentioned that when Adolf Kolmodin became professor in Uppsala, he succeeded Waldemar Rudin, one of the founders of the SEM in 1856. Rudin was also the first principal of Johannelund and, like Kolmodin, a man with a strong interest both in the Bible and in mission work among non-Christian peoples.

As far as the SEM, and indeed the work of Adolf Kolmodin, is concerned, his greatest contribution probably relates to foreign mission – Christian mission appears to be the most appropriate label for his work within the SEM. Adolf Kolmodin was theologically Low Church Lutheran pietist,[10] but above all he was a man of mission and evangelism – in Sweden and in other parts of the world.

In 1862, the board of the SEM decided to start mission work in Africa. The goal was to reach the Oromo people of central Ethiopia. In the course of pursuing this goal – it took some 40 years before the first missionaries reached the Oromos – the SEM decided to start mission work in what is today Eritrea.[11] From

---

9 For a short biography of Adolf Kolmodin, see Lundqvist, Karl Axel, *Organisation och bekännelse: Evangeliska Fosterlands-Stiftelsen och Svenska kyrkan 1890-1911* (Skrifter utgivna av Svenska kyrkohistoriska föreningen. II. Ny följd 25), Uppsala 1977, pp. 55-8. For a presentation of Adolf Kolmodin as a theologian, see *idem*, pp. 221-43.

10 See for an example of this characterisation Bengt Sundkler's article about Adolf Kolmodin in *Svenskt biografiskt lexikon 21*, Stockholm 1975-77, p. 478.

11 For a short but engaging introduction to the earliest history of the SEM mission in Africa, see Hellström, Ivan, *Bland faror och nöd i Kunama*, Upsala: EFS-förlaget 1989, second edition 1996. For a scholarly presentation of the early mission history, see Arén, Gustav, *Evangelical Pioneers in Ethiopia: Origins of the Evangelical Church Mekane Yesus* (Studia Missionalia Upsaliensia XXXII), Stockholm: EFS-förlaget 1978.

Johannelund missionary school as built in 1867

Ivan Hellström: *Johannelund 125 år*, Uppsala: EFS-förlaget, 1987, p.21

the very beginning, missionaries were educated at Johannelund, the training institute for missionaries founded in the same year as the decision was made to take
up foreign mission. As we have already seen, it was here that Adolf Kolmodin
was a teacher and later principal; and it was here that Johannes Kolmodin grew
up. Certainly, he was from early childhood keenly aware of the history and fate
of the first missionaries to Eritrea.

The Mission Institute Johannelund

When Johannes Kolmodin wrote his report of the study tour to Africa in 1908-
10, he explicitly mentions Johannelund as the place where he first heard about
the Swedish mission on the coast of the Red Sea and where he came into contact
with three young men from Eritrea among the students at the institute.[12] The
questions therefore are: What did he hear? Who were the three men?

The second question should be fairly easy to answer, since Kolmodin mentions
them by name in his article,[13] even if in one case it is doubtful that he actually
remembered the young man from his childhood.

The first man mentioned is Pastor Markus Germei. He was born in 1862 in
Asmara, Eritrea, studied at Johannelund from 1884 to 1888, was ordained in
Uppsala in 1889 before he returned to Eritrea, where he worked as a missionary
and teacher for several years.[14] He was married to a Swedish missionary, Regina
Johansson, whom he probably first met at Johannelund during his period of study
there. In his sixties, he moved with his wife to Sweden, where he died in 1924.
Markus Germei must have been an interesting acquaintance for Johannes

---

12 Johannes Kolmodin calls them "three young Abyssinians" (drei junge abessinier), "Meine studienreise,"
p. 230.

13 Ibid., p. 231.

14 Rodén, Nils, *Johannelunds Missionsinstitut genom 75 år: Jubileumsskrift 1863-1938*, Stockholm:
Evangeliska Fosterlands-Stiftelsens Bokförlag 1938, p. 144.

Markus Germei

Twoldo Medhen

Haile Mikael Kidano

Natanael Hagena Djigo

Nils Rodèn: *Johannelunds Missions-*
institut genom 75 år, Stockholm 1938

Kolmodin, since the Eritrean pastor and teacher had a great knowledge of different languages and played a role in translating the New Testament into Tigrinya.

The second person mentioned by Johannes Kolmodin in his report is Twoldo Medhen. He was born in Eritrea in 1860 and was a deacon in the Ethiopian Orthodox Church before he came into contact with the Swedish missionaries and became a pupil at the mission school in Gheleb. He studied at Johannelund from 1883 to 1887, after which he returned to Eritrea, where he worked for the Swedish mission. During the visit of Adolf and Johannes Kolmodin in 1908-09, Kolmodin senior ordained Twoldo Medhen a minister in the Eritrean church. This took place on New Year's Day 1909 in Asmara.[15] Twoldo Medhen became one of the leaders of the Eritrean church and participated in the translation of the New Testament into both Tigré and into Tigrinya.[16]

The third person mentioned by Johannes Kolmodin is Haile Mikael Kidano. He was a student at Johannelund from 1881 to 1886,[17] and it is not very probable that Johannes Kolmodin actually remembered him from that time, since Johannes was only two years old when Haile Mikael Kidano returned to Africa to serve in the mission in Eritrea. But Johannes Kolmodin calls him his old friend, and expresses his thanks to him for helping him with no less than 50 songs in local language.[18]

Now there was another young man from Eritrea who studied at Johannelund while Johannes Kolmodin lived there with his family. His name was Natanael Hagena Djigo, and he was a student at Johannelund in the years 1884 to 1888, but died in Stockholm before he could return to his home country. His background is almost unknown, except that he was born in 1864 and had been a slave, but was freed by the Egyptian government and accepted as pupil in the mission school in Massawa before he was sent to Sweden to study.[19]

So these are the three – or four – men from Eritrea that Johannes Kolmodin met as a young boy at Johannelund. They made an impression on him, as he himself states, and it is not difficult to imagine how they excited the boy's imagination.

Mention should also be made of some of the Swedish students at Johannelund. Several of them Johannes

---

15 Adolf Kolmodin's own account of the ordination can be found in his book *Några minnen,* pp. 207-09.

16 Rodén, Nils, *Johannelunds Missionsinstitut,* p. 143.

17 Ibid., p. 141.

18 Kolmodin, Johannes, "Meine studienreise," p. 235.

19 Rodén, Nils, *Johannelunds Missionsinstitut,* p. 144.

Kolmodin would meet on his journey in Eritrea between 1908 and 1910, and they would help him in many ways, as he himself also notes in his report. Some of the missionaries in Eritrea at the time of Kolmodin's field trip had been students at Johannelund before Johannes Kolmodin was born. That is true of Karl Winquist, who was a student at Johannelund between 1870 and 1877, and who would be known for his translation, together with among others Markus Germei, of the New Testament into Tigrinya.[20] Johannes Kolmodin calls him "the great authority on the Tigrinya language,"[21] and notes that he obtained some 30 poems in Tigrinya from him.

In Eritrea, Johannes Kolmodin also met with Anders Svensson, student at Johannelund from 1869 to 1874, long before Johannes was born. When Kolmodin arrived in Eritrea, Svensson was chairman of the SEM mission's work in that area, and Johannes Kolmodin seems to have been rather impressed by the missionary's depth of knowledge. According to Kolmodin, there was probably no one who knew as much as Svensson about the recent history of Ethiopia and Eritrea.[22]

Yet another missionary who had studied at Johannelund before the birth of Johannes Kolmodin was Karl Gustaf Rodén. He was a student there from 1879 to 1883 and had an impressive knowledge of the Tigré language,[23] and he also helped Johannes Kolmodin in his research.[24]

Several others could be mentioned. Karl Cederquist studied at Johannelund from 1879 to 1885. Through his contacts at the Ethiopian court, he helped Johannes Kolmodin to obtain the permits necessary for travel in certain areas of northern Ethiopia.[25]

Three missionaries in Eritrea whom Johannes Kolmodin most certainly had met while they were students at Johannelund were Johan Magnus Nilsson (student 1887 to 1893),[26] August Andersson (student from 1893 to 1898),[27] and Jonas Iwarson (student from 1894 to 1896).[28] All three were to work for long periods in Eritrea, and they are all mentioned with gratitude and affection in Kolmodin's short account of the journey.[29] Iwarson told of his travels in Tigray with Adolf and Johannes Kolmodin in his own book.[30] A missionary not mentioned by Johannes Kolmodin is Olle Eriksson (student at Johannelund from 1898 to 1903), who worked in Eritrea between 1904 and 1915.[31] He had a great interest in languages and would likely have been of help to Kolmodin.

---

20 Ibid., p. 128.

21 Kolmodin, Johannes, "Meine studienreise," p. 233.

22 Ibid., p. 234.

23 Rodén, Nils, *Johannelunds Missionsinstitut*, pp. 135f.

24 Kolmodin, Johannes, "Meine studienreise," p. 235.

25 Ibid., p. 236.

26 Rodén, Nils, *Johannelunds Missionsinstitut*, p. 147.

27 Ibid., pp. 148f.

28 Ibid., p. 153.

29 Kolmodin, Johannes, "Meine studienreise," pp. 231, 238.

30 Iwarson, Jonas, *På färdevägar i Ostafrika: Ur minnet och dagboken*, Stockholm: Evangeliska Fosterlands-Stiftelsens Bokförlag 1935, pp. 155-88.

31 Rodén, Nils, *Johannelunds Missionsinstitut*, p. 157.

As to what Johannes Kolmodin heard about mission work while he was a boy at Johannelund, it is not too difficult to get at least a fairly accurate picture of the kinds of information and stories that were circulating. Some of the letters sent to Johannelund and to the mission director were published in SEM periodicals. Moreover, we know from different accounts that the reading of letters from missionaries was a recurrent and frequent element in the so-called mission evenings at Johannelund. One student provides the following picture of such occasions at the institute:

> Every Friday, we gathered in the home of the principal for so-called mission evenings. During the evening, we listened to newly received letters from the missionaries together with accounts about the work among heathens in different mission fields. While listening, we worked at various crafts like painting on glass, woodcarving, manufacturing Bible cases, etc.[32]

It is reasonable to assume that the young Johannes Kolmodin took part in these evenings together with the rest of his family. The strong impression created of life at the institute is that it was more or less like the life of an extended family. Adolf and Nelly Kolmodin probably were like father and mother to many of the students at Johannelund. Several of them were quite young when they came to Stockholm, and most of them could not afford frequent visits to their homes in distant parts of Sweden. Johannes and his brothers and sister were probably like younger siblings to some of the students. One has to remember that the total number of students at the institute was not great. During the years 1884 to 1895, the period when Johannes Kolmodin lived there, a total of 72 students were admitted. The normal duration of study was four years: with an average of six new students per year, there would on average be a total of 24 active students present at the institute at any one time. We also know that in some years there were even fewer students at the institute, since students weren't admitted every year.[33]

I have chosen examples of the kind of letters from missionaries that Johannes Kolmodin might have heard as a young boy by perusing the foreign mission magazine of the SEM – *Missions-Tidningen* – for the year 1890,[34] when Johannes Kolmodin was six years old. The magazine was published twice monthly and had as its primary aim providing information and inspiration about foreign mission work, with special focus on the work of the SEM in other countries, including work among seamen in foreign ports.[35]

---

32 P. A. Gustafsson in *Hälsning från Johannelund: Minnesskrift 60 år*, ed. Carl Olsson, Stockholm: Evangeliska Fosterlands-Stiftelsens Bokförlag 1923, p. 51.

33 See Hellström, Ivan, *Johannelund 125 år*, Uppsala: EFS-förlaget 1987, pp. 285f.

34 The magazine was at that time edited by mission director Knut Johan Montelius with the help of Adolf Kolmodin.

35 As a note of curiosity, it can be mentioned that the first port in which the SEM began work among Swedish seamen was in fact Constantinople, where the SEM worked between the years 1869 and 1879. Only two pastors were sent to Constantinople by the SEM: Per Johan Svärd (1869–73) and Jonas Linus Aspling (1874–79). Rodén, Nils, *Johannelunds Missionsinstitut*, pp. 119f., 121. When Aspling died in 1879, no further missionaries were sent to Constantinople. Aspling, therefore, also became the last Evangelical chaplain of the Swedish chapel in the city. The chapel itself can still be found just below the Swedish consulate and the Swedish Research Institute in Istanbul. For information about the chapel, see Theolin, Sture, *The Swedish Palace in Istanbul: A Thousand Years of Cooperation between Turkey and Sweden*, Istanbul 2000, pp. 149-56.

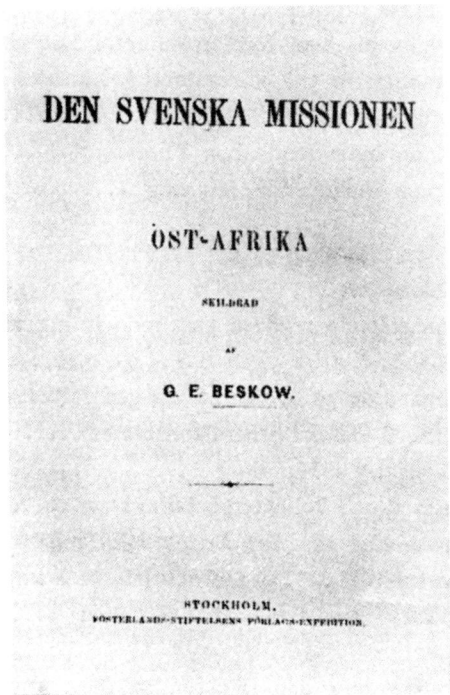

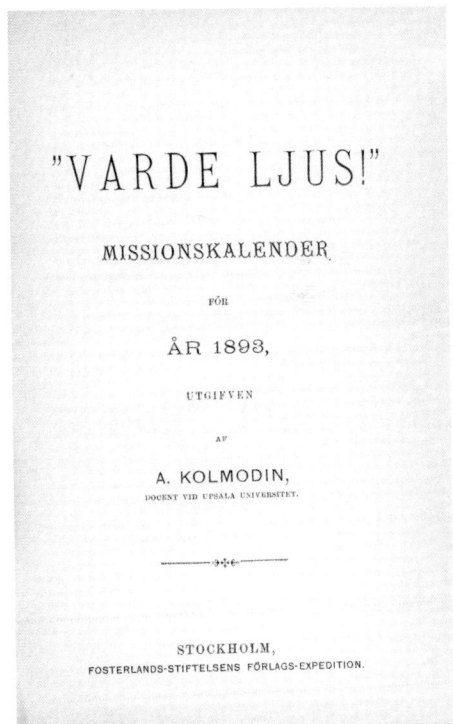

Selected missionary publications.

In the first issue of the magazine for 1890 there is a fairly substantial article with excerpts from letters from missionaries in Eritrea. It tells of the health of the missionaries, the building of houses in Gheleb, conflicts with the people in a village, an epidemic of smallpox in and around Asmara, with as many as 100 dead each week, wishes for prayer, etc.[36] From India, a letter includes a report from the

36 *Missions-Tidningen* 1/1890, pp. 2f.

conference where most of the missionaries had gathered, excepting Lars Erik Karlsson and one other missionary, who had gone to Bombay to meet Karlsson's prospective wife. This, says the letter-writer, was very appropriate. The young bride had been seriously ill during the latter part of the voyage to India and was in such poor health that she had to be carried ashore. In order to make it possible for Karlsson to take care of his young bride in the best manner possible, the two were married that same day. After good care by her husband, Mrs. Karlsson soon recovered, the writer continues.[37] Immediately following the account of the missionary conference in India there are two letters from Johan Ruthquist, also in India. In the first, he tells of the birth of their daughter; in the second letter he tells of her death. And he concludes: "Today we experience a feeling of emptiness and deeply miss our little child, but the thoughts and the ways of the Lord are not ours; and we know that what he does always is the best."[38]

These are only samplings. A substantial part of the magazine's content is taken from missionaries' letters. In the second issue in 1890, Anders Svensson writes briefly on the political problems in Hamazen,[39] Regina Johansson, who was later married to Markus Germei, pleads in a long letter for support for the work among children,[40] and from different missionaries in India there are no less than four long and informative epistles.[41] Alongside the letters are longer and shorter accounts of mission work in different parts of the world, many of which are signed A. K., i.e., Adolf Kolmodin. An example of such accounts is a fairly substantial report on the political situation in Uganda after a series of revolutions and the dethronement of King Mwanga in 1888, and the consequences of this for Christian mission.[42]

Johannes Kolmodin's father also edited a yearly publication, a mission calendar called *Let there be Light!* (in Swedish, *Varde Ljus!*) from 1893 to 1910. If one assumes – which there is good reason to do – that much of the material in the publication, or that similar material, was also presented at mission evenings at Johannelund, one can arrive at a likely picture of what young Johannes heard besides the contents of the letters from the missionaries.

By way of further example, I present the contents of the first volume of *Let There Be Light!* from 1893. In this volume, there are among the contributions a poem about the Oromos, a short biographical sketch of the mission bishop Hans Peter Hallbeck, a report about a mission conference at Johannelund, a report from South Africa and on the work of the Church of Sweden Mission among the Zulu people, an account of the work of the SEM in India, a report on the Swedish Covenant Church's work in the Congo, a report on mission work in China and a translation of a field report from a trip to the Oromos in Somalia.

It is striking from the content of this first volume – and the impression is confirmed when the content of the following volumes is taken into account – that the scope of interest is Christian mission at large, not only the missionary enterprises of the SEM. There is an evident ecumenical interest by the editor of the calen-

---

37 Ibid., 1/1890, pp. 6f.

38 Ibid., 1/1890, p. 7.

39 *Missions-Tidningen* 2/1890, p. 9.

40 Ibid., 2/1890, p. 10.

41 Ibid., 2/1890, pp. 10-13.

42 *Missions-Tidningen* 3/1890, pp. 21-3. The article is continued in the following two issues of the magazine.

dar, and there is reason to believe that Johannes Kolmodin was also exposed in early in his childhood to this side of mission work. Later, in his cooperation with the Swedish Archbishop Nathan Söderblom, this aspect would of course become important in a special way.[43]

When, one comes to Johannes Kolmodin's particular interest in the Ethiopian and Eritrean languages and cultures, there is reason to believe that this had its basis in what he heard as a young boy growing up at Johannelund. That, I imagine, is the correct interpretation of his own words: "So wurde in mir ein lebhaftes interesse für diese rührige, halbbarbarische welt erweckt."[44]

The Weekly Chronicles of Johannelund

Mostly out of curiosity, I have skimmed through some of the weekly chronicles (a kind of notebook diary) written by students at Johannelund as part of their duties. The period covered is from 1884 to 1903, and I have especially looked out for comments about the Kolmodin family.

Every student at Johannelund had to write in these chronicles according to a running schedule. They were to note news of interest and to comment on this. It is evident that the students' interest in this assignment varied greatly. Some simply write that nothing of special interest has taken place, while others provide long summaries of sermons given by their teachers and by visiting preachers at the institute. Once in a while, there is a short comment on the world outside the institute, but most reports are of the life at Johannelund. The chronicles resemble a family diary for those living at the institute.

Johannes Kolmodin was born on 22 February 1884 and was the oldest son of Adolf and Nelly Kolmodin. The family was living at Johannelund at that time, but there is no trace of the birth of Johannes in the chronicles. The notes from this period are short and rather uninteresting. What is of interest, however, is that the students from Africa evidently took part in keeping the diary on the same terms as Swedish students. In September 1884, there is a short note that when the fall semester began there was a new class with "black" students, including two new ones: Markus Germei and Natanael Hagena Djigo.[45] Twoldo Medhen, Haile Mikael Kidano, the South African Josef Kamataka, and the Zulu prince Josef Umkwelantaba were already in the class at that time.[46]

During the following years, the chronicles say nothing about the Kolmodin family. The only mention is of Adolf Kolmodin. In October 1885, it was noted that he had been ill – "seriously ill" even – for a week.[47] Often the students noted that everything was proceeding as usual. Sometimes, classes were cancelled because of the teacher's absence or because of practical duties for all the students, e.g., harvesting potatoes.

In March 1893, Kolmodin is welcomed as the new principal of Johannelund,[48] and from then on he and his family are mentioned more often. On 22 November

43 See further Sundkler, Bengt, *Nathan Söderblom: His Life and Work*, Lund: Gleerups 1968.

44 Kolmodin, Johannes, "Meine studienreise," p. 230. For translation, see quotation on first page of this chapter.

45 *Väktarkrönikan*, September 1884.

46 Hellström, Ivan, *Johannelund 125 år*, pp. 54f.

47 *Väktarkrönikan*, 16 October 1885.

48 *Väktarkrönikan,* 26 March 1893.

1894, mention is made of the death of Kolmodin's young son Karl Fredrik, and on 26 November lessons are cancelled because of his funeral.[49] In the fall of 1895, Jonas Iwarson, who would later become a missionary in Eritrea, writes in the chronicles that Nelly Kolmodin has left Johannelund together with Johannes, who is moving to Strängnäs where he will begin his studies at the secondary grammar school (*läroverk*).[50] One can sense a special understanding in the lines of Iwarson: "Mrs. Kolmodin left with little Johannes for Strängnäs, where J[ohannes] will take up studies at the secondary grammar school. This is the first time he is separated from his home for a longer period of time. May the Lord raise him, and if that is his wish, make him a great missionary to the Oromos!"[51] Later that same fall, on 7 October, Adolf Kolmodin celebrated his 40th birthday. The following day, he has his first lessons in Greek for the semester.[52] A week later, Johannes visited his home, an event noted by the student who wrote the chronicles for that week.[53]

Several times during the following years the chronicles contain small notes about the Kolmodin family. The impression is confirmed that the students formed a big family together with Dr. and Mrs. Kolmodin. When Nelly Kolmodin celebrated her birthday in early December, the students were all invited,[54] and on Christmas Eve all the students staying at the institute had dinner together with the principal's family and a group of other guests.[55] I have, however, not been able so far to find any further notes about Johannes Kolmodin.

Conclusions

It is easy to understand that Johannes Kolmodin carried with him lasting impressions from his home at Johannelund and the milieu created by his parents and the institute. The Swedish Evangelical Mission was the broad background to the life and work of his father and mother. The interest in foreign languages and cultures, especially in Eritrea, was passed on to Johannes through his parents and through what he heard and encountered at Johannelund. And Johannes Kolmoldin himself became part of an extended family at the institute. He made friends for life there, and had the privilege of being reunited with these friends later in life, when he pursued some of his own research in Eritrea, and later again, in Ethiopia.

---

49 *Väktarkrönikan*, 22 and 26 November 1894.

50 For a discussion about the reasons for choosing Strängnäs, see Carl Gustaf Kolmodin's chapter "An Ill-matched Couple" in this book.

51 *Väktarkrönikan*, 28 August 1895.

52 *Väktarkrönikan*, 7 and 8 October 1895.

53 *Väktarkrönikan*, 18 October 1895.

54 *Väktarkrönikan*, 7 December 1895.

55 *Väktarkrönikan*, 24 December 1895.

Zanta Tsazzegan Hazzegan: Johannes Kolmodin's Contributions to an Understanding of Eritrean Highland Culture

EZRA GEBREMEDHIN

Johannes Kolmodin's history of Hamazen according to the traditions of Tsazzega and Hazzega was first published in *Archives d'études Orientales* (Uppsala) in 1912 in the Tigrinya language. His doctoral thesis, containing a fuller version of the same material, was published in the same series in 1914, and in 1915 a French translation of the work was published.[1] There is also a later edition in Tigrinya, *Zanta Tsazzegan Hazzegan*, based on the 1912 and 1914 publications and edited by Fre Woldu Kiros.[2] In this chapter, this later 1989 Tigrinya edition, here referred to as *Zanta,* will be used. The focus will be on Eritrean history and culture, with particular reference to the role of narrative and the use of different literary types.

Zanta is the only work by Kolmodin available in print in Tigrinya. As such, it is known and quoted by Eritreans high and low, learned and less learned. I have seen references to it both in its printed form and in texts distributed by Eritreans over the Internet.[3]

Kolmodin's collection of Tigrinya songs is not available in Tigrinya yet,[4] but 36 of them that deal with childbirth have been translated into Swedish as *Barnsängssånger* by Carl Gustaf and Birgitta Kolmodin. There is also an unpublished translation into Swedish of "Traditions de Tsazzega et Hazzega." Publication of these Swedish translations carries the promise of a happy reception among younger Eritreans, not only in Sweden, but also in the whole of Scandinavia.[5]

---

1 Kolmodin, J., "Traditions de Tsazzega et Hazzega. Textes tigrinja" (Preface in French), *Archives d'études Orientales* 5:1, Uppsala, 1912; Kolmodin, J., "Traditions de Tsazzega et Hazzega: Annales et documents," Ph D. Thesis, *Archives d'études orientales,* 5:3, Uppsala, 1914; and Kolmodin, J., "Traditions de Tsazzega et Hazzega. Traduction francaise," *Archives d'études Orientales* 5:2, Uppsala, 1915.

2 .Kolmodin, J., *Zanta Tsazzegan Hazzegan,* edited by Fre Woldu Kiros, Stockholm: African Triangle, 1989, in this chapter referred to as *Zanta.*

3 Johannes Kolmodin's various works in Swedish, German and French are treasures waiting to be made available to those Eritreans who are not equipped with Europe's main languages.

4There are 889 such songs, according to Carl Gustaf Kolmodin. See, Kolmodin, J., "Tigrinska Barnsängssånger," (unpublished translation from German to Swedish by Birgitta and Carl Gustaf Kolmodin, with an Introduction by Carl Gustaf Kolmodin).

5 Kolmodin, J., *Berättelser från Tsazzega och Hazzega. Muntliga traditioner från Hamasens högland i Eritrea, upptecknade av Johannes Kolmodin.* Unpublished translation from French into Swedish by Birgitta and Carl Gustaf Kolmodin.

Background

Carl Gustaf Kolmodin has aptly summarised the background to my topic in his book *Johannes Kolmodin i brev och skrifter.*[6] Kolmodin arrived in the highlands of Hamazen and in Tsazzega, the main town at that time, in 1908. The town was the home and residence of a princely family that had played the leading role in this Eritrean province for over 200 years. Kolmodin was to stay either there or in Asmara, when he was not on his research-related journeys to other parts of the country. Gradually, he became fascinated by the oral history of Däqätäscim, the children of Attäscim and he decided to record this tradition in Tigrinya. At the same time, he started thinking about a subject for his doctoral thesis.[7]

In Tsazzega, Kolmodin met a most fitting helper and co-worker in the person of a young man by the name of Bahta. With his help, he could contact a wide cross-section of people well-versed in the province's oral tradition, including people who could provide Kolmodin with material from as far back as the 10th century.[8] His "Traditions de Tsazzega et Hazzega" *(Zanta)* is therefore a compilation from various sources.

Glimpses into Kolmodin's Work as a Scholar

The thoroughness of Kolmodin's mode of working is reflected in his notes in notebook II of *Tigrinja sånger.*[9] One encounters notes, references and cross-references about names, places, historical background and the dating of documents, etc. Many of the *awlo* (the short poetic compositions that dot the *Zanta*) are annotated and explained in these notebooks, which served as the workshops in which Kolmodin did his demanding preparatory work before different texts received their final formulations.

In a notebook containing *Ge'ez sånger* (songs in Ge'ez) collected in Eritrea in 1909, there is a lovely letter (a eulogy, really), written in Ge'ez to Qes Menson by a certain Haleqa Kidanä Mariam. The letter was in fact addressed to Pastor Anders Svensson, field director of the Swedish Evangelical Mission in Eritrea at the time of Kolmodin's visit. Kolmodin has discreetly included the following note about the composer of the eulogy above the letter: "Went to Jerusalem in March 1909; wanted some help for his journey."

This note and the eulogy itself give us a glimpse into a highly refined culture of begging, which uses as a literary vehicle the poetic form known as *qiné* (literally composition or song). Here follows the eulogy in a translation from Ge'ez, the last line of the text being in Amharic, a language which Svensson used regularly:

Sent by haleqa Kidanä Mariam. May it reach the honoured and exalted Qes Menson!

Knowledgeable and wise man of God!

---

6 Kolmodin, C.G. *Johannes Kolmodin i brev och skrifter,* Kungl. Vitterhets Historie och Antikvitets Akademien (Filologiskt arkiv 41), Stockholm: Almqvist and Wiksell International, 1999, p. 21.

7 Ibid.

8 Ibid, p. 26.

9 UUB Manuscript Collection Q.15:24e. Notes on rites connected with weddings and funerals are available under Q 15:24a-p. Kolmodin's letters are found under Q 15. Letters to his parents are also available in T 3 l:18 and 19.

Elected from his mother's womb, like John the Baptist

And like Job the righteous one, a lover of God!

You whose mind is like that of the prophets, incomparable

Gentle as a dove

Delicious like milk

Bright as the sun

Receiver of generations like Abraham

You who have received all these things

How are you?

Johannes Kolmodin: A Man Beloved

A great admirer by the name of Mäsmär, the son of Yikunolom, dedicates a whole eulogy to Yohannes! The poem has the title *Yohannes* and is headed with the words, "Given to me by Mäsmär wäddi Yekunälom." I have translated the gist of the eulogy, which, though somewhat artless as a literary piece, reflects how highly Eritreans regarded this Nordic scholar among them.

Yohannes

You are advanced in the things of the Gospel

Son of Kolmodin, revealer of truth

You are advanced in the books of the New

Advanced too in the books of the Old

You who activate the country through prayer and faith

The unbendable tree trunk, Yohannes!

Recognised[10] by Italian authorities!

Recognised by British authorities!

Recognised by Swedish authorities!

Recognised as far as Shäwa [i.e,. Ethiopia]

All love you as they love food and drink

You are as precious as a crown of diamonds

Acquired [bought] here, so far from Sweden!

Kolmodin's contribution to Eritrean culture consists not only of his arrangements for the recording of the stories, but also in the enormous amount of preparatory and analytical work that must have gone into the compilation of this work. A look at his well-filled and annotated notebooks in the Manuscript Collection of Carolina Rediviva, Uppsala University Library (UUB), provides evidence of this fact.

It is obvious that he was interested not only in paper work and research but also in human relations. Among his papers, I discovered some letters that he had received from the treasurer's office of the Syrian Protestant College in Beirut. They are about a certain Mikael Uqbagabir and acknowledge receipt of money sent to the college. One of them specifically acknowledges a Christmas gift. Something of Kolmodin's good-heartedness and concern as a person comes through in his letters. This personal contact must have been the fruit of his long contact with Eritreans and his two years of research in the country.

---

10 Literally means "registered."

His reports and writings and lectures on Eritrea in Sweden and in other countries contained material not only about documents but also about people, including specific persons who had acted as his informants and become his lifelong friends. Among his collection of Tigrinya songs in one of his notebooks is a beautiful eulogy on Bahta Tesfa Yohannis, his right-hand man, written in the form of a poem. The poem is entitled, "A Poetic lamentation, containing wisdom, on our beloved brother Bahta Tesfa Yohannes."[11]

Johannes Kolmodin must have been a man who gave both his heart and mind to Eritrea. But now to a closer look at the *Zanta*!

Zanta's General Content and Character

It should be pointed out that *Zanta* is a compilation of material bearing on the history and culture of a section of the highlands of Eritrea. It basically deals with traditionally Christian areas that once had close links with Ethiopia, its church and royal house. This fact, of course, limits the scope of the material presented and commented upon, even though the narrator tells his story with great abandon and a sense of freedom. Around this centrepiece, the regions of Tsazzega and Hazzega, he gathers the history of mankind and the histories of those races and tribes who came knocking or rushing at Eritrea's doors, be they Turk, Egyptian, British, Italian or other Abyssinian.

A Gallery of Literary Types

However, *Zanta* is more than history and narrative: it is a gallery of literary types shared over several centuries by people in what is now Eritrea and Ethiopia, in church and society, on common days and on special occasions.

In his book, *A History of Tigrinya Literature,* Ghirmai Negash points out some "generic labels" as far as Tigrinya poetic compositions are concerned. These are the *masse,* the *melkes* and the *dog'a.*[12] The *masse* poems are performed by highly respected oral poets, the *masseniyas,* at special social gatherings. They include the commemoration of local chiefs or national figures and marriage ceremonies. *Masse* poems are, according to Negash, also the medium for expressing collective wishes, expectations, fears and hopes, especially in times of social and political change.[13]

The *melkes* share most of the traits of the *masse,* but "… unlike the generically festive and prototypically panegyric content of the *masse,* the poems in this category are exclusively performed to mourn a dead person, during a funeral."[14]

---

11 Johannes Kolmodin, "Tigrinja sånger," UUB Manuscript Collection Q15:24e.

12 This he does in his comments on Conti Rossini's collection, "Tigrinya Popular Songs" (Canti Popolari Tigrai), published in three parts in *Zeitsschrift für Assyriologie und Verwandte Gebiete,* volumes 17, 18, 19 (1903-06). See Negash, G., *A History of Tigrinya Literature in Eritrea. The Oral and the Written 1890-1991,* Leiden: Research School of Asian, African and American Studies (CNWS), Leiden University, 1999.

13 Ibid., pp. 98-9. In a footnote on p. 98 Negash states, "These terms are those commonly used by the Tiginya communities in Eritrea and Tigray. Other terms for the *masse* are *awlo* and also, particularly in Hamasien region of Eritrea, *hilay* … *Masse* also designates all three genres of oral poetry collectively, as an umbrella name."

14 Ibid., p. 99.

In the Ethiopian and Eritrean Orthodox traditions, there is the *Mälke'a*, a genre of praise that describes almost every part of the body of the person in question. The word *Mälk* itself means face or feature. *Mälke'a Iyyäsus* consists of praises directed at the different parts of the body of Jesus. It begins with the words, "Hail to the memory of thy name ..." and then goes on to Jesus' hair, head, etc. Deep theological thoughts are interwoven into the enumeration of the different parts of the body. There is also *Mälke'a Maryam,* a deeply emotional collection of praises in poetic form to the different parts of the body of the Virgin. This collection is, in all likelihood, of Ethiopian composition or an adaptation of a work probably of Syrian provenance. One can speculate about how much the *folk* tradition of composing *mälke*s has affected the *mälke*s, and vice-versa.

The third category of poems mentioned by Negash, the *dog'a*, also eulogises the dead. Negash writes, "What mainly distinguishes this genre from the *melkes,* however, is that it is composed sometime after the death has taken place. Other differences from the former are that this genre allows, relatively, more room to lament several deaths together in one poem; the poems are more nostalgic and romantic, and are freer in their commentary on socio-political issues of contemporary society."[15]

The Zanta as a Repository of Literary Genres

According to Negash, the major forms of poetry represented in Kolmodin's *Traditions of Tsazzega and Hazzega* are *masse, melkes* and *dog'a*. Negash continues: "There are also other types of poems belonging to the genre: *fekera* (boasts) and writings in prose called *terekab-zereba* (witticisms)."

An example of *fekera* attributed to the chief of Tsazzega, Deggiat Hailu, a rival of Ras Weldemichael, the two main figures in Kolmodin's *Zanta,* reads as follows,

> *He, who if he gazes to the right overwhelms the earth*
> *He, who if he gazes to the left overwhelms the earth*
> *Pluck courage hyenas; your Master is coming*
> *A banquet for the vultures*
> *I, Gommorrah, the brother of Illen!* [16]

Here Hailu was evidently seeking to induce courage in his troops by underscoring his prowess in battle. He is the warrior whose exploits result in so many deaths that hyenas can count on a rich table of human flesh.

There is also the liturgical category of poems and compositions known as *deggwa*, which seems to be a secular variant of what Negash calls *dog'a*. *Deggwa* means singing, song and praise. The liturgical book that bears this designation is attributed to Saint Yared of Axum. Composed in poetic form, the *deggwa* contains songs for the whole year. Traditionally, eight types of musical notations were used. The liturgical handbook *Tsomä Deggwa* contains compositions for Lent that are believed to have been extracted and compiled separately by or under

---

15 Ibid.

16 This poem from Kolmodin, *Traditions de Tsazzega et Hazzega* is reproduced in a translation by Negash, *A History of Tigrinya Literature in Eritrea,* pp. 101-2.

Abba Giorgis zä Gassecha, theologian and ascetic, known both in Ethiopia and present-day Eritrea. The Sundays in Lent have their specific designations, depending on the texts allotted to each.

There are also *deggwa* compositions for the seasons of the year. These cover *Keremt,* the rainy season from 26 säné (June) to 20 mäskäräm (September); *Mätse,* the time of wind, from 26 mäskäräm until 25 tahsas (December); *Hagai,* which means dry, or sunny, and extends from 26 tahsas 26 to 25 mägabit (March) and *Tsäday,* the season of sowing and harvesting and extends from 26 mägabit to 25 säné. Once again, it would be interesting to establish relations among the *deggwa* compositions in different spheres of social life.

Literary Characteristics in Zanta

The *Zanta* is, in short, a flowing fast-moving narrative, told with facility and rhetorical elegance. The memory of the narrators appears to be unfailing, and they are ever on the alert. What is impressive is the fact that the narrator reproduces not only accounts of events and occurrences, but also rich poetic skills.

Zanta abounds in a wealth of literary idioms no longer in frequent use in Tigrinya. One interesting idiom involves the use of the verb to sleep (*mädeqäs*) for settling and staying at a place for a longer period. Furthermore, to cause unrest among a people is expressed in terms of depriving them of sleep. The narrator states:

> Hänäshim left Tsazzega and made his sleeping place at a place called the ruins of Hänäshim, at Jan tekel. He threw his weight to the left and to the right, raiding at will. He deprived Akäläguzai of sleep.[17]

Consider the following interesting expressions, which are no longer common in every day Tigrinya and which should be of interest to younger Eritreans: they dropped a leaf on him (they voted for him or elected him to an office); carrying the sun on his back (with the sun behind him, p. 227); take control of a neck (occupy a strategic position or a bottleneck); he did not hang or mount a drum (he did not take over power, p. 186); and, today is not our bird (today is not an auspicious day for us).[18]

We also have the literary phenomenon known as *awlo*, the art of summarising an event of importance in short, pithy rhymed verses. *Awlo* is basically a vehicle for the expression of praise and admiration. However, not only victories and success but also sorrows, defeats, tragedies, losses, grief and joys were expressed in terms of *awlo*.

Even curses are expressed in poetic language. Consider the curse that was pronounced against *ChalouQ* by his brothers for being deceitful in his dealings:

> *May you not amount* [even] *to a small village*
> *May your number be so low that your kith and kin can easily take shelter under an oak tree!*
> *May you not lack supper for the day!*[19]

---

17 Kolmodin, *Zanta,* p. 56.

18 Ibid., p. 226.

19 Ibid., p. 10.

The narrator continues with this comment:

Therefore, the tribe of ChalouQ has not succeeded in establishing other villages or regions because of the curse of their brothers. In their totality they never manage to exceed the limited number of the members of the tribe of *Gäshinashim*. Even if all of them were to gather, they could still sit under the shade of one oak tree. They have food for the day. However, they don't have land enough to be able to boast or become rich. Therefore, the curse of brothers is indeed effective.[20]

Zanta is a collection of narratives and comments where language is used on several levels. There are cryptic references to events. The literary phenomenon known as wax-and-gold (an expression or word with an outer and inner meaning), so common in the rest of Ethiopia, permeates the narrative and comes forth in the *awlo* tradition.[21]

The *Zanta* is not only a record of events, although it purports to be so. It is a story interspersed with interpretations and comments. Once in a while, the narrator brushes aside claims briskly with comments like:

Likewise, here in MetaHit the children of Levi have brothers, namely Tor'A, the House of Mensa'e, Marya QeyiH and Maria Tsellim. Now, however, those who have become Muslims say, "No! We are relatives of Mohamed who have come from Arabia." They are lying.[22]

Amharic words are rare in the *Zanta* but crop up here and there. Expressions like *aynä quranja* (spy, p. 206); *ferdi yebqa* (let the judgment stand or suffice, p. 219); the rhyme "*Endet sänäbäteh, Gäbru Webät*" ("How have you been, Gäbru the handsome one!"), a short eulogy to the Tigrean Wakshum Gäbru who had been appointed over Hamasén, (p. 212), are examples of the occurrence of Amharic expressions in the text of the narrative.

History, the Main Concern

Notwithstanding this description of literary types in *Zanta*, it must be stressed that the narration of history is the main concern of this work. The narrator or informant may embellish his stories with niceties of language, but his main interest is, however, to tell a story.

The work is an example of a tradition in which "history" is remoulded in the minds and mouths of storytellers. This is the sort of material that would make for a rich field of research for scholars of oral tradition and its relationships with recorded history. Kolmodin was fully aware of this possibility and deals with it in his doctoral thesis.

Here is history woven in minds fertile with imagination out of a great variety of sources: the Bible, Israel, Ethiopia and her kings and legends, the *AdimHara* (the land of the Amhara), *Gondär, negus, baHregasi* (Bahri Nägassi, i.e., "the king of the region of the sea"). Here is a world without any boundaries separating Ethiopia and Eritrea from Israel.

---

20 Ibid., pp. 10-11.

21 For the literary phenomenon of wax-and-gold (*sämna wörq*) in Amharic, see Levine, D., *Wax and Gold: Tradition and Innovation in Ethiopian Culture.* Chicago: Chicago University Press, 1965.

22 Kolmodin, *Zanta*, p. 31.

And in the telling of a story, one must begin at the beginning. A question of primary concern in this regard is genealogy. Thus the first chapter of *Zanta*, entitled *The Genealogy of Hamazen,* begins with the words, "This is the genealogy of Hamazen, which we have arrived at by inquiring from the great and the knowledgeable."

The chapter then continues with the first paragraph, which has the title: "The Queen of Sheba Goes to King Solomon."

Then follows the text itself,

> After Abba Jigo[23] had destroyed his entire creation through the flood, he let one called Noah, a chosen one, survive with his three children, Shem, Ham and Japheth, in order that there wouldn't be a gap in mankind's genealogy. Afterwards, Noah gave Shem Egypt and all countries to the East as an inheritance. He gave Japheth all the country to the West as an inheritance. And to Ham he gave the place where we are, as an inheritance. But about Jerusalem he said, "Let him who is chosen among you inherit it!"

The fact that Jerusalem didn't exist (in the form that it took later) in the days of Noah doesn't seem to worry the narrator. There is something artless about the way "history" is reproduced in this narrative. Legend is narrated with the certainty that accompanies fact. Imagination and fantasy reign supreme. This trait comes forth in the way the story of the visit of Ethiopia's Menelik to his "father" Solomon is narrated.

> King Solomon received him and honoured him. He appointed him saying, "Go and reign over your mother's home region." In his company Solomon sent some members of Ruben's, Mosef's [Joseph's], Minab's [Binyam's, i.e., Benjamin's], and Judah's tribes. He also sent some of Levi's children so that they may take care of priestly functions. He gave them the Ark of the Covenant named after Minki'el [Michael] to show them the way home. However, the sons of Levi, who knew the ins and outs of the temple, exchanged the ark named after Minki'el for an ark named after Mary. After bidding the king farewell, they started on their way. Shortly after that the king discovered that they had taken Zion with them and followed them in hot pursuit. Menelik and his family crossed the Red Sea at the place where the children of Israel had done so before. Upon arriving at the crossing, Solomon remembered the fate of Pharaoh and didn't dare to follow them![24]

The fact that the Ark of the Covenant belonged to the period of the Old Testament and that Mary the Mother of Jesus belonged to that of the New Testament does not bother the narrator. He is not concerned with logic.

Women of Wealth and Might

Zanta gives us glimpses of women of wealth and might. An example of the first category is of *Imbäbet* (Lady) Säbänägergish. She was a daughter of Emperor Iyassu (1730-55) and the wife of *Deggiat* Gäbrä Kristos, who had won the emperor's favour. *Zanta* describes her wealth in the following words:

---

23 A colloquial designation for God.

24 Kolmodin, J., Traditions de Tsazzega et Hazzega, textes tigrinja (Preface in French), *Archives d'études Orientales* 5:1, Uppsala, 1912, p. 5.

Deggiat Gäbrä Kristos took his wife, Säbänägergish, and travelled all the way from Gondär to Hammasen, granting every place where she put her feet and where she spent the night, left and right, to her as property. Furthermore, she went out from Se'Azega as her base, appropriating much land, wherever she went or spent the night. All these places became the property of the couple.[25]

It was not uncommon for such women of birth to retire to a monastic style of life, with fasting and prayer, after the death of close relatives or husbands. Such became the fate of Säbänägergish after the death of a son:

After the death of Deggiat Tesfatsen, grief caused his mother, *Imbäbet* Säbänägergish, to assume the lifestyle of a nun. She left her mansion and moved into a small house. The house still stands. In fact, Woizero [Mrs.] Mersha, the daughter of Deggiat Hailu, lives there now, she too having become a nun.[26]

An example of a woman of might is *Woizero* Illen, the sister of Deggiat Hailu, prince of Tsazzega. The fact that Hailu "swore" in the name of his sister shows that she was a woman of dignity. In her simmering anger against a chieftain in her region, Kentiba Wolde Gabir, a male nobleman who had offended her on several counts, Illen went to war and defeated him. He had to flee.[27]

Interesting local modifications in the voicing and spelling of non-Tigrinya names are preserved for us in abundance in the *Zanta*. Joseph is called Mosef, Benjamin (Binyam) is designated Minab, and Merdokios is called MerKedios. Ras Alula, the favourite general of Emperor Yohannes, who was sent to present-day Eritrea in 1879 as governor of Mereb Milash (another designation for Eritrea), is called *Ras Alla*. The Swiss Pasha Werner Münzinger (1832-75), once French Consul in Massaw and later a collaborator with General (later Sir) Robert Napier in the campaign against Emperor Teodros (1868), is called Bashai Bishinjir. General Antonio Baldissera, who occupied Asmara on 3 August 1899, is called Jinenar Bandisera.[28]

A Glimpse into Taboo Thinking

The reader is given glimpses into customs that border on the superstitious. One example has to do with the relationship between the group of people known as *Jin* and the *deqeteschim*. The *Jin* were latecomers to Hazzega and belonged to the category of the so-called *ma'ikälay bet* (middle house, i.e., not original natives). The narrator says:

Where people are gathered for a marriage feast, the Jin don't eat or drink before having asked, "Is there a son of ateschim here?" Likewise, the deqeteschim don't eat or drink before having asked, "Is there a son of Jin here?" There is no intermarriage between the Jin and deqeteschim. They say, "If we eat ahead of them, we become sick. If we take one of their daughters in marriage we don't get children."[29]

---

25 Kolmodin, *Zanta,* p. 72.

26 Ibid., p. 77.

27 Ibid., pp. 160-1.

28 Ibid., pp. 20, 116, 246, 220 and 250 respectively.

29 Ibid., p. 19.

A Special Eye to the Swedes

The narrator or narrators knew that they were telling things to a Swede with connections to the Swedish Evangelical Mission. They therefore add sympathetic touches to what is narrated about Swedish-Eritrean relations. A Swedish missionary by the name of Lager was one of the casualties of the fierce battles between Tsazzega and Hazzega in July 1876 at Addi Qontsi. In a surge of innocent curiosity, he had asked his Eritrean friends, his evangelical co-religionists (the *kenisha* in his company), if he couldn't witness an "Habesha battle." His curiosity was to cost him his life. A furious warrior who belonged to Wäldänki'el's camp discovered him and his co-religionists hiding in St. Michael's Church. Lager and one of his companions were dragged out and beheaded. The narrator states: "But he [Lager], believing that things functioned according to the rules of his country, said, 'As for me, I would like to witness a Habesha battle, if possible.'"

A little later, the narrator has the following to say on Lager's death: "As of that day the blood of Tsä'Azzega and that of the *känisha* flowed together and their lives and deaths became one."[30]

Cruelty and Mercy

Cruelty was part of this whole landscape, exotic and bleak as it was and marked as it was by instability, fear and changing fortunes for high and low. Fear, flight, vengeance were the order of the day, with mercy shown to the one who came begging for it, repentant and broken. We have the remarkable picture of the one who comes to Woldenki'el with a rope around his neck or a knife or a boulder on his head, and pleads:

> *Take, here is a knife for my mutilation*
> *Take, here is a rope for my hanging*
> *May my bones be broken to pieces*
> *May my body be splintered*
> *Never have I reckoned it, to end like this*
> *You are far-famed oh, "Slasher"!*[31]

Woldenki'el was so impressed with the poetic skill of the petitioner that he had mercy on him. This creative pleader is believed to have given Ras Woldenki'el the nickname *Gomida*, which means "the Slasher"!

Mercy or appointments to office were awarded either for courage or quick wit in the composition of clever verse! There are some moving passages that show both the folly and the tragedy of this fratricidal conflict between two fraternal clans of Tsazzega and Hazzega.

Not all chieftains were as "warlike" as Woldenki'el and Hailu. A certain *Deggiat* Mäkonnän, a member of the Hazzega clan who had been appointed over Tsazegga, addresses his subjects with the words:

---

30 Ibid., pp. 229-30. *Känisha* is the designation for Eritrean Evangelical Lutheran Christians. Their church owes its birth to Swedish missionaries.

31 Ibid., pp. 234-5, based on a translation by Ghirmai Negash. See Negash, *A History of Tigrinya Literature in Eritrea*, p. 102.

We are brothers from two [branches] of the house of Täsfatsen. We are brothers and sisters of one man [father]. It is most appropriate for us to live in love and brotherhood. As far as appointments to office are concerned, these are from God. We should acknowledge the one who is appointed by God, be he from our ranks or your ranks. As for the rest, let us watch over and preserve our country and fight our enemies.[32]

The Zanta and Later Eritrean Political Ambitions

Kolmodin's *Zanta* provides a rich background for an understanding of Eritrea's independence as the result of a cumulative process to which local ambitions and struggles have contributed. Persons like Bahri Negasi Yishak, Ras Wolde Mikael Solomon and Bahta Hagos are prominent figures in the gallery of Eritrean heroes.

As Gustav Arén has put it: "In the early 1890s there was widespread discontent with the Italian settlement scheme and agricultural policy. Bahta Hagwos's revolt in Akeleguzai in December 1894, was the signal for extensive fighting between the malcontents and the colonial power."[33] In urging his hesitant brother Sängal to join him in revolting against the Italians, Bahta used the following *awlo*:

> *O Sängal, my brother, believe, don't be a deceived!*
> *There is no remedy for the sting of a white snake!*
> *However diligently you seek.*[34]

The exploits of these Eritrean fighter spirits are believed to have provided some of the ideological fuel for more recent Eritrean efforts to obtain independence.

Bahri Negasi Yishak, a governor of the Kingdom of Medri Bahri ("land of the sea," as Eritrea was once known) under Ethiopian suzerainty, defended his territory from incursions by Turks. But there were also times when he made common cause with them to oust his Ethiopian overlords, who were often only grudgingly recognised by him and his like. He died in 1578 in an insurrection launched in concert with Turkish troops against his Ethiopian overlords.

Ras Wolde Mikael Solomon of Hazzega was and is regarded by not a few of Eritrea's "freedom-fighters" as a forerunner of Eritrea's aspirations to self-determination.[35] He was the most prominent and powerful ruler in the highlands in the 19th century, having had a formidable and well-organised army. Eritreans are quick to point out that Emperor Yohannes of Tigray and his right-hand commander, Ras Alula, objected to Wolde Mikael's growing military and influence.

---

32 Kolmodin, *Zanta*, p. 214.

33 Arén, Gustav, *Evangelical Pioneers in Ethiopia. Origins of the Evangelical Church Mekane Yesus*, Stockholm and Addis Abeba: EFS-förlaget, 1978, p. 336. Arén refers to Pankhurst, Richard, *A Brief Note on the Economic History of Ethiopia from 1800 to 1935*, Addis Ababa: Haile Sellassie I University, 1967, pp. 165-74 as a further source.

34 Kolmodin, *Zanta*, p. 162.

35 This sentiment is clearly reflected in Yishaq Yosef's book in Tigrinya, *Imbi Yale Woldu ... (?)Gomida*, (A life history of Ra'isi Wolde Mikael), Asmara: MBY Printing Press, 1999. The term "Imbi Yale" means, literally "He said 'I refuse!' "

Wolde Mikael, who inflicted a crushing defeat on one of Yohannes's commanders, Ras Bariyu, in 1878, was, according to the opinion of practically all
Eritreans, deceived into negotiating with Ras Alula. He paid dearly for that mistake. In September 1879, he was captured and sent to languish in a prison in
Adua. This led to the creation on the Eritrean highlands of a power vacuum,
which Tigrayan Ethiopians were quick to fill.[36]

The last phase of *Zanta*, the story of Italy's creeping ascent from the coast to the
Eritrean highlands, presents a massive shift of loyalties, a collapse of faithfulness
to the Ethiopian throne or *AddimHara*. One by one, Eritrea's noblemen fled to the
coast or rushed into the bosom of Italy. It was an Eritrean who led the Italians into
Asmara. Soon, however, Eritrea's warlords were to learn that their new masters
were not to be trusted. Soon there would be rebellion in the air! *Zanta* narrates how
Italy tightened its noose around the necks of its previously unsuspecting Eritrean
subjects, and how the Eritrean nobles revolted one after the other.[37]

At the same time, it must be said that a great number of the participants in the
Eritrean struggle for self-determination, with their once strongly Marxist emphasis on the interpretation of history, regarded Wolde-Michael and his counterparts
in Tsazzega simply as destructive feudal lords.

This was also the view, at least in part, of At Wolde-ab Woldemariam, one of
the fathers of the Eritrean struggle for independence. In an interview given to the
present writer in Sweden in 1988, he said:

> Eritrea's weakness was that it had no leaders. Leaders like Woldenki'el were cruel and ambi-
> tious. They destroyed each other. Woldenki'el was not a national leader — he was a tribal
> leader. He had no national concept of leadership [...] There is nothing wrong with the Eritrean
> people. They have been unfortunate enough not to find leadership of a national magnitude in
> their recent history.

Thus the memory of the performance of some of the leaders mentioned in
Zanta led to a critical evaluation of Eritrea's local history and provided something of a tacit guideline for its growing political ambitions. The liberation struggles did in fact fall, from time to time, prey to the temptation to idolise "tribal"
or "religious" leaders. However, the stated goal of all Eritrean liberation struggles was the development of national leadership. Thus, *Zanta* can be said to have
become an inspiration in providing not only models of courage but also warnings
against the risks involved in allowing power-hungry individuals to take centre
stage in the struggles of a nation.

In Closing

To listen attentively and to record what one has heard faithfully is to find a
way into the heart and soul of a people. And language is an indispensable vehicle for such a listening experience. The collection known as *Zanta Tsazzegan
Hazzegan* is the fruit of such listening and recording. What makes it special is
that it is the result of a cooperative enterprise between several Africans and a

---

36 This is the general sentiment reflected in the introduction to the recent book by Denison, E., Ren, G.Y.,
and Gebremedhin, N., *Asmara. Africa's Secret Modernist City,* London and New York: Merrell, 2003, pp. 20-7.

37 Kolmodin, *Zanta,* p. 257 ff.

European, who join their native and learned skills in bringing about a collection of oral traditions that is rich in linguistic, historical and cultural memory and imagination.

Kolmodin's contribution to an understanding of Eritrea's culture consists in his having made available already existing *oral* material from the lips of children in the areas under study. His studies and comments on this and similar materials, particularly in his doctoral thesis, have been instructive for the scholarly world in Sweden, Germany, and Italy and among French-speaking people.[38] Eritreans with knowledge of the main languages of Europe have shared in the benefits of his studies. It is to be hoped that more is to come. Kolmodin's *Zanta* is the spearhead as far as his influence among Tigrinya-speaking people is concerned. It has become a *mahdär* (a treasure house) for the memories of a significant part of the population of Eritrea.

---

38 Kolmodin, Johannes, "Traditions de Tsazzega et Hazzega: Annales et documents," Ph D. Thesis, *Archives d'études orientales,* 5:3, Uppsala, 1914.

Friends and Compatriots: Sven Hedin, Sven Lidman and Nathan Söderblom[*]

CARL GUSTAF KOLMODIN

Johannes Kolmodin had a large circle of friends, both as a researcher, intellectual and activist in Uppsala and as a diplomat in Constantinople. This is clear from, among other things, his extensive correspondence. In the present chapter[1] I will describe Kolmodin's relations with three contemporaries who were especially close to him: Sven Hedin, Sven Lidman and Nathan Söderblom.[2] It is difficult to find more controversial and mutually contrasting personalities in Sweden's intellectual world at the beginning of the last century. The fact that Johannes Kolmodin kept their friendship throughout his varied life says, therefore, a good deal about himself. His correspondence with these friends is an indispensable source if one wishes to become better acquainted with Kolmodin. The period in question covers primarily the years from 1911 to 1926.

Sven Hedin

Kolmodin was active in the conservative student association Heimdal, at times as its chairman. The group was strongly influenced by Harald Hjärne – the man who "gave Sweden back Charles XII,"[3] and whose role can hardly be overestimated. Heimdal was "a debate forum for the young, to whom the dissolution of the union [with Norway] in 1905 was traumatic."[4] Their guiding principle was duty to one's country. They staunchly opposed the so-called "company philosophy or utility philosophy,"[5] the same outlook that President J. F. Kennedy would express fifty years later in his famous dictum: "Ask not what your country can do for you; ask what you can do for your country."

The activities were intensified when the matter of defence arose, just after the election in the autumn of 1911. The newly appointed liberal Staaf ministry then decided to reduce the costs of defence and cancel the construction of an armoured ship (the "F-boat"), a decision that was taken by the previous Parliament some months earlier. Instead, the Staaf ministry wanted to investigate the issue and, pending the results, to postpone the ship's construction. Many protested against this decision, not least the Heimdal group. Loudest was the voice of Sven Hedin, who wrote in the polemical pamphlet *A Word of Warning*:

---

[*] This chapter is translated from Swedish to English by Jon van Leuven.

1 This chapter is mainly based on: Carl Gustaf Kolmodin, *Johannes Kolmodin i brev och skrifter* [Johannes Kolmodin in letters and writings]. Kungl. Vitterhets Historie och Antikvitets Akademien, Filologiskt arkiv 41, Stockholm 1999.

2 See the index of persons at the end of the book.

3 Jan Olof Olsson, *1914*. Stockholm 1964, pp. 50-53.

4 Sigrid Kahle: *H. S. Nyberg*. Svenska akademiens handlingar från år 1986:16. Stockholm 1991, p. 78.

5 Johannes Kolmodin: *Fosterlandet och vi* [The fatherland and we]. A lecture [13 March 1915]. Uppsala 1915, p. 13.

It is with certificates of deposit and committee reports that we are expected to meet enemy armoured fleets! When the 30-centimetre cannon thunder outside our shores, we should answer with the clinking of heaps of gold. When the invading army crosses the sea to land wherever he pleases, he shall face a coastal flotilla made of paper.[6]

This 70-page pamphlet appeared in a million (!) copies, an unbeatable record at that time. The distribution was efficient and quite unconstrained. Hedin himself comments on it:

The pamphlet...is printed in a mass edition – say over a million copies, and is inserted into *all* rightist newspapers and so many moderate ones as can be persuaded to accept it. When the subscribers open today's morning or evening newspaper, the little pamphlet tumbles out handily onto their knees and you can be certain that they will look for what the completely cost-free publication has to tell. That it is something important can be taken for granted and, in any case, one has to read the message.[7]

Not only was the press relied upon to spread *A Word of Warning*. The country's clergymen were also exploited. Each of them was sent 25 copies for distribution "to suitable members" of the congregation, "particularly those who would not be in a position to read rightist or moderate newspapers."[8]

The main purpose of *A Word of Warning* was to depict the threat from the east:

Recently the Finnish railroad network has been connected with the Russian... The track gauge is the same in Finland and Russia. Now troops from the heart of Russia will be thrown at any moment straight up to Torneå, without a single trans-shipment...

Have you seen in your newspaper that the Finnish military has been suspended, and that the Finns' barracks, built with Finnish money, are quartering only Russian troops...

Is it not true that during the past two years, time and again, new troop units from innermost Russia have been transferred to Finland and gradually, quietly, shifted ever farther up to the north?[9]

With great imagination Hedin described how life in Sweden would be "under a foreign yoke." He answered the question "Could we defend ourselves?" with an unreserved affirmation, and ended by insisting: "Before the year's Parliament breaks up, the keel of the first truly seagoing armoured ship of the new type must be laid." And he added: "Therefore we ask of all who stand apart from political quarrelling...that during the days while [the question] is discussed in the chambers, the battle between right and left be called off."[10] Unfortunately, he forgot to specify *how* this could be achieved, but Sweden's most intensive political debate until then was the sequel. Several meetings of opinion were held in the country, urging the Swedish people to take part in a national collection for building the so-called F-boat. There were two successful collections and, already in May 1912, a total of 15 million crowns had been donated, easily enough to carry out the construction.[11]

---

6 Sven Hedin, *Ett varningsord* [A word of warning]. Stockholm 1912, p. 70.

7 Sven Hedin, *Försvarsstriden 1912 - 14* [The defence dispute]. Stockholm 1951, p. 10.

8 Ibid., p. 14.

9 Sven Hedin, *Ett Varningsord* [A word of warning]. Stockholm 1912, p. 15.

10 Ibid., p. 70.

11 Jan Olof Olsson, *1914*. Stockholm 1964, p. 62.

Heimdal invited Sven Hedin to address the students in Uppsala on 3 November 1913. This was perhaps the first time Johannes Kolmodin met Hedin. The latter spoke to a large assembly of students, and it proved to be a great meeting with shouts of exultation. Immediately afterward, some Heimdal students started to publish a weekly newspaper "for enlightenment and agitation on the defence question." It was entitled *Vårdkasen* [*The Beacon*] and soon acquired 130,000 subscribers.

At the centre of events stood Olof Palme (the later Prime Minister's paternal uncle) and Johannes Kolmodin. Much later it was written of Kolmodin that he "lived and acted in our midst. We in the deep ranks were captivated by his elegant repartees, clear style of delivery, quick understanding and swift decisiveness."[12] But he was not only a representative leading figure: he was also the persevering worker who wrote brochures and handbooks, participated in debates and organised elections and expressions of opinion.

The political unrest culminated in the "farmers' march" on 6 February 1914, which led to the famous – or notorious – castle courtyard speech, given by King Gustaf V but written by Sven Hedin and Carl Bennedich (a lieutenant on the General Staff). The speech ended with the king stating his definite view that the defence question should be resolved "now, without delay and coherently." Thereby he came into conflict with the government, whose resignation turned out to be the only possible solution.

Two days after the farmers' march, Heimdal arranged a new general meeting in order to "close ranks behind the King's call to a coalition." Olof Palme then proposed that the students seek a royal audience, and was assigned to prepare it. After the meeting, there was a social gathering of the Heimdalites at the Gillet restaurant. This had gone on for a while when Johannes Kolmodin appeared, not having been seen previously during the evening, and announced:

His Majesty the King has promised to receive the students on Wednesday 11 February at 1:30 in the afternoon. The students at Stockholm and Lund have declared themselves willing to take part...an extra train to Stockholm has been arranged, leaving at 11:30 in the morning, and the return ticket costs 1 crown. Then the cheering broke out! They rejoiced that the King would receive them, that members of the other student associations had accepted the proposal, and – not least, I think – about the rapid execution and grand organisation that have emerged here.[13]

How Johannes Kolmodin managed all this in such a short time is unknown in detail to us, but a qualified guess is that Sven Hedin had a hand in it. The two were by now familiar with each other and had met on several occasions – and Hedin, of course, had close contacts with the royal family. The students left on schedule, numbering 1,200 of Uppsala's 1,800 male ones (the 200 female students were naturally not allowed to come along).

Just after the royal audience, the activists continued their national conservative policy and created a new organisation, the *Constitutional Union*. It was founded on 16 February 1914 with the aim of conducting lecture and agitation tours all

---

12 Gunnar Hesslén, Några minnen från den "politiska" vårterminen 1914 [Some memories from the "political" spring term of 1914]. *Bland professorer och studenter. Hågkomster och livsintryck 19.* Uppsala 1938, pp. 316-317.

13 Ibid., pp. 322-324.

over the country, as support for retaining the King's authority under the Constitution of 1809, and against the introduction of parliamentarism. In great haste a "strictly secret" guide was formulated. The students commonly called it the "Gospel according to Johannes,"[14] so there was little secret about its main author. "He sacrificed everything for the national work," wrote his Orientalist friend H. S. Nyberg (see the chapter by Sigrid Kahle), "even his personal career here at home, his scientific path for which he was brilliantly endowed."[15]

In the meanwhile, Kolmodin completed his doctoral dissertation, *Traditions de Tsazzega et Hazzega*, and defended it on 29 May 1914. He had collected the material during a year and a half of field work in Eritrea. It built upon oral traditions from the medieval period until his day, recorded and for the first time written down in the country's own language. He upheld an entirely new principle: "that the oral tradition in question is far more reliable (*beaucoup plus exacte*) than one is at first inclined to believe by the view which has won adherence in historical science."[16]

Next to the historical writing itself, the emphasis on oral traditions' significance was the most important aspect of the dissertation. Kolmodin thus became "the primary inspirer" of H. S. Nyberg's revolutionary research long afterward in regard to translation and interpretation of the Old Testament, where he argued that the oldest sources had been oral and often metrical for ages before they were put in writing.[17] Nyberg passed the following judgement on Kolmodin's work:

> Lönnrot was the originator of the *Kalevala*. Kolmodin and his Abyssinian disciple Bahta were the originators of "Traditions de Tsazzega et Hazzega." The materials for composition were obtained by Lönnrot from the East Karelian professional singers, and by Kolmodin and Bahta from thirteen native old men. In the same manner, the authors of the Pentateuch had taken up material transmitted from the most diverse directions according to an arranged plan.
>
> [...] The Pentateuch was organised on a unified plan, which was not any worse executed than in other great compositions from older times; it not only *could*, but *should* be attributed to an individual author's personality, and the most natural explanation for the richness and variety of material in the Pentateuch is that the author used the same method as h, Kolmodin and Bahta.[18]

This assessment was made in 1948, but let us return to 1914, the year of Kolmodin's disputation. For his licentiate degree in 1908, Kolmodin had two subjects – history (with Professor Harald Hjärne) and Semitic languages (with Professor K. V. Zetterstéen) – and earned the highest mark ("three") in both. But his doctoral dissertation was nearly disallowed with an indifferent "two." In a statement to the marking committee, Zetterstéen wrote:

> The actual purpose of licentiate Kolmodin's dissertation is to illuminate, within a given area, the question of the significance of oral tradition as a historical source, and the work's value should

14 *Konstitutionella förbundets handbok. Mars 1914* (tr. as manuscript). Uppsala 1914.

15 H.S.Nyberg, Högtidstal vid Föreningen Heimdals 50-årsjubileum. *Svensk Tidskrift 1941,* p. 257.

16 G.Wk. [G.Wittrock], 'Johannes Kolmodin, Traditions de Tsazzega et Hazzega. Annales et documents' [A review.] *Historisk Tidskrift 34* (1914), p. 142.

17 Sigrid Kahle, *H. S. Nyberg.* Svenska akademiens handlingar från år 1986:16. Stockholm 1991, p. 234 ff.

18 Ibid., p. 334.

thus be judged more in historical than philological terms... The work's purely philological side, however, seems to have interested the author less than the historical...[19]

Why was Zetterstéen's assessment of a previously perfect student so hard? Did Zetterstéen think that Kolmodin devoted too much time to political activities? Or was he a severe guardian of subject divisions who regarded an "interdisciplinary" initiative as a weakness? Zetterstéen was right about the dissertation's strictly historical character, but it could not have been written without the author's profound knowledge of Ethiopian languages in speech and writing. In other words, Kolmodin used the language as a means for his historical research and not as an end in itself.

In any case, Johannes Kolmodin was now a doctor and received a stipend as senior lecturer in Semitic languages. He lectured on this subject and later also "on the history of the ancient Orient." No bitterness was revealed about the indifferent assessment of his dissertation, but he felt that a further academic career in Uppsala was inconceivable. He began to seek new fields for his research and his activist interests. To the joy of posterity, he now began to engage in lengthy correspondence, which is witnessed by the collections in the Carolina (Uppsala University Library), the Royal Library and the National Archives. These are letters full of thoughts, knowledge, ideas and intellectual discussions – and especially of friendship.

Among all the preserved letters, those to his parents are of course the majority. But almost as many were written to Sven Hedin, who came to play an active role in Kolmodin's subsequent plans. In one of the first letters to Hedin, Kolmodin writes of a mutual friend's death "in the imagery of the old desert travellers," as translated by the German poet Rückert:

> Was sind die Menschen anders? Ein
> Zeltplatz und sein Häer,
> und wann das Zelt sie räumen, so
> bleibt die Wüste leer.[20]

Hedin answers with thanks (on a visiting-card) "for your so friendly letter and for the noble desert verse."[21]

Already in 1910, during a brief visit to Constantinople, Kolmodin had oriented himself in Turkish archives and libraries,[22] and the chairman of the Caroline Union (Professor Stille) had encouraged him to do research on Charles XII's time in Turkey. But this required money, as well as and special permits from the Sultan's new Young Turk government. Sven Hedin stepped in and arranged most of it. In 1916 he had made a trip to Baghdad and, true to habit, written a book (*Bagdad, Babylon, Ninive* – with help from Kolmodin on the history in one chapter). On the way back he passed some days in Constantinople and met members of the Young Turk government:

---

19 Johannes Kolmodin, *Biographica*. UUB, Kaps. fol. Q 15:13.

20 Johannes Kolmodin to Sven Hedin. Uppsala 21/2 1917. RA, SHA, vol. 341. "What else is human life? A tent-place people are in, and when they leave the tent, the desert's empty again."

21 Sven Hedin to Johannes Kolmodin, undated, UUB, Q 15:3.

22 Johannes Kolmodin, *De turkiska arkiven. En orientering*. [The Turkish archives. An orientation.] KFÅ 1910. Lund 1911, pp. 154-165.

Thanks to Djemal Pasha and the letters he wrote to the Interior Minister – Talaat Pasha, later the Grand Vizier – and a couple of other potentates in Istanbul, I managed to obtain permission for a Swedish historian, Dr Johannes Kolmodin, to spend two years in the Old Serail's archive looking for sources from Charles XII's residence in Turkey. The costs were covered by the general consul, Axel Ax:son Johnson...[23]

The summer of 1917 brought Kolmodin to the famous *Orientalisches Seminar* in Berlin to refresh his knowledge of Turkish. Here he met Professor Enno Littman, who had done research in Ethiopia a couple of years before Kolmodin. "By the way I am studying Turkish 10 to 12 hours daily," he wrote home.[24] In the autumn of that year, he travelled home to prepare for a longer period abroad. He took time to meet the Foreign Minister, Arvid Lindman, resulting among other things in a telegram from Lindman to the legation in Constantinople, where Kolmodin was appointed *honoraire attaché,*[25] a title intended as support for his research.

Johannes Kolmodin reached Constantinople late in the autumn of 1917, and a totally new life began for him. He immediately wrote to Sven Hedin:

Had the luck to get an excellent two-room flat with an Armenian family... It is a mother and four girls – i.e. the oldest, mademoiselle Philomène, has recently married. One of the other three, Mathilde, boasts of having met you at the house of Miss [illegible], and even asserts that you promised never to forget her – or perhaps it was only her name. Another is called Emilie; she bears, seen in profile, no slight resemblance to Charles XII, and I usually call her Charles-Douze.[26]

Kolmodin is grateful to Hedin for arranging all his affairs, and reciprocates with letters and reports about his activities. Only ten days after the first letter came the second, in which he wants "to wish you Merry Christmas and at the same time to thank you for helping me come here. I have the best hopes – more should perhaps not be said now."[27]

The research in the archives started instantly. Yet Sven Hedin's letters to the Grand Vizier were not enough to give an infidel access to the documents. Kolmodin therefore allied himself with a Turkish historian, Ahmed Refik, who could check out documents and give them to him. This enabled the work to continue, alongside the correspondence with Hedin. There were many long letters about work and politics, but Hedin's replies were at least as numerous and voluminous. Kolmodin writes as follows at the beginning of his stay in Constantinople:

Regarding my research I want to mention now that I have brought together a rather verbose amount of material into a special little lexicon, meant to comprise all the Turks and Tatars who play a role in the Carolines' history down here. It was an almost unavoidable preparatory measure...[28]

23 Sven Hedin, *Stormän och Kungar II* [Great Men and Kings]. Stockholm 1950, p. 336.

24 Johannes Kolmodin to Pappa. Berlin 23/6 1917. UUB, T3 1:18.

25 Foreign Minister Arvid Lindman to the Swedish legation in Constantinople (telegram). RA, Beskickningen i Cpl, P1, 1917.

26 Johannes Kolmodin to Sven Hedin. Cpl 22/11 1917. RA, SHA, vol. 341.

27 Johannes Kolmodin to Sven Hedin. Cpl 3/12 1917. RA, SHA, vol. 341.

28 Johannes Kolmodin to Sven Hedin. Cpl 4/1 1918. RA, SHA, vol. 341.

Kolmodin's work at the legation commenced with modest tasks, but these soon became more qualified and the duties took ever more time. His finances were terrible and eventually he was forced into debt, both to the Mälar Bank with his father's guarantee and to Sven Hedin.

In other respects, however, Johannes Kolmodin flourished in Constantinople. He sought a synthesis between research and practical action, and the city offered him opportunities to contribute. It should now be noted that he came fairly soon in Constantinople to adopt quite different attitudes than his earlier ones. He wrote to his parents of a new political life:

> So Pappa writes in his letter about Åland, Finland...etc. What's the point of thinking about such things? ... As far as I can understand, nothing is conducted at present that deserves to be called Swedish foreign policy. ... The thought of the country there at home lies like an awful pressure over me, but I also feel clearly that I could not be of any use there now.[29]

Developments in Finland during 1918 were followed by Kolmodin with great anxiety. The reports from home spoke of Finland's hard battle for independence and Sweden's refusal to intervene. He wrote to Sven Hedin:

> I have not worked well in recent days – you probably understand why. The kingdom's dishonour burns us all – it is difficult to think of anything else. Ultimately I am inclined to trace it all back to Charles XII's death – I have never doubted that he was murdered. The curse of the unsolved and unpunished royal assassination, whose accomplices succeeded in taking power and shrouding themselves and petty Swedishness into the gown of the Council of State and acquiring a reputation for being the rightful Swedes, has weighed heavily upon us ever since. It ushered in the victory of dark forces – the murder of Sweden's history, which evidently is now on the way to completion before our eyes. 1718–1918.[30]

A little later he writes to Hedin: "When it comes to gathering strength, nothing beats disappearing for a while – well, you know that best, having practised it deliberately."[31]
Furthermore:

> Wasn't it Frederick the Great who once said that, in his opinion, Sweden was really the strongest of all states, since the Swedes have long customarily worked on their own ruin and still not managed to do away with themselves?[32]

If the reports to the Foreign Ministry could be hard to read (see the chapter "An Ill-matched Couple"), the reporting to Hedin was much simpler:

> The conflict of *nationalism* versus *imperialism* has, I think, only passed the initial stage as yet – there surely remain many acute and galloping stages, and it seems to me far from certain that imperialism has even gained much of a lead through the World War. National consciousness is arising just about everywhere, with one new nation after the other discovering itself. Here in Turkey it was the Greeks' occupation of Smyrna that gave the impetus: the Turks, who last

---

29 Johannes Kolmodin to Mamma. Cpl 4/1 1918. UUB, T 3 l:18.

30 Johannes Kolmodin to Sven Hedin. Cpl 9/3 1918. RA, SHA, vol. 341.

31 Johannes Kolmodin to Sven Hedin. Cpl 16/4 1918. RA, SHA, vol. 341.

32 Johannes Kolmodin to Sven Hedin. Cpl 29/4 1918. RA, SHA, vol. 341.

spring appeared ready to let anything whatever be done with them, have now awakened, and Anatolia has acquired in Mustafa Kemal Pasha's personage an Engelbrekt or Charles IX.[33]

The correspondence with Sven Hedin, which was so extensive during Kolmodin's first period in Turkey, eventually began to dwindle. In the autumn of 1922 Kolmodin received a letter that did not delight him:

> Thanks for the payment. It came to 505:80 crowns. How are your archive studies on Charles XII going? I have spent some days this summer with Axel Johnsson in Avesta and he asked again when something will be published. Considering that it was I who pressed him for 25,000 crowns to this end, it is uncomfortable for me not to be able to give him positive news. I would therefore be grateful if you could tell me, when convenient, how things stand.[34]

This naturally made unpleasant reading. Much of the research was finished, but a completed manuscript and printing were far off. Diplomatic reports and consular assignments at the legation now took all day at work and there was simply no spare time. Kolmodin's only writings on Charles XII and his stay in Turkey were four articles in the newspaper *Svenska Dagbladet*. One of them, *Mazeppa in Turkey,*[35] is worth studying even today. It is cited, for instance, by Ragnhild Hatton in her detailed and thorough synthesis of the research on the age of Charles XII.[36]

The relationship between Hedin and Kolmodin became strained for a while, but the two were reconciled later when Kolmodin had paid off his debt to Hedin (with 299:45 crowns). Hedin sent his recently published book *From Peking to Moscow* with a letter saying, among other things, that "it has aroused, due to my sympathetic statements about Russia, quite a lot of bad blood here in rightist circles. It will be fun to hear in time what you think."[37] Kolmodin answered:

> [...] I do understand that, among those rightists who lack enough mental flexibility to get along without the traditional arguments, people could resent what you have said. But the revision of our arguments on policy and especially defence policy, which you have thereby begun, was and is necessary in the highest degree, if we do not want to stand like the blind in the world where we live. Besides, it is of vital interest for us, in view of the unanticipated and unfamiliar situation that the World War has put us in. Don't they even see from the Danish disarmament that, unless we watch out, we shall slowly but surely be pushed into the framework of "The British Empire" and that it may be appropriate for us not even to shrink from conferring with Russia, naturally while observing all the considerations that our tradition of independence and our self-esteem demand of us, about the best way to avert this danger?
>
> As you can tell, I may be going further than you did in your book; but I believe that one must get there if one seriously puts the kingdom before the doctrines. For that matter, Charles XII himself, during the interesting Görtzian period, gives us an example of a Swedish policy that did not hesitate to make use of Russia when the main danger threatened from another direction.[38]

---

33 Johannes Kolmodin to Sven Hedin. Cpl 7/12 1919. RA, SHA, vol. 341.

34 Sven Hedin to Johannes Kolmodin. Stockholm 1/9 1922. UUB, Q 15:3.

35 Johannes Kolmodin, *Mazeppa i Turkiet. Debatten om hans och Karl XII:s utlämnande* [Mazeppa in Turkey. The debate on his and Charles XII's extradition]. Sv.D. 16/1 1925.

36 Ragnhild Hatton, *Karl XII av Sverige* [Charles XII of Sweden]. London 1968 and Köping (Swed. transl.) 1985, p. 649.

37 Sven Hedin to Johannes Kolmodin. Stockholm 12/5 1924. UUB, Q 15:3.

38 Johannes Kolmodin to Sven Hedin. Cpl 29/11 1924. UUB, Q 15:3.

This is the last letter to Sven Hedin with political content. More letters and cards exist, but only about ordinary things of no relevance in the present context.

Sven Lidman

Johannes Kolmodin knew Sven Lidman well since the latter's scarcely successful years of study in Uppsala at the beginning of the last century. They became friends in Heimdal and through evening conversations in student rooms, but then Lidman moved to Stockholm and pursued a turbulent life in the capital city's social circles. Like Kolmodin, he grew strongly engaged in "Swedish activism." This was a movement which played a great role in Swedish debate, if not also in official politics. The activists were a heterogeneous group, with no really common programme point except the liberation of Finland. The principal members were Hjärne's disciples who had been involved in the defence movement and the weekly *Beacon*, with cool sympathy for Germany and with Olof Palme and Johannes Kolmodin as their chief representatives. To their right stood the almost fanatical supporters of Germany, at first led by Adrian Molin and Rudolf Kjellén. These were "all convinced that the danger can be averted only in one way: through brave solidarity on Germany's side."[39] A third main thread consisted of young Finnish academics, who regarded a military showdown with Russia as inevitable and sought support for it in Germany and Sweden.

In 1915 a letter reached Kolmodin from Lidman:

Now, comrade Kolmodin, I come with a greedy request. I have taken it upon myself to be editor and responsible publisher of a Swedish national weekly paper, which is to conduct *healthy* activist propaganda. I greet you as a co-worker. *Svensk Lösen* [*Swedish Watchword*] is to be its title.[40]

Kolmodin was not hard to persuade to write articles for *Swedish Watchword*. Lidman wrote to him:

… You yourself, dear Johannes, I need not beseech for help. In the name of *Swedish Watchword*, when I think or speak of you, I always say:

Tu es Petrus.
Your pieces I hope are ever on call:
I wait for the large, I wait for the small,
but none of them sugary sweet at all.[41]

And the pieces arrived. Kolmodin wrote several articles with activist aims. He compares, for instance, England's and France's autocracies with Russia's and finds similarities. He warns against England and Russia, asserting that Central Europe "nowadays is nearly smothered in the English-Russian embrace, rather as

---

39 O. Järte, R. Kjellén, Y. Larsson, A. Molin, *Sveriges utrikespolitik i världskrigets belysning* (*"Krigsboken"*) [Sweden's foreign policy in the light of the World War ("The War Book")]. Stockholm 1915, p. I.

40 Sven Lidman to Johannes Kolmodin. Stockholm 17/12 1915. UUB, Q 15:4.

41 Sven Lidman to Johannes Kolmodin. Stockholm 10/3 1916. UUB, Q 15:4.

the ancient Greek culture was about to be crushed between Persia and Carthage."[42]

In *The Prince of Peace* he employs Jesus, perhaps with some risk, to argue against those who equate a Christian outlook with a pacifist one:

[…] even Jesus rejected physical violence as a means of achieving his ends, and [the pacifists] fail to see that he regarded this as a consequence of his great and immortal discovery, that his Father's kingdom was *not* of this world and that its living conditions were thus quite different from those of worldly nations. […] Here, as so often otherwise, liberalism has trivialised the issue and striven to delete this central point in a vital Christian view of God's kingdom – since it has never been able to understand that Christianity is not a moral teaching (still less a liberal one) but a doctrine of redemption, and that no one can grasp its essence who has not himself, with his entire personality, experienced the need for a foothold outside of transient existence.[43]

Kolmodin's articles display abundant knowledge and viewpoints that have partly retained their topicality. He wrote numerous articles on the same subject, and also had *Swedish Watchword* publish selected excerpts from Isaiah, in his own translation and with the original metre.[44]

After a stormy marriage that ended in divorce, Sven Lidman experienced a deep crisis with severe religious brooding and no relief. The crisis was so profound that his friends were afraid he would do something rash and irreversible. They organised an emergency watch to ensure that he was not left alone day or night. On the evening of 17 March 1917 his friend the psychologist Pehr Norrmén was sitting with Lidman and observing his poor condition. Norrmén went out for a bit, and

once back, finds that something has happened: Sven Lidman has written a poem. Full of light, transformed to light, he has versified. God has written four stanzas with his hand, and he himself has written a fifth that is worse. Two of those by God contain the great psalm tone.[45]

Lidman continued the account on his own in one of his memoir books:

Some hours later my unforgettable friend came, Johannes Kolmodin, he who died as a political adviser to the Negus of Abyssinia.

Johannes Kolmodin was not merely an Orientalist by scientific profession, but an Oriental diplomat by endowment. He had telephoned a few days earlier and said that he wanted to spend the night with me when he came to Stockholm on Saturday. I had thought it a curious request from my dear Johannes, who gladly stayed at hotels during all his Stockholm trips. But I had naturally accepted his request without guessing what lay behind them. It was arranged with a bed in my library.

We chatted and I mentioned that I had written a poem, and read it aloud. I shall never forget his response, or the little accompanying laugh as if tickled forth by his palate: "Which newspa-

---

42 Johannes Kolmodin, Den stora synvillan [The great illusion]. *Svensk Lösen* 1916:50.

43 Johannes Kolmodin, Fridsfursten. Kristendomen och pacifismen [The Prince of Peace. Christianity and pacifism]. *Svensk Lösen* 22/12 1916.

44 Johannes Kolmodin, translations of Isaiah in *Svensk Lösen* Nos. 36, 38, 40, 42, 43, 45, 47, 51/52, all in 1916.

45 Knut Ahnlund, *Sven Lidman – Ett livsdrama* [Sven Lidman – a life's drama]. Stockholm 1996, p. 227.

per are you thinking of publishing that poem in?" I answered immediately that I had not intended to publish it anywhere.[46]

Lidman did not yet perceive the depth of the experience which had shaken him
that night, when he thus found "salvation." In the beginning of the new year 1918
he wrote to Kolmodin with a blend of religious revival and activism:

> Dear old Johannes! More than usually missed friend and supporter! You have no idea how
> much trouble and talk there has been about and with the financing of *Swedish Watchword*.
> Those were different times when you, with masterful elegance and no nonsense, plucked ten
> thousand from thankful patrons' pockets. To be sure, I now have a commitment of 10,000 from
> L.H. [initials uncertain] but no cash is in sight yet. Talking has been done, though. Old
> Johannes, you linger far away among the lithe *houris*, when your place would be here among
> careless and thoughtless financiers. You pillar of *Swedish Watchword*, you pole in the light
> bedouin tent of activism!
>
> Now I am living in the valley of the shadow of death and say my evening prayers each night
> like a sad, poor little child.[47]

Kolmodin senses what has happened to his friend and answers in a moving letter:

> Written words – there are times when one feels that they are not good for much. It would be
> otherwise if I could walk in on you one evening and continue that little séance – an unsuitable
> term, but I can't find any other – which you and I had once, in the late winter of 1917. It's an
> evening I never forget, because we both (even I, as I recall) were more sincere that time about
> ourselves than we poor actors on life's stage usually are to each other. Since then I have felt it as
> though there were a special, secret bond between us – and I know you have felt the same. […]
>
> I want only briefly to tell you that, also for me, the past month has involved a dreadful cri-
> sis. What has actually held me above water until now, though, has been my innermost faith in
> Sweden – but it wavers, it seems to have been hay and straw that I've built upon. I play bridge
> – passionately – in the evenings to avoid thinking – I feel that certain things must grow ripe
> inside me without being disturbed by the hard-handed intrusion of wilful thinking. However,
> perhaps in the end a higher and stronger hand than my own shall take me by the hair and pull
> me up on solid ground – deep in my heart I have always believed in the miracle.
>
> Your mystical authorities are not very familiar to me, yet I have others, possibly more naive,
> but good enough for me.[48]

In his letter Kolmodin quotes Junus Emre, whom he describes as a "Turkish
mystic, probably from the thirteenth century, author of popular hymns (*ilahi*),
which are sung at the gatherings of the dervish orders." He attaches an *ilahi*
which was to be published long afterward with commentaries by Gunnar
Jarring.[49] Jarring maintains that Kolmodin was the first European who devoted
attention to Junus Emre. The latter subsequently had a renaissance in Turkey and
became something of a cult figure in Europe during the 1970s.

---

46 Sven Lidman, *Stjärnan som tändes på nytt* [The star that was lit anew]. Stockholm 1950, pp. 62-63.

47 Sven Lidman to Johannes Kolmodin. Stockholm 23/1 1918. KB, L 83:8.

48 Johannes Kolmodin to Sven Lidman. Cpl 8/4 1918 [wrongly dated to "1917" by Johannes Kolmodin].
KB, L 83:8.

49 Gunnar Jarring, Johannes Kolmodin som översättare av turkisk lyrik [Johannes Kolmodin as a translator
of Turkish poetry]. *Svenska forskningsinstitutet i Istanbul. Meddelanden* No. 1. 1976, pp. 40-47.

By the year's end, Kolmodin has regained courage, at least enough so that he can work again. He remains bitter about the developments at home, but there is still hope – the new Finland's declaration of independence on 6 December 1918 is certainly one of the reasons. In his (last) letter to Lidman he writes:

>...devoured your book [*The House of the Old Maids*] – or rather, it sucked me in. There was so much that went directly into me – also much that made me recognise myself. Your Euridike Berg lives in a world that has quite a few traits in common with the one I have come from, and which I may one day succeed in returning to in my fashion. The same post brought me a letter by my father from mid-November; at that time my family had not heard from me in ages, and hardly hoped to do so for a long time more. Among other things he then wrote: "Regardless of all obstacles and difficulties, there is one road which no revolutionary storms have been able to close: that of prayer. For it there are no obstacles, since for it there are no distances. And when we bear you forth in prayer to our heavenly Father in Jesus' name, it does not feel that you are far away, but near. Thus we seek in our weakness to envelop you with invisible but strong, protecting walls. May God deal with you and us as He wishes. Then it will be to our eternal benefit."
>
> You understand what I mean...
>
> I know almost nothing about the developments there at home, as the telegrams published here and the French newspapers that have arrived until now contain nothing about it. Sometimes it feels a bit hard, but one must comfort oneself that the very silence shows at least that Sweden continues to exist. "The stone still stands in the green valley." As for women's right to vote and the like, it need not matter nowadays – since the compulsory military service's bankruptcy through Bolshevism. And when all is said and done, a higher hand has ensured that our own shortcomings will perhaps not prove too dangerous. I believe that, despite everything, we are right to take up work with fresh courage:
>
>> through perils and dismays
>> renewed and *re-renewed.*[50]

Towards the end of 1918, the First World War was finished. So were activism and *Swedish Watchword*. The obituary of activism has been formulated by, for instance, the political scientist Mats Kihlberg:

>...The central motive in the activism of *Swedish Watchword* was the perspective of cultural struggle towards the east. Insofar as one can speak of a common ideology and programme, it consisted of this historically traditionalistic, chauvinistically Swedish outlook. This was characteristic of the chief editor Sven Lidman, of the leading co-workers Otto Järte, P. H. Norrmén, Hjalmar Haralds, Erland Hjärne, Johannes Kolmodin and Nils Ahnlund – and it occupied as dominant a place in the newspaper's last issue as in the first.[51]

In the middle of April 1918, Olof Palme fell while leading the Swedish Brigade outside Tammerfors. At the funeral in Uppsala Cathedral, the archbishop Nathan Söderblom concluded his speech with these words:

---

50 The closing lines are quoted from Rudyard Kipling. Johannes Kolmodin to Sven Lidman. Cpl 31/12 1918. KB, L 83:8.

51 Mats Kihlberg, Aktivismens huvudorgan Svensk Lösen [Activism's main medium *Swedish Watchword*]. In: Kihlberg, M. & Söderlind, D., *Två studier i svensk konservatism 1916 - 1922* [Two studies in Swedish conservatism 1916-1922]. Skrifter utgivna av Statsvetenskapliga föreningen i Uppsala, 41. Uppsala 1961, pp. 12-13.

...The future is shaped out of conflicts, which have never been more bloody and disturbed than now. Seldom do people act on such unified and clear grounds as did the students we now uncomplainingly lament. Different motives often mix together in the same heart. They are still more mixed within a single group or movement in history. Murky and clear waters meet in the same stream. Violent currents stir up mud from its bottom. But once it has come to rest, it can reflect the stars in heaven.[52]

Nathan Söderblom

This brings us to the last of the three personalities who are discussed here in relation to Johannes Kolmodin. Chronologically, the friendship with Nathan Söderblom was oldest. Johannes' father, Adolf Kolmodin, had long been acquainted with him, and they later worked in the same faculty.

Already two months after Johannes Kolmodin arrived in Constantinople, Söderblom wrote to him about a planned ecumenical conference. The archbishop resolved that his conference would take place at Uppsala in April 1918. On 26 January he writes:

It is certainly a remarkable and peculiarly favourable dispensation that you are in Constantinople... [The conference] is to be in Uppsala and have a core of Nordic evangelical Christianity including Finland and Estonia. I do not know whether the patriarch is still in Phanar, but surely you can easily find there some reliable person belonging to the synod or joint council. Presumably it is easier to get someone from Constantinople than from Athens. We must have a bishop, Greek, here by 14 April. Preferably two... The Greek Church must appear to its full advantage at this meeting. I can guarantee that the Greek Orthodox Church's representatives would be honoured in a worthy and proper way. It is not fitting that Orthodox Christianity is represented only by Russians, however valuable they are... The synod has plenty of archbishops, why can't one of them travel. He wouldn't regret it. If a good Armenian representative can come, he will get a unique chance to put forward his views and wishes.[53]

This letter initiated an extensive correspondence between Söderblom and Kolmodin. Most of the letters are rendered as in Professor Bengt Sundkler's presentation. He first gives a commentary which he thinks irrelevant to his framework, but it suits our own:

We shall not speculate here on the causes of the fact that this brilliantly talented man with his enormous capacity did not receive more attention from the Swedish foreign ministry at the time. That Kolmodin's chauvinistically Swedish declarations – and admittedly his declamations – between 1910 and 1916, about F-boats and the like, hindered his promotion in a Swedish diplomatic career long afterward ought to be an easily defensible hypothesis. He also stood out from the mass of manicured – and barely occupied – copyists and was probably unsuitable for just that reason.

The interesting – and indeed rather instructive – point in this connection is to note how Kolmodin, at his post in one of the most exposed and complicated sectors of world politics,

---

52 Nathan Söderblom, Minnesord vid båren. *Till minnet av Olof Palme.* [Commemorative words at the bier. *In Memory of Olof Palme.*] Uppsala 1918, p. 101.

53 Bengt Sundkler, Ärkebiskopens ambassadör hos Österns patriark. *Nathan Söderblom och hans möten.* [The Archbishop's ambassador to the patriarch of the East. *Nathan Söderblom and his meeting.*] Gummessons 1975, p. 101f.

came to adopt quite different attitudes than those which his fairly nationalistic Swedish past would have led one to expect. But the potentates of varied colours in Stockholm were not eager to concern themselves with such nuances among their lower civil servants in the landscape beyond Europe.[54]

Kolmodin began his negotiations immediately and succeeded in establishing a decisive contact with Patriarch Damianos V. He reports to Söderblom in a long, amusing letter:

His Holiness, the ecumenical patriarch...I called upon down in Phanarion [Fener]. Through a number of curious passages, upstairs and downstairs, I was first brought into a sort of anteroom, where two popes received me and inquired in very broken French as to my errand. As I thought it unwise to get on the wrong side of subordinates – this is in my experience what one should chiefly avoid in the East – I took out your letter and let them read it, at the same time naturally emphasising that I wished to deliver it into the hands of His Holiness. Now and then I was able to interject some other explanation – I pointed to Sweden and Uppsala on a map that hung on the wall... The Patriarchate's second *kapu-kihaja* [substitute delegate to the Sublime Porte] was summoned... Accompanied by him, I was taken through yet another corridor into a humbly furnished little office where the patriarch, with a long grey beard and an ankle-length caftan, sat at a work-table. I presented my errand as eloquently as I could, explaining that the Archbishop of Uppsala believed himself to find in the head of the venerable old Eastern church a very special resonance for the idea that just now, during the World War's pressing times, a great demonstration of Christiandom's essential unity was needed, etc.

The patriarch expressed his interest, but stressed that the matter must first be considered by the Synod.

His Holiness then wanted to know something about the Archbishop of Uppsala's position: "is he independent?" he asked (presumably he wanted to verify that no Papal intrigue lay behind it all). I gave as good an account as I could in a few words of the ecclesiastical conditions in Scandinavia; possibly it gave the patriarch a rather exaggerated notion of the power of the Uppsala see, and no doubt he now regards it as a kind of Nordic-Baltic patriarchate, which of course we have a while yet to attain. But since the Bulgarian separation has left hardly two million souls under His Holiness himself nowadays, I thought it could not hurt him to hear that this was an Archbishop who holds the worthy post alone among 12 to 15 million, and is no ordinary archbishop either.[55]

Söderblom is grateful for the letter: "The brilliant manner in which you have evidently conducted this affair enhances the ecumenical conference's prospects and raison d'être."[56]

Söderblom's assignment to Kolmodin was, as Sundkler writes, anything but simple. There were several reasons for that:

First, Söderblom's ecumenical programme had just taken shape, and he wanted to invite several Orthodox clerics to a preparatory ecumenical conference at Uppsala in 1918. He wrote to

---

54 Ibid., p. 97f.

55 Ibid., p. 102f.

56 Ibid., p. 103.

Kolmodin on 8 March 1919: "The goal must be [an] ecumenical church council with the Patriarch and Canterbury as obvious participants, and other selected representatives of orthodox and evangelical Christianity." Due to the world political situation in 1918, the conference had to be postponed repeatedly, and finally became a reality in 1920 at Geneva. These delays inevitably caused uncertainty, but the man on the spot, Kolmodin, was constantly forced to act on the assumption that the conference in question would take place at a stated time.

Second, the political situation in Turkey. To be sure, the Ottoman caliphate was not definitely abolished until 1924, but it had long been falling apart, "ever since that 'man of destiny', Kemal Atatürk, gathered his forces in 1919 and, at the end of January 1920, set forth a national pact on whose basis a new Turkey was to be built."

Third, in order to survive, the orthodox patriarchate in Phanar had to establish some kind of *modus vivendi* with the secular rulers in Turkey. Instead of striving for this, the patriarchate broke with the Sublime Porte in 1919 to orient itself toward Greece, and then it managed to bet on the wrong horse, namely Venizelos in Athens. The latter fell already in November 1920, rendering the patriarchate's position even more critical. It was foreseen that the patriarch could not keep himself in Constantinople and would be forced to seek asylum in Jerusalem.

Through this explosive political minefield, Johannes Kolmodin was to lead Söderblom's ecumenical interests. They would face catastrophic consequences with any wrong step to right or left. Each enthusiastic word about the Christians' ecumenical cooperation could be fatally misunderstood by the Turkish political leaders.[57]

There were many letters and several postponements, but these only stimulated Kolmodin, and he was fascinated by the grandness of Söderblom's programme. They both stimulated, encouraged and influenced each other in equally high degree.[58] Kolmodin's many fascinating letters were sent alternately to the Archbishop's house and to the Fjellstedt School, where Adolf Kolmodin was the rector. They were studied and shared by the two addressees.[59] After a year, Johannes Kolmodin writes to his father: "Constantinople, Canterbury, Uppsala – it is, of course, a rather beautiful combination, which deserves to be promoted. Greetings to the Archbishop."[60]

It would be too far afield to go into all the negotiations Kolmodin pursued for the purpose, not least with the Turkish foreign minister Halil Bey, where his entire diplomatic skill was called upon. "Halil Bey must have known on the whole that the conversation with the young Swede was a diplomatic exchange of ideas on a quite different level than what he was used to in talking with Westerners. He encountered a Western emissary with great opinions on the meeting of religions."[61]

A further amusing ecumenical document must, however, be reproduced. In July 1920, the World Alliance in the United States sent an "American mechanical engineer" to Constantinople. Kolmodin guided him around the city and reported to Nathan Söderblom:

You will probably meet him in Switzerland, and you know the type: [...] enterprising, naïve, but educable. [He] had, on arriving, a number of impossible thoughts about forming some sort of

---

57 Ibid., p. 100f.

58 Sundkler, personal communication 1994.

59 Sundkler, ibid., p. 100.

60 Ibid., p. 203.

61 Ibid., p. 104.

joint committee of the World Alliance for the Ottoman Christians, with representatives of the Orthodox, Gregorians and – Protestants (from the American schools). Already on the first evening I cleaned him up thoroughly on this point and got him so far that his talk with the person in question only distantly touched upon this suspicious idea which could have completely compromised not only the World Alliance but also the ecumenical conference. Here one must stick to every confession in itself since the confession also has the character of a nation (*millet* is the Arabic-Turkish term for both); a collaboration can certainly be conceived in a wider context, but not within the Ottoman "nationality," which is a nineteenth-century illusion. Make sure that this question is treated with the necessary delicacy in Geneva and Beatenberg. Not to mention the madness of putting the ecumenical patriarch on a level with the director of Roberts College.[62]

The letter shows that Kolmodin had a good command of these issues. In fact, here he made a contribution to ecclesiastical history,[63] consisting of the Patriarchate's publication in January 1920 of an encyclical which proposed the formation of an all-Christian *League of Churches*. Söderblom thanks Kolmodin for the help:

The letter and proposal from Dorotheos [i.e. the current substitute for the Patriarch] and the Holy Synod are particularly attractive, intelligent and surprising in their sense of reality. You have the satisfaction which belongs to the greatest and purest a person can have, of finding your own thoughts and ideas in others, after an imperceptible and unconscious influence on them![64]

It may well have occurred to Kolmodin that the same was true of Söderblom's influence on him.

Söderblom's meetings took place and culminated in the ecumenical conference at Stockholm in 1925. The Orthodox Church's participation can largely be attributed to the activities of Johannes Kolmodin. As a sign of his appreciation and friendship, Söderblom made a spontaneous handwritten addition to a dictated letter: "Imagine if you had any idea of being ordained and becoming vicar of Constantinople." It was actually a post that Söderblom himself had considered during his time in Paris, since the post had long been vacant.[65]

In 1924 a letter arrived from Nathan Söderblom after meeting Ras Tafari, the crown prince who would later become Emperor Haile Selassie I of Ethiopia:

Dear Friend!

Ras Tafari is a pleasant person with clear and solid judgement, Oriental dignity, personal refinement, and the best intentions of benefiting his country and people. At dinner here we spoke of the educational institution he wants to found eventually in Addis Ababa. I told him about you, what you can do and have done, while his interest and amazement grew, which finally released a liveliness I have hardly otherwise noticed in him. He wanted to see your portrait, and it was immediately requested from Järnbro Street. He wondered whether you would like to come down to Abyssinia, and I could not answer. But I know your interest in this whole world, which your knowledge and judgement and linguistic abilities command, where Asia and Africa and Europe meet. He greatly

---

62 Johannes Kolmodin to Nathan Söderblom. 11/7 1920 on board a ship between Piraeus and Alexandria. UUB, Q 15:6.

63 Sundkler, pp. 106-107.

64 Ibid., p. 107.

65 Ibid., p. 107f.

appreciated my pointing out that you do not belong to any of the land-hungry colonial powers. Perhaps, I suggested, he might enjoy starting the institution of higher education. "No," was the reply, "he must become my *conseiller politique*. I look upon it as a gift of God that you have mentioned this man." [...] A response to his proposal, that you visit him this autumn at his expense, you can send directly to His Imperial and Royal Highness the Crown Prince and Regent Ras Tafari, or else to me and, in that case, I shall forward it together with further information. [...][66]

Kolmodin answered Ras Tafari through Söderblom that he was willing to come and discuss the conditions, but then the matter took a different turn and had to wait awhile. Some time later, Kolmodin writes to Söderblom about the offer:

To tell the truth, I think that by now in my life I have worked enough for free or for insufficient remuneration, and that it is no more than right if the Ethiopian government has to pay quite well if it wants to be sure of me. [...] If I am to go on suffering economic difficulties, I naturally prefer to do so in Swedish service.[67]

Thus, nothing came of Ethiopia on this occasion and doubtless it was for the best.

In the summer of 1924, Johannes Kolmodin became engaged to an old friend from childhood, Eva Forsslöf. Married at home in Sweden on 6 January 1925, they moved into the upper storey of the consulate building. On 24 January 1928, the couple was blessed with a son, Lars Olof Togrul. He would naturally be baptised, and Söderblom had given a half-promise to do this during a planned journey to Jerusalem. But time went by and no news came from Uppsala. Then Kolmodin wrote to him:

My wife and I are now very anxious to know whether and when the Archbishop can be expected – since otherwise it is time for the boy to be baptised soon by someone else. We have thought about sending a telegram as follows:

The Archbishop   Uppsala   Matt. 11:3.

For the present, though, we have decided to wait for a written message. We would of course be very glad if we could count on having him baptised by you.[68]

Söderblom unfortunately did not come, and the baptism had to be done by "someone else."

In 1929 Ras Tafari became *Negus* (king) in Ethiopia and wanted to have a Swedish political adviser. Polite as he was, he took the official path and wrote to King Gustaf V. The Swedish government replied in April the same year, regretting that it had been unable to find any suitable candidate(!).[69] In Addis Ababa, *Negus* Tafari became "rather ill-humoured with this categorical refusal whose cause he certainly did not understand."[70]

The Swedish consul in Addis Ababa, Knut Hanner, who was a physician at Haile Selassie's Hospital in the city, travelled to Sweden that year at the request

66 Nathan Söderblom to Johannes Kolmodin. Uppsala 12/6 1924. UUB, Q 15:6.

67 Johannes Kolmodin to Nathan Söderblom. Cpl 29/6 1924. UUB, Q 15:6.

68 Johannes Kolmodin to Nathan Söderblom. Cpl 15/3 1928. UUB, Q 15:6.

69 Viveca Halldin Norberg, *Swedes in Haile Selassie's Ethiopia 1924 - 1952.* Uppsala 1977, p. 127.

70 Ibid., p. 127.

of the *Negus*. He made a stop in Istanbul, where he informally spoke with Wallenberg about Kolmodin. The latter learned of this after a year and wrote to Nathan Söderblom:

> His [Wallenberg's] fear of losing me has also emerged in other ways, for example during Dr. Hanner's visit last year when, taking advantage of my being here in Ankara, he took care to direct him towards filling a possible post in Abyssinia with an officer employed in the Greek-Turkish population exchange commission, who can scarcely have believed in his own suitability for the special assignment that would be faced down there. [...]
>
> I, of course, am first and foremost Swedish, even if it is perhaps prescribed for me to make my main contribution to *Africa's* history.
>
> With the best of greetings and, once more, thanks for your interest in me, which I know to be my best and surest support. [...][71]

As soon as Hanner returned to Addis Ababa, he spoke with the Emperor and suggested that an attempt be made to engage Kolmodin through Söderblom without any mediation by the Swedish Foreign Ministry. Then things happened fast. After new contacts between Söderblom and the Emperor, Kolmodin said that he was ready to travel to Ethiopia. He explains his reasons to Arvid Richert at the Foreign Ministry:

> [..] Apart from my old interest in Ethiopia, whose history and relations I have followed ever since childhood and where I spent a couple of pleasant years in youth, it may be sufficient to mention that I now consider myself to have fulfilled my Swedish "political conscription" and to have the right of looking around for an assignment that could be my personal one. That it is to some extent a leap into the unknown, I am naturally aware; but since on the other hand I am still "supernumerary" and thus relegated to self-pensioning (which I will never manage here) and cut off from ordinary opportunities of promotion, it cannot be said that by daring to leap I would deny myself any more important measure of security.[72]

Such were circumstances in the last generation. It was Sven Hedin who arranged for Kolmodin to come to Constantinople. And it was Nathan Söderblom who enabled him to go on to Addis Ababa.

Johannes Kolmodin's constitutional ideal was a strong, enlightened monarchy – and undoubtedly nothing else was left of his former Great Swedish activism. Back then, the problem was that Gustaf V could not, with the best will in the world, be called a strong monarch. But elsewhere in the world, two leaders appeared who fulfilled his ideal: Mustafa Kemal in Turkey, and Haile Selassie in Ethiopia. He served both of them faithfully.

---

71 Johannes Kolmodin to Nathan Söderblom. Ankara 25/2 1930. UUB, NSA, Kolmodin.

72 Johannes Kolmodin to Richert. Istanbul 4/12 1930. KUD, Beskickningen i Cpl, P1, Kolmodin V.

Contradictions of Modernity: Cultural Life in Sweden during the First Decades of the Twentieth Century

INGA SANNER

There is an interesting tension – or perhaps even a contradiction – within the personality of the young Johannes Kolmodin. This tension arises from the fact that he was at one and the same time a conservative nationalist and a cosmopolitan being with a great curiosity about and open-mindedness towards non-Western cultures. The combination of these two aspects can be seen as one reason for his leaving Uppsala for Constantinople. His visit Constantinople was made possible by a scholarship awarded to him to undertake research on the Swedish King Charles XII in Turkish archives. Kolmodin's interest in Charles XII was part of the conservative and nationalistic ideology he – and others – subscribed to at the beginning of the 20th century. But Kolmodin would hardly have travelled to Constantinople were it not for his interest in the languages and cultures of this part of the world. Unlike many others, Kolmodin, when he later became involved in diplomatic circles in Constantinople, chose to live in a quarter of the city where the natives lived, rather than in the parts inhabited by other Western diplomats. His ambition to become integrated into the foreign culture seems to have been something fundamentally different from his nationalistic ideas.[1]

How could these seemingly contradictory tendencies combine in one personality? While this may seem strange, it becomes less so when considered in a broader context. In this paper, the two aspects of Kolmodin will be interpreted as a reaction to modernity, a reaction that was a central feature of cultural life during the decades surrounding the turn of the 20th century.

The times during which the young Johannes Kolmodin spent in Sweden were quite turbulent. He was born in 1884, and the 1880s are sometimes labelled "the modern breakthrough" in Sweden. He left Sweden during the First World War, a war often regarded as a line of demarcation in the history of Sweden as well as in the Western world as a whole. The period between "the modern breakthrough" and the war can be described in different ways. On one hand, it can be seen as the final phase of the old pre-war world, before the innovations after the war. On the other hand, the same period can be seen as the starting point of modernity in Sweden. The decades around the turn of the century were a time of preparation, with many demands for social and political reform being made. It is not surprising that the period was characterised by intense argumentation for and against modernity.

But what is modernity? Needless to say it is a problematic concept that can signify many different things. Whatever the definition chosen, there seems to be a

---

1 Biographichal information about Johannes Kolmodin can be found in Carl Gustaf Kolmodin, *Johannes Kolmodin i brev och skrifter*, Filologiskt arkiv 41, Stockholm: Almqvist and Wicksell, 1999.

close connection to the ideas of the Enlightenment. In his famous article, "What is Enlightenment?" published in 1784, Immanuel Kant equated enlightenment with the courage of each person people to use his or her reason. Kant believed that human reason could be used as a critical weapon against all kinds of conventions in society. Although he was eager to give warning of revolutionary activities – the article was published a few years before the outbreak of the French Revolution and Kant praised the stability of social institutions – his statements contained a message that could appeal to radical thinkers. Kant's ideas could be used as an argument in favour of education and political influence for people in general. These demands became a vital ingredient in the political messages of liberals and socialists in the 19th century.[2]

Enlightenment ideas were questioned by conservative thinkers. A prominent opponent of these ideals was the British author and politician Edmund Burke, who wrote a comprehensive critique of the French Revolution, *Reflections on the Revolution in France*, published in 1790, in the middle of the revolutionary ferment. In this book, Burke criticised the revolutionaries for being too theoretical in their approach to society, constructing an outline of a new society from their desks rather than out of reality. "History" and "tradition" were key words for Burke. He believed that what had endured for a long time must be of great value. Burke was not hostile to the idea of historical progress – quite the reverse – but he emphasized that progress must be organic, that is, in accordance with tradition. Compared to Kant he was much more pessimistic about the intellectual capability of – at least most – humans. Burke did not consider people to be generally very rational: on the contrary he thought them to be in great need of authority. He stressed the importance of strong societal institutions and argued against widespread education and democracy. Another difference between Kant and Burke was their view on war. According to Burke, wars were necessary as the only way of solving conflicts between nations. Kant believed that progress and rationality would result in eternal peace, with all nations living harmoniously.[3]

Many of Burke's ideas were similar to those held by German idealists within the Romantic Movement. Since Romanticism was critical of Enlightenment ideas, it can be described as an early reaction to modernity. Not every Romantic thinker was conservative, but some were, and their way of describing history shared similarities with the ideas of Burke. Hegel is probably the best known of the conservative philosophers of this period, although he is not a typical Romantic thinker. In Hegel's system, there is a strong connection between political ideas on one hand and a certain view of history on the other. Just like Burke, Hegel worshipped tradition and preferred to talk of the rationality of history as a whole, rather than of the reason of single persons in history. Hegel advocated strong nations and regarded wars as the necessary means of solving conflicts between nations.

The view of history held by Hegel and other German historians is sometimes called historicism and is associated with the University of Berlin, founded in 1809. The historians within this tradition claimed that each historical epoch must be understood in its own right by taking account of its unique conditions. They also

2 Franklin Baumer, *Modern European Thought. Continuity and Change in Ideas, 1600-1950*, New York: Macmillan, 1977, pp. 140-59.

3 Ibid. pp. 288-95.

developed methods for the use of historical sources in order to create a true under-standing of earlier epochs. This was a way of approaching history that became influential throughout Europe, including Sweden – and including persons of great importance to Johannes Kolmodin.[4] So let us turn to the situation in Sweden at the turn of the 20th century, a period of intense political and intellectual activity.

Industrialisation had changed the conditions under which most people lived in Sweden. Many moved to the large cities where they could find work. The greatest expansion took place in Stockholm, where many new factories were established. In the Swedish capital the double character of industrialisation was obvious. There was, on one hand, a marked optimism related to high expectations of material and technical improvement. Technical development was rapid in many fields, such as in communications, with innovations like the telephone and the telegraph and expansion of the railways and – in the cities – tramways. The material standard in many houses was markedly improved with the laying on of water and electricity. Illumination of city streets with electric lamps can be seen as concrete correspon-dence with the enlightenment proclaimed by Kant concerning public discussions.[5]

The1897 Scandinavian Art and Industry Exhibition in Stockholm can be regarded as a manifestation of the optimism related to industrialisation. At the exhibition, one could see examples from different sectors in the newly industri-alised country. Many investments were made in science and technology during this period. The founding of the *Stockholms högskola* is one example, with its ori-entation towards science, mathematics and modern languages. This institute was regarded as the polar opposite of the University of Uppsala, which represented a more classical form of education. Related to these new forms of education was the higher evaluation afforded new professions, such as the physician, the engineer and the scientist. The men who set out for the North Pole were regarded as heroes, representing mastery of the whole world through knowledge and technology.[6]

But there was also a dark side to industrialisation. Working conditions in the factories were often extremely harsh and social misery was extensive. In the large cities, many people had no decent places to live, hygiene was deplorable and dis-eases spread quickly. Working days were long, salaries low and even small chil-dren were used for hard work. Alcoholism was a serious problem.

The so-called social question was highly debated. The need for improvements in the conditions of the lower classes was obvious, but there was no consensus about the means to attain this goal. The kind of philanthropy practised earlier in the 19th century was often criticised, the most famous example of criticism being August Strindberg's satirical description in his novel *Röda rummet* (1879) of well-mean-ing upper class ladies visiting workers in the poor districts of Stockholm.

---

4 Ibid., pp. 294-302.

5 This is a theme in Inga Sanner, "En stad i ljus och mörker. Stockholm 1870-1900," Erland Sellberg (ed), *Den skapande staden. Idéhistoriska miljöer*, Stockholm: Carlsson, 2003. The expression "the new enlighten-ment" has been used to characterise the period by, for instance, Anders Ekström in *Den utställda världen. Stockholmsutställlningen 1897 och 1800-talets världsutställningar*, Stockholm: Nordiska museets förlag, 1994, pp. 95-104. The following description of the cultural and intellectual life of Sweden at the turn of the twentieth century is based on Tore Frängsmyr, *Svensk idéhistoria. Bildning och vetenskap under tusen år. Del II 1809-2000*, Stockholm: Natur och kultur, 2000, "Utvecklingstrons epok (1866-1914)," pp. 101-209.

6 Frängsmyr, *Svensk idéhistoria*, pp. 102-34. On higher education during the period, see Bo Lindberg, "Från prästskola till högskola," *17 uppsatser i svensk idé- och lärdomshistoria*, Stockholm: Carmina, 1980.

Strindberg, and many others like him, believed that the struggle for a better society had to be initiated by the workers themselves. Working associations had been founded earlier in the 19th century and by the end of the century had grown large and developed into modern trade unions. In mid-1880s, the first social democratic association was founded in Stockholm and soon the Social Democratic Party played an important role in Swedish politics. One of the main issues for the new party was the suffrage question. Behind the arguments in favour of the right to vote was a conception of every (male) human being as rational and capable of taking part in questions concerning the government of the country – a conception in line with Kant's Enlightenment ideas.[7]

Many conservatives questioned this line of thinking. They argued that, generally, people were not capable of taking part in political life and – like Burke – they emphasized the importance of authority. Democracy was seen as a threat to social stability and suffrage as something that would create division and disorder in society.

In the cultural field, the turn of the century was a period of upheaval. There was tension between different kinds of ideas – a tension that was sometimes described as a polarisation between old ideas and new. In any event, this description was common among those who identified themselves with the new ideas. The word "modern" was frequently used, for instance in the expression "the modern breakthrough" used by the Danish critic Georg Brandes. He influenced a whole generation of young authors in Scandinavia, men as well as women, who criticised what they regarded as old-fashioned ways of writing and out-of-date modes of thinking. They pleaded for a new kind of literature in keeping with a more modern way of looking at man and society. By this they meant a more realistic – or even naturalistic – literature, describing human beings as they actually were, without idealisation. These authors were highly influenced by modern sciences such as biology, and above all by Darwinism and physiology. The influence of these sciences was combined with a strong optimism concerning the development of humanity. Darwinism could be used to support a belief in moral and cultural progress, and the future was often described as an earthly paradise – almost as an alternative to the Christian one.[8]

The authors gathered around Brandes mounted critical attacks on established institutions like the state, the church and the university. They criticised political conservatism, religious orthodoxy and philosophical idealism. Strindberg – a model for the radical authors – had in one of his books, *Från Fjerdingen till Svartbäcken* (1877), characterised the intellectual atmosphere of Uppsala as representing an old fashioned way of thinking, and he regarded the system of the conservative and idealistic philosopher Christopher Jacob Boström as prototypical of this.

But Stockholm did not escape Strindberg's criticism. In the novel *Röda rummet,* he attacked the old and new authorities in the Swedish capital. The fact that the principal character in the novel is a journalist is significant, since the expanding press became an important platform for social criticism during this period. Critical views were also expressed in a variety of associations that were estab-

---

7 Frängsmyr, *Svensk idéhistoria*, pp. 187-90.

8 A general characterisation of the ideas of "the modern breakthrough" is given by Gunnar Ahlström in *Det moderna genombrottet i Nordens* litteratur, Stockholm: KF, 1947, pp. 113ff.

lished at this time, such as the women's movement, the peace movement, associations for religious freedom and many others.

In many of these associations, belief in the possibilities and capabilities of humanity was a central feature. This can be seen in the religious field, where the state church and orthodox Christianity were criticised for being too focused on ideas of sin and punishment. The church was also regarded as hierarchical and as leaving too little room for activity by individuals in the parishes. This was one reason various alternatives to the state church were initiated during the 19th century. In many of these communities, personal engagement was highly esteemed. *Evangeliska fosterlandsstiftelsen* (Swedish Evangelical Mission, SEM), in which Johannes Kolmodin was brought up and in which his father was a leading personality, was an example of an inward church reform movement that became quite successful during this period.[9]

"The modern breakthrough" is associated with the 1880s, but the following decade is often characterised in terms of romanticism and a *fin de siècle* atmosphere. The author Verner von Heidenstam is sometimes seen as a symbol of a literary movement associated with the 1890s, which – compared to the realistic and naturalistic literature described earlier – had a more introverted character. It also placed greater emphasis on nationalistic themes.[10]

Nationalistic ideas became stronger at the turn of the century and were expressed in many ways. One manifestation was the building of *Skansen*, an open-air museum in Stockholm where a mosaic displayed the different parts of the Swedish nation. The use of flags became more frequent at the end of the century, and discussions were held on a national day as well as a national anthem. In the 1897 Stockholm exhibition, many flags bedecked the exhibition area, and portraits of the king and his family could be bought in many stalls. This is one example of the connection between nationalism and industrialisation, and there were many other kinds of nationalism during this time – one cannot talk of only one form of nationalism.[11]

One type of nationalism was directed at the internationalism associated with socialism. At the end of the 19th century, the use of the red flag and the celebration of the first of May was introduced into the socialist movement and can be seen as a counterpoint to national celebrations. The relationship between socialism and nationalism was, however, not a simple one, since nationalistic values were also of great importance to many socialists. This became obvious by the outbreak of the First World War in Europe, when many socialists remained loyal to their own nations rather than to socialists in other countries.

For Swedish Social Democrats, it was important to show loyalty to the nation as a means of gaining respectability as well as support from as many sectors of society as possible. When *Folkets hus* (the People's Palace) was inaugurated in Stockholm in 1901, the red socialist flag hung side by side with the national flag as the manifestation of a will to compromise. Another expression of the ambition

9 Frängsmyr, *Svensk idéhistoria*, pp. 184-7. About SEM, see Stefan Gelfgren, *Ett utvalt släkte. Väckelse och sekularisering – Evangeliska fosterlandsstiftelsen 1856-1910*, Skellefteå: Artos and Norma bokförlag, 2003.

10 An exhaustive description of the nationalism of Heidenstam can be found in Staffan Björk, *Heidenstam och sekelskiftets Sverige. Studier i hans nationella och sociala författarskap*, Stockholm: Natur och kultur, 1946. See also Frängsmyr, *Svensk idéhistoria*, pp. 150-61.

11 Ekström, *Den utställda världen*, chapter 6, "Behovet av nationen," pp. 264-95.

to gain acceptance was the eagerness shown by many Social Democrats to criticise anarchists, since the latter were associated with anti-parliamentarianism and could thus be seen as a threat to national values.[12]

The reverence for national values was common to various political groups. The same can be said of the widespread vision of the progress of humanity. Such views may have been inspired by a new "science," eugenics, formulated by Francis Galton, cousin of Charles Darwin, in the 1880s. Galton was concerned with the evolution of the human race and feared that there was degeneration taking place in the Western world because people with a supposedly poor inheritance – people living in the slums and in so called non-civilised cultures – were the ones giving birth to most children. The purpose of eugenics was to investigate differences between races and individuals and to discuss how to improve the qualities of humanity. Later in the 20th century, sterilisation – mostly of women – was used as a means to attain this goal.[13]

Eugenic ideas were gaining purchase all over the Western world, including Sweden, and were connected with visions about the progress of humanity. One important spokesman – or rather woman – was Ellen Key, an influential author and intellectual of the period. For Key, eugenic ideas were part of a comprehensive vision of the progress and evolution of society and of humanity as a whole. She attacked Christian ideas about salvation of the individual as dreams that, according to her, led people away from trying to reform their earthly conditions. Key wanted to replace Christianity with a belief in life (*livstro*) in which belief in the progress of humanity was a cornerstone.[14]

The role of women was a crucial part of this vision. According to Key, female characteristics – and by this she meant characteristics like peacefulness, morality and the ability to take care of other people, especially children –should be afforded a more prominent place in society. Key emphasized the importance of the mother, since mothers were the carriers of the future of mankind. She believed that the most gifted children were born to couples that loved one another and she regarded love as more important than the matrimonial institution. For Key, love between the sexes attained an almost sacred dimension, since it was seen as a vehicle for personal fulfilment and a better future for mankind.[15]

Key was a controversial personality and her ideas were attacked from many directions. *Fredrika Bremerförbundet*, the most important women's movement at the time, criticised her for emphasizing the inequality between the sexes and for her attacks on Christianity. Another critic was the conservative philosopher Vitalis Norström, educated in the tradition of Boström, who considered Key's ideas to be typical of contemporary radicalism. The basis of her philosophical system was, according to him, a naturalism that considered nature as in itself normative. But nature is, according to Norström, neither good nor evil and it is

---

12 Frängsmyr, *Svensk idéhistoria*, pp.187-90.

13 Gunnar Broberg and Mattias Tydén, *Oönskade i folkhemmet. Rashygien och sterilisering i Sverige*, Stockholm: Gidlund, 1991.

14 Key's development from Christianity to a belief in life has been described by Ulf Wittrock in *Ellen Keys väg från kristendom till livstro*, Uppsala: Appelbergs boktryckeri, 1953.

15 On Key's theories of love, see Claudia Lindén, *Om kärlek. Litteratur, sexualitet och politik hos Ellen Key*, Eslöv: Symposion, 2002 and Inga Sanner, *Den segrande eros. Kärleksföreställningar från Emanuel Swedenborg till Poul Bjerre*, Nora: Nya Doxa, 2003.

impossible to talk about values without some kind of metaphysical belief. Furthermore, Norström held that Key had a much too optimistic view of human nature. According to him, human beings might be rational, but more often than not they are led by selfish instincts. The consequence for Norström – as well as for Burke more than a century earlier – was that people in general were in need of authorities, religious as well as political.[16]

Norström was worried about the condition of Western culture as a whole and expressed a profound sense of discontent with modernity. In the book *Masskultur*, published in 1910, he attacked industrialisation for creating a society in which economic and materialistic values became dominant. Norström regarded the mechanical work of the new industries and mass production as a threat to spirituality and culture as a whole. Socialism was not an alternative, since he saw it as an ideology based on the interests of one specific class rather than on a concern for society as a whole. In this respect, his views were similar Key's. Like Norström, she was sceptical of socialism because it was too much concerned with the interests of a certain class. But – in contrast to Norström – she was positive towards socialism, although she pleaded for a socialism based on the individual rather than on class.[17]

Norström's criticism of modernity is interesting in yet another way, since it can be seen not only as the expression of nostalgia, but also as a forerunner of the criticism of industrialisation from different political standpoints later in the 20th century. His book was published a few years before the outbreak of the First World War, a period of turbulent political discussion. In those disputes, King Charles XII was used as a political weapon. One of the leading personalities with an obvious admiration for the king was the history professor Harald Hjärne, teacher of Johannes Kolmodin during his studies in Uppsala.

Hjärne was a conservative thinker and, as has been pointed out by Nils Elvander in his dissertation on Swedish conservatism during this period, for Hjärne, as well as for Hegel, there was a close connection between his views on history and his political ideas. Elvander relates that there existed an old kind of conservatism in Sweden before 1866 – the year of great parliamentary reform – in which defence of the old system of representation was the most important issue. This kind of conservatism faded after the reform of parliament had taken place. In the 1880s – again according to Elvander – a new conservatism emerged, a conservatism that can be characterised by its criticism of "the modern breakthrough" – or "the new enlightenment" – of the time. This kind of conservatism was close to the ideas of Burke and Hegel and was to a great extent influenced by German thinkers – although Swedish conservatives quite often referred to domestic philosophers such as Boström.[18]

Criticism of modernity was a central feature of this conservatism. The conservatives were critical of industrialisation and capitalism and were sceptical of

16 Vitalis Norström's criticism of Ellen Keys is in *Ellen Keys tredje rike. E n studie öfver radikalismen*, Stockholm: Hierta, 1902 and *Radikalismen ännu en gång*, Stockholm: Hierta, 1903. About Vitalis Norström, see Mats Persson, *Förnuftskampen. Vitalis Norström och idealismens kris*, Stockholm/Stehag: Symposion, 1994.

17 Vitalis Norström, *Masskultur*, Stockholm: Hierta, 1910, pp. Ellen Key, *Socialism och individualism. Några tankar om de få och de många*, Stockholm: Verdandi, 1891.

18 Nils Elvander, *Harald Hjärne och konservatismen. Konservativ idédebatt i Sverige 1865-1922*, Stockholm: Almqvist and Wicksell, 1961, pp. 19-39.

democracy and the new representation system. They pleaded for a strong state and strong royal power. Their nationalistic ideas were in sharp opposition to socialism, with its internationalist character.

Elvander distinguishes between two kinds of conservative ideologies that emerged at the turn of the 20th century in Sweden: one represented by Hjärne and the other by Rudolf Kjellén. Both were professors, Kjellen in social sciences and Hjärne, as we have seen, in history, and both were active as members of the Swedish parliament. The conservatism espoused by Kjellen was more biologically oriented than Hjärne's. Kjellén was influenced by Darwinism, and described the state as an organism with the different organs cooperating with one another. Kjellen used evolutionary theory as an argument for the necessity of war – according to him, wars led to a natural survival of the fittest. He was also keen on describing foreign cultures and nations in racial terms. Hjärne – and Kolmodin as well – was much more critical of those ideas than Kjellén. Both Hjärne and Kolmodin regarded cultural differences as much more important than racial ones.[19]

Hjärne was of great importance to what has been called the Carolinian renaissance at the beginning of the 20th century in Sweden. As early as in the 1880s, he had shown an interest in and had stressed the importance of historical memories in the form of statues and other types of celebration. In a speech in 1882, he criticised Swedish historians for being too negative towards historical tradition and historical memories.

However, much attention had already been paid to Charles XII some decades earlier in connection with the raising of a statue to him in the centre of Stockholm in 1868. The plans for a statue had first been laid at a feast in 1862 at which the loss at the battle of Poltava was being celebrated. The seeming paradox of celebrating a military defeat can be understood as an expression of the re-evaluation of the king during that period. Magnus Rodell has shown how the former negative estimation of the king changed into more positive assessments by this time because of contemporary political issues. In a period when Russia was seen as a threat to European nations, Charles XII's opposition to the Russian tsar was interpreted as a crucial act of resistance. In light of the political situation in the mid-19th century, this Swedish king could even be seen as a symbol of national freedom. At this time, there was a tendency to explain the warlike side of the king's personality and his position as an absolute ruler in light of the historical conditions of his lifetime. Many different assessments were made of the king, but a common trait was the value placed on his moral character and his simple habits – attributes regarded as typically Swedish.[20]

Later, the picture of the king changed and he became associated with a conservative ideology. The interest shown by Hjärne was an example of this. In 1897, he wrote an article about Charles XII, which, according to Elvander, was the starting point of the Carolinian renaissance in Sweden. From this time on, this king was regarded as a symbol of a strong Swedish nation, a view that still prevails.[21]

In the case of Hjärne, the celebration of historical memories was a vital part of conservative ideology. The interest in Charles XII grew constantly after the turn

---

19 Ibid. pp. 258-79.

20 Magnus Rodell, *Att gjuta en nation. Statyinvigningar och nationsformering i Sverige vid 1800-talets mitt*, Stockholm: Natur och kultur, 2001, chapter 4, "Den svenskaste svensk som någonsin funnits," pp. 133-214. The Poltava feast was a reaction to the proclamation by the Russian tsar to celebrate the victory at Poltava.

21 Elvander, *Harald Hjärne*, pp. 341-50.

of the century and reached its peak between 1908 and 1912. Among the king's admirers, historical and political motives were intertwined.

In 1908, a vast work on Charles XII was published with the historian Arthur Stille as the editor. Stille wanted to restore the reputation of the king as a commander. One of the contributors was the young lieutenant Carl Bennedict, who the following year wrote another essay on the king. The writings of Bennedict had a clear political message, namely that the Swedish people of the 20th century could and should be inspired by the great deeds of the king. Bennedict sent this article to Hjärne and the famous professor was quite satisfied with the message.[22]

In the same year, Stille contacted Hjärne and suggested the founding of a Carolinian Society to promote research on Charles XII and the Carolinian epoch of Swedish history. The association was established in 1910 with Hjärne, Stille and Bennedict as members and Prince Charles as president. In a speech, the prince expressed a wish that the association would contribute to the rebirth of the nation. Among its members were many historians and officers, and from the start there were tensions between the scientific and historical objectives on one hand and the political objectives on the other.[23]

This association can be seen as a reaction to modernity in a period when modernisation was a strong force in Sweden. The political situation was rather unstable at this time, and the fact that different governments replaced one another in quick succession could be used to argue against parliamentarianism, and against democracy itself. There were several conflicts between workers and employers during this period and 1909 saw a general strike in Sweden. Political life was polarised and the Social Democratic Party became more and more influential. Charles XII was regarded as a symbol of a different kind of society, gathered around a common national goal and not torn between the interests of different groups. No wonder the king was attacked by persons such as August Strindberg who held political ideals fundamentally different from those of the members of the Carolinian Society.[24]

The admirers of Charles XII expressed discontent with modern culture and a longing for a pre-modern period in Swedish history, before "degeneration" had taken place. But there was no future for this world-view. After the First World War, there was even less room for such nostalgic ideas. Modernisation was victorious. The Swedish welfare state was constructed. All men as well as women were now allowed to take part in political life. Intellectual life changed rapidly and new sciences and ideas were introduced into cultural life, such as psychology and sociology. In the field of philosophy, idealism had come to an end and new alternatives were being formulated.

By this time, Kolmodin had left Sweden. What do we really know about his motives? Was his leaving Sweden a way of escaping modernity in search of a premodern society? Among Romantic thinkers, the Orient represented a counterpoint to Western modernity, since it was associated with unity and wholeness in contrast to what was regarded as a disunited Western civilization. It is tempting to suggest that Kolmodin, when he went to the Orient to do his research on the Swedish king, was searching for an alternative to the Western society he had left. What he actually experienced in the new environment is quite another story.

---

22 Ibid., pp. 419-24.

23 Ibid. pp.419-24.

24 Frängsmyr, *Svensk idéhistoria*, p. 169.

Swedish Foreign Policy at the Time

TORSTEN ÖRN

Johannes Kolmodin joined the Swedish legation in Constantinople in the autumn of 1917 and left for Addis Ababa in the spring of 1931. In historical terms, this meant that he arrived towards the end of the First World War, when the communists had just taken power in Russia, and left during the Great Depression, when the Nazis were knocking at the door in Berlin.

In order to judge his performance on the Bosphorus, it might be of interest to know what Swedish foreign policy looked like during those years. After all, as a member of the Swedish legation in Constantinople, Kolmodin was an instrument for implementing that policy.

Paradoxically, the most important change regarding Swedish foreign policy during those 14 years was probably domestic. The conditions under which foreign policy was made changed fundamentally as part of the breakthrough of democracy during the years 1917–20. Compared with revolutionary events in other countries during the same period, the evolution of Sweden as a democracy was rather undramatic. At the centre of this evolution was a change in the law governing municipal and provincial elections. Previously, the right to vote and the number of votes cast in those elections had been dependent on wealth and income. Now, a universal and equal right to vote was introduced, for women as well as men. This determined the composition of the indirectly elected first chamber of parliament, in which the Conservatives had hitherto enjoyed a privileged position. The political coloration of the two chambers now became almost identical and the monarch had to accept the popular will without any possibility of playing off one chamber against the other. The same principle applied to foreign policy, where the king had hitherto enjoyed a relatively free hand in communicating with his fellow monarchs (many of whom had lost their thrones after 1918 anyway). The king retained only the chairmanship of the new advisory council on foreign affairs created in 1921 to give the government an opportunity to discuss foreign policy issues confidentially with leading members of the other major political parties in parliament before making decisions. Henceforth, no foreign policy could be decided upon without the support of a parliamentary majority.

Between the resignation in 1920 of the Liberal-Social Democratic coalition under the Liberal Professor Nils Edén, who carried through most of these reforms, and the assumption of power by Per Albin Hansson at the head of a stable Social Democratic government in 1932, Sweden had 11 governments and nine foreign ministers. That would appear to be a prescription for a short-sighted improvised foreign policy, but the reality was different. Once the decision was taken in 1920 to join the League of Nations, there was considerable consensus on broader issues. One of the contributory factors to this consensus was the fact that leading politicians from all democratic parties participated in the elaboration of Swedish foreign policy not only in the council on foreign affairs in Stockholm but also at the League of Nations in Geneva. The continuity and homogeneity of the professional foreign service also played its part. The only notable exception was the Conservative Foreign Minister Carl Hederstierna, who had to resign in 1923 after suggesting a defence alliance between Sweden and Finland without previously reaching an understanding with either the government or the council on foreign affairs.

With regard to that other pillar of security policy, national defence, the situation was rather different. In 1925, Liberals and Social Democrats pushed through reductions in the armed forces that went far beyond what the Conservatives and the Farmers' Party felt justified by the international situation. This decision caused what was by Swedish standards a rather harsh debate, which was to continue until the formation of the National Union Government in 1939.

The change of government in the autumn of 1917, just as Kolomodin arrived in Constantinople, also led to important changes in foreign policy. Within the framework of neutrality, the policy shifted from a relatively pro-German stance to one that was much more attuned to the Allied powers, foreign trade considerations being important in those days of economic blockade. Relations with Russia were also important, as always in Swedish foreign policy. It was to a large extent the traditional fear of Russian ambitions that had lain behind the previous pro-German bias. With the Russian Revolution in 1917, the situation had changed, at least momentarily. What now engaged Swedish public opinion was Finland's chance to gain independence from Russia, and the possibility that the Åland Islands might revert to Sweden. The former was to prove more attainable than the latter.

For Swedish legations abroad, the First World War meant a lot of additional work, particularly as Sweden acted as protecting power for a great number of warring countries, 15 in all. In Constantinople, Sweden looked after the interests of the United States, Belgium and Serbia and, towards the very end of the war, also of Germany and Bulgaria. Refugees wanting to come to Sweden created another workload. In Constantinople, many of them were White Russians escaping from the new Red Russia.

The first major issue after the end of the war was whether Sweden should join the new organisation for universal peace, the League of Nations. For Liberals and Social Democrats it was self-evident that Sweden should, in a spirit of international solidarity, join in efforts to prevent new armed conflicts. The Conservatives, on the other hand, argued that the League of Nations – particularly as long as Germany was not allowed to join – merely constituted a prolongation of the "entente" and that the stipulations on sanctions could endanger traditional Swedish neutrality in times of conflict. The various Communist groups that had made it into parliament saw the League of Nations as a capitalist conspiracy against the new Russia, which was at the time also excluded from the League. In the first chamber, 86 members voted in favour and 47 against. In the second chamber, the figures were 152 for and 67 against. Underlying the votes were the different attitudes towards the major powers. Liberals and Social Democrats sympathised with the Western democracies, the Conservatives with Germany, irrespective of that country's political system, and the extreme leftists with Communist Russia.

Once the decision was taken, however, even leading Conservatives, such as the former Prime Minister Ernst Trygger and the former Foreign Minister Erik Marks von Würtemberg, were to play a major role in Geneva. The potential conflict between solidarity and neutrality soon faded from day-to-day politics. When it resurfaced, it was usually in connection with defence policy. How much could Sweden – and Finland – rely on international solidarity in case of war and how much did they need to rely on their own military strength?

What, then, did the international scene look like from Stockholm's perspective after the end of the First World War and Sweden's entry into the League of Nations? What part did Turkey, where Kolmodin was working, play in Swedish foreign policy considerations?

With regard to military security, there had been a sea change for the better since 1914. Both the major powers that had dominated the Baltic Sea region, Russia and Germany, had collapsed and were to pose little military threat for a long time to come. Like Finland, Estonia, Latvia, Lithuania and Poland had gained or regained national independence. Sweden was seen as a central regional power in a way that had not been the case since Charles XII 200 years earlier.

But Sweden was not to play such a leading role. There were, of course, many reasons for this. After the remarkably peaceful dissolution of the union with Norway in 1905, there were few Swedes who wanted such an ambitious foreign policy. Satisfaction over Finland's independence was for a number of years somewhat overshadowed by the conflict over the Åland Islands and the dispute within Finland regarding the use of the Swedish and Finnish languages. The three Baltic republics were viewed with considerable scepticism both with regard to their domestic policies and their international future. Poland's efforts to establish itself as a great power during the period of weakness in both Russia and Germany attracted little Swedish sympathy or support. In Denmark, security policy remained a matter of observing German ambitions, the more so since Denmark had now regained northern Schleswig from Germany. In Sweden the matter of principal concern was exclusively Russia, and continued to be so until Hitler came to power in Germany in 1933. Consequently, there was little convergence of views around the Baltic Sea.

Sweden's diplomatic energy was, rather, directed towards the broader issues of international peace and security, with an emphasis on disarmament and on arbitration as a favoured means to secure the peaceful resolution of conflicts. If these efforts were successful, military threats would obviously also recede in the neighbouring regions.

Great power rivalry, however, blocked genuine disarmament, and when a major conference on disarmament finally met in Geneva in 1932, the Nazis were already close to assuming power in Berlin.

Swedish diplomatic efforts were directed even more towards the peaceful resolution of various local or regional conflicts, which, if neglected, might develop into serious threats to international peace and security. The dispute between Poland and Lithuania regarding Vilnius, the Italian occupation of the Greek island of Corfu, the question of whether the province of Mosul should belong to Turkey or Iraq, were some of the main concerns in the 1920s. Another controversial matter in which Sweden played an active part, was the entry of Germany into the League of Nation after the Locarno agreements in 1925 and its right to a permanent seat on its Council.

The dominating personality on the Swedish side was the Social Democratic leader Hjalmar Branting, whether as prime minister, foreign minister, both or neither. In fact, he won the Nobel Peace Prize for his mediating efforts. After Branting's death in 1925, Östen Undén, legal adviser to the foreign ministry and foreign minister from 1924 to 1926, played a prominent role. After an arbitration between Greece and Bulgaria, he even had a mountain named after him in Bulgaria. The Liberal Eliel Löfgren, who was foreign minister from 1926 to 1928, was the first of many Swedes to be engaged in a mediatory capacity between Jews and Arabs in Jerusalem.

What part did Turkey play in Swedish diplomacy? The often very amicable Swedish–Turkish relations were, of course, based on both countries' fears of Russian ambitions to reach out towards warmer waters in both north and south. Romantics cultivated the memory of Charles XII, who spent five years in Turkey after his defeat by the Russians at Poltava in 1709. The Swedish legation in Constantinople was then established on a permanent basis at the same time as those in other major European capitals after this military debacle. The site for the Swedish legation – the present location of the consulate general and cultural institute – was acquired in 1757, which makes it the oldest Swedish state property abroad.

With the ending of the First World War, and before the eyes of Kolmodin, the multicultural Ottoman empire vanished and was replaced by Kemal Atatürk's Turkish national state. Sweden was present at the international conference in Lausanne in 1922–23 that confirmed this development. Kolmodin was, in fact, called in as an adviser to the Swedish delegation. As usual, he argued in favour of Turkey's integration into Europe.

The new Turkey was one of the first countries to normalise its relations with the Soviet Union, in 1920-21. Sweden and most other European countries waited until 1924. It is hard, however, to establish that Turkish considerations played any noticeable part in the formulation of broader Swedish foreign policy in the 1920s.

In Geneva, the dominant issue as far as Turkey was concerned was the status of the Mosul region, i.e., where the new border between Turkey and the then British-dominated Iraq would be. Far-away Sweden was drawn into the dispute as a temporary member of the League's Council.

Those involved from Swedish side were Mr. Branting, as the Council's rapporteur on the matter in 1924, Mr. Einar af Wirsén, as chairman of the commission of experts that was to look more closely into the local circumstances, and Professor Undén, who, after Branting's death took over as rapporteur and brought the matter of the Council's competence to the Permanent Court of International Justice in the Hague. This was an extremely complicated issue. In the absence of clear ethnic indicators, the Swedes tried to recommend a solution "*ex aequo et bono*" that both sides could live with. Incidentally, Mr. af Wirsén had served as Swedish military attaché in Constantinople during the war and had become one of Kolmodin's closest friends there.

The efforts of the new Turkey to modernise and Europeanise itself were looked upon with great sympathy by Sweden. Kemal Atatürk was compared to Gustav Vasa, who had created the Swedish national state in the 16th century. The visit to Turkey of Crown Prince Gustaf Adolf in 1934 was a significant event. To that understanding and sympathy Kolmodin contributed actively through his diplomatic dispatches and his frequent correspondence with leading Swedish cultural personalities. He also helped the Lutheran Church of Sweden to remain in touch with the Orthodox Patriarch in Constantinople.

Reviewing Swedish foreign policy in the 1920s, when Kolmodin worked at the Swedish legation in Constantinople, one is struck by the similarities with

Swedish involvement in the United Nations after the Second World War. There are also obvious similarities regarding the situation in the Baltic Sea region then and after the Cold War. However, this is not to say that history repeats itself. Suffice it to mention the existence of the European Union and the much warmer international reception given the three Baltic republics the second time round. Today it is also from a EU perspective rather than from a Russian one that we view our relations with Turkey.

I think Johannes Kolmodin would have liked that.

"The Swedish Palace" - The Swedish Embassy during Ottoman times. Today the Swedish Consulate Generale

Åke E:son Lindman

An Ill-matched Couple:
The Envoy Gustaf Wallenberg and
the Dragoman Johannes Kolmodin[*]

CARL GUSTAF KOLMODIN

In 1920 Gustaf Oscar Wallenberg (1863-1937) took up the duties of *ministre plénipotentiaire* and head of the Swedish legation in Constantinople. This was to bring great changes in the life and work of Johannes Kolmodin.

It is hard to imagine two men more different than these. Wallenberg belonged to Sweden's leading financial family and never lacked money. Kolmodin came from a large family in which strict austerity was essential. His father, once a teacher and director of the mission school in Johannelund, became a professor at Uppsala University. Johannes Kolmodin had a rich intellectual life in Uppsala and, at the same time, an extensive involvement in conservative politics. History and Semitic languages were his main subjects, and he took a special interest in Turkish[1] and Ethiopian languages. During 1908–09 he conducted field studies of Ethiopian languages in Abyssinia. In 1914 he obtained his doctoral degree and a senior lectureship in Semitic languages, and began to lecture in that discipline as well as "on the history of the ancient Orient."

Wallenberg lived in a grand style and sat temporarily on the board of Stockholms Enskilda Bank until his brother Marcus persuaded him to resign. Known for his enormous energy, he became a naval officer, ship owner and railroad builder. In 1900–06 he was a Liberal representative in the second chamber of Parliament, then entered service as Sweden's first ambassador in Tokyo and later in Peking. He devoted himself diligently to Swedish trade relations with the Far East and to copious correspondence, but with varying success. A shortage of diplomatic tact earned him influential enemies, and even a warning from the Foreign Minister. His Germanophile tendencies in word and deed were the last straw, and in 1918 he was called home. Yet in 1920 a new ministerial post befell him: Constantinople.

When Wallenberg arrived in Constantinople, Johannes Kolmodin had been there just over two years, working as a researcher and an honorary attaché at the legation. The latter appointment had been made to support his studies on the his-

---

* This chapter is translated from Swedish to English by Jon van Leuven.

1 His interest in the Turkish language had awakened already when he was a pupil at the secondary grammar school of Strängnäs, where he lived with his maternal aunt and her husband, Karl Uno Nylander. Being a Semitist, Nylander had for some time been acting professor in Semitic languages at Uppsala University, but when he found out that he would never get the permanent position he resigned and became dean of Strängnäs, a position he held, when Johannes was staying with the family. Nylander was knowledgeable in the Turkish language and was the editor of Michael Eneman's *Resa i Orienten 1711-1712* (Travel in the Orient, Uppsala 1889). From Nylander's Turkish interests we can assume that Johannes, already as a young secondary school student, was stuffed with information about Turkey and the Turkish language.

tory of Charles XII in Turkish archives, for which he had acquired a grant in 1917 through the mediation of Sven Hedin, the well-known explorer. According to Archbishop Nathan Söderblom, his "unique capacity for orientation in world politics and interest in religious politics"[2] had enabled him to carry out extremely complicated negotiations with the Orthodox patriarch and the Young Turks' government, which allowed Söderblom's ecumenical conference in Stockholm to take place with the Orthodox Church's participation.

Apart from his political activities in Uppsala, Kolmodin had previously been occupied only with science. Now he sought a synthesis between this and practical action, and the Royal Swedish Legation in Constantinople provided him with an opportunity. His command of history and languages – he spoke almost every tongue used in the city – equipped him well for new tasks. While he started with modest assignments at the legation, his chief, Ambassador Anckarsvärd, soon discovered his ability to make current political analyses on the basis of solid historical knowledge. After scarcely half a year, Anckarsvärd launched Kolmodin at the Foreign Ministry (UD) by asking him to write a memorandum on "Turkey and the Black Sea Issues." However, Anckarsvärd could not let it take the form of an official report, since he – like every head of a legation then and now – he had to "sign all outgoing writings." He solved the formal problem elegantly by writing to Hellner, the Foreign Minister, to "direct your Excellency's attention to the attached memorandum with two appendices, composed by Senior Lecturer Kolmodin at my suggestion."[3] Kolmodin evidently won the Ministry's approval, and considerable appreciation from Anckarsvärd. The collaboration between these two was clearly good, and Anckarsvärd entrusted Kolmodin with further and more qualified tasks, such as writing drafts for the legation's reports.

After two years, Kolmodin could be regarded as well-established in the city. In December 1919 he wrote, "I may be so bold as to claim that, at the moment, I am the most respected foreigner in Constantinople." In the same letter he adds that it is "only the economic aspect that weighs on me."[4]

In 1920 Anckarsvärd resigned and was replaced by Wallenberg. Anckarsvärd almost never appeared in Kolmodin's letters home, but Wallenberg did so frequently. Now it was two quite different personalities that would collaborate for better or worse during the next ten years. From the very outset they had trouble in understanding each other. Financial problems pursued Kolmodin through the years, even until he reached Abyssinia. He had no salaried post at the legation, but his duties remained and were greatly increased when Anckarsvärd gave way to Wallenberg. His stipend was running out and only short-term paid work there could be counted on. No help came from Wallenberg: "for rich folks it is so difficult to grasp such matters," he wrote home. One controversy after the other arose, about things big and small, mostly small – yet without diminishing Kolmodin's spirit of civil service: loyalty to leaders and to labours. In spite of their conflicts, they had the same aim: Sweden's interests and image in the East.

Another important change occurred in 1920, when Kolmodin moved out of his

---

2 Bengt Sundkler, *Ärkebiskopens ambassadör hos Österns patriark. Nathan Söderblom och hans möte*, Stockholm: Gummessons, 1975, p. 100.

3 Report No. 65 to Foreign Minister Hellner regarding Turkey and the Black Sea Issues. Constantinople 21/5 1918. UD, HP vol. 1149. RA.

4 Johannes Kolmodin to Sven Hedin. Constantinople 14/12 1919. RA, SHA, vol. 341.

room in the consulate building (Dragoman House) at the legation quarters in Pera. He rented a four-room apartment with a balcony and a view over the Sea of Marmara, in the midst of the purely Turkish district of Stamboul, "where the two streets named after Claude Farrère and Pierre Loti meet." The household was managed by a "pious and devoted" old Turkish woman who spoke only her own language. Here he built up "a friendly circle of Turks with literary and cultural interests, who expanded over the years to include the leading Turkish personalities in culture, science and politics."[5] Wallenberg clearly disliked this choice of residence, since he believed that diplomats should consort with diplomats and not Turks. A reminder to this effect was sent from the Foreign Ministry (!) to Kolmodin who, for once, got angry and answered with a letter explaining that it suited him to live there, and adding:

I would next like to make a little mark in the margin at the passage where I am denied representational duties. On the contrary I have done not a little "representing" in years past – and if those attending my small intimate suppers have not generally been of the sort who constantly go to tea parties at the legations, they have instead been as a rule more valuable from the viewpoint of information. Nor do I wish it in any way to be said that a good number of members of the diplomatic corps – namely the more serious ones – have not learned the way to my home. How this intercourse has been possible for me is not hard to elucidate: the secret is simply to maintain a certain style and avoid making any adventures out of it. Besides a few specialties – Swedish or Turkish – little more is needed. (The costs are entirely different, of course, for a legation chief's official dinners.)[6]

Kolmodin's letter with the last parenthesis shows how splendidly the Swedish representation was conducted in Constantinople: Wallenberg playing the charming host at grand banquets in the *Palais de Suède* with its famous wine cellar, and Kolmodin's intellectual company of poets and politicians in modest surroundings. Surely these two complemented each other, regardless of all else.

Reporting was the legation's primary task. And plenty of reports were produced – not only quarterly ones to the Foreign Ministry, but many about Turkish foreign policy in particular, as well as Turkish and Bulgarian domestic affairs (the Swedish minister was also accredited in Sofia). Relations with other European countries, the issue of the Patriarchate, the fall of the Sultanate, Kurdish uprisings, and other current events were analyzed and described so carefully that the reports give a good picture of contemporary Eastern history from the vantage point of Turkey. Gunnar Jarring wrote of the reporting that "it is so comprehensive, detailed and well-informed as to exceed by far what one could expect to be of interest for such a small and remote land as Sweden."[7]

There is reason to wonder how all these reports originated. Einar af Wirsén, who was military attaché at the legation until the autumn of 1919, told in his book of memoirs, "Memories from peace and war," that Kolmodin at the time "wrote most of the legation's reports."[8] More specifically, I can imagine that the report writing began with Kolmodin producing a draft at the consulate house or, most

---

5 Gunnar Jarring, 'Johannes Kolmodin', *Svenskt Biografiskt Lexikon* 21, Stockholm, 1977, p. 480.

6 Kolmodin to Eric E. Ekstrand, UD. Constantinople 26/5 1923. UUB, Q 15:2.

7 Gunnar Jarring, 'Den första svenska diplomatiska rapporteringen om Atatürk', *Svenska Forskningsinstitutet i Istanbul, Meddelanden* No. 6, 1981, p. 53.

8 Einar af Wirsén, *Minnen från krig och fred,* Stockholm, 1942, p. 256.

often, at home in his Stamboul apartment. The former place seldom gave him any calm for coping with the numerous duties involved, which were often "acute." Actually the reporting was so extensive that it is a mystery how Kolmodin found enough time alongside his other assignments, not least the consular ones. Undoubtedly he needed many late evenings and nights. It is also obvious that his research on Charles XII in Turkish archives suffered, to be completed by others after his death. Still, he managed nearly to finish "the notably demanding endeavour of a translation into Swedish of the parts of Rashid's and Dil-aver-Aga-zade's works which are of interest to Swedish historians."[9]

That it was Kolmodin who wrote the great majority of the reports becomes ever plainer when reading the vast material. He drafted them all by hand on closely written double folio sheets. Then followed discussions with Wallenberg and consequent corrections. The drafts survive at Carolina Rediviva in Uppsala[10] and a study of some of them reveals how the work proceeded. They are full of deletions, alterations and additions, in Kolmodin's or sometimes Wallenberg's handwriting, both easily legible. Most of the corrections are definitely results of discussions with the chief, even if later couched in Kolmodin's language. But the main point is that the reports owed to a collaboration, although it was not free of friction.

Kolmodin's style made difficult reading, to say the least of the continual parentheses, dashes, double negatives and so forth. He wrote in an academic manner where parentheses and subordinate clauses were supposed to meet all possible and impossible objections. Probably he had learned it from his highly esteemed teacher in history at Uppsala, Professor Harald Hjärne, whose style was similar but even more tedious and is considered antiquated today. Kolmodin's style is fairly easy to identify, especially in comparison with Wallenberg's, which is much lighter and commoner, at times to the degree that Kolmodin could not conceivably have used it in diplomatic reports.

The effort of reading these reports is, however, repaid with brilliant political analyses and insights into Turkey's fascinating history during 1921–1929. Nathan Söderblom wrote in 1922 to Prime Minister Hjalmar Branting that, already a couple of months after the Versailles peace treaty, he had received from Kolmodin "a presentation of the situation in Asia Minor, which in the most remarkable way has been confirmed at every step by the events."[11] Another and truly expert judgment of the reports came from Ambassador Gunnar Jarring, who wrote:

> The reporting from Constantinople would never have looked as it does if the undersigned themselves had written; everything bears Kolmodin's touch and is extremely informed, terminologically and linguistically and scientifically correct. Sometimes one senses a certain despair in Kolmodin that the person concerned has taken to "rectifying" his manuscript.[12]

---

9 Stig Jägerskiöld, 'Ur Johannes Kolmodins litterära kvarlåtenskap', *Karolinska Förbundets Årsbok*, 1935, p. 19.

10 Johannes Kolmodin, *Diplomatiska rapporter.* UUB Kaps. Fol. Q 15:12.

11 Nathan Söderblom to Hjalmar Branting. Uppsala 21/9 1922. KUD, Beskickningen i Konstantinopel, P1, Kolmodin. See also Carl Gustaf Kolmodin, *Johannes Kolmodin i brev och skrifter.* Kungl. Vitterhets Historie och Antikvitets Akademien, Filologiskt arkiv 41, Stockholm, 1999, p. 83.

12 'Gunnar Jarrings excerpter', uncatalogued material at LUB.

A further description of Kolmodin's activity is by the author Knut Ahnlund in a commentary in *Svenska Dagbladet* in 1999: "Behind the scenery he applied a master's hand to our diplomatic transactions with that great country, meekly concealing his superiors' relative incompetence."[13]

Although one can hardly do full justice to all these sharp-eyed writings in the present space, some brief excerpts should be cited from a tiny portion of the many long reports that deal with important phases of the Turkish revolution and renovation.

An example of the legation's versatility is given by Kolmodin at the end of a letter to Sven Hedin:

P.S. My work at the moment comprises – besides my essay Caroline Grand Viziers –

1. A survey of the interior development in Anatolia under Mustafa Kemal Pasha.
2. The situation in Constantinople after the armistice. A review.
3. The legation's (political) quarterly report (for the Parliamentary standing committee on foreign affairs).
4. An investigation of the need and plans for a debated Swedish humanistic research institute in Constantinople.

During the past week I have finished:
1. A survey of Persia's conditions since 1918.
2. The Armenian question's development since the armistice.
3. A report on the film service in Turkey (!).
4. A small article for Le Monde Oriental.[14]

Einar af Wirsén, the military attaché in Constantinople until 1921, related in his report (to the Rural Defence in Stockholm) that, at a certain time in 1919, he and Kolmodin were perhaps the only Europeans aware of Mustafa Kemal's revolt in Anatolia. Kolmodin had connections with Turkish circles around Kemal, and could translate the Turkish congress's decisions in Erzerum and Sivas. These reports do not exist at the Foreign Ministry, but one does from the spring of 1921 when the situation in Anatolia was becoming clear, while the rest of Europe still lounged in ignorance and continued to regard Turkey as "the sick man." The report from the legation, "i.e. without doubt Kolmodin,"[15] to Foreign Minister Herman Wrangel on the state of affairs in the East, with Wallenberg's signature, is long and exhaustively reasoned, but leads to a summary:

1. The Anatolian national defence government, which in Europe was once popularly viewed almost as a pack of bandits, has gained recognition as a legitimate expression for a nation's right to live,
2. Greece, which once counted rightly or wrongly as the Powers' mandatory, now stands alone against Turkey,
3. That the Treaty of Sèvres cannot be carried out has been conceded; it is now clear that little more of the original peace treaty than its heading will survive.

---

13 Svenska Dagbladet Understreckare, 23/8 1999.

14 Johannes Kolmodin to Sven Hedin, Constantinople 8/12 1921. Sven Hedins Arkiv, vol. 341, Riksarkivet.

15 Jarring, 'Den första svenska diplomatiska rapporteringen om Atatürk', p. 55.

The picture is supplemented in a key respect by the separate French–Turkish agreement on the question of Cilicia, whereby Turkey has been freed of the only remaining front except the Greek.[16]

Somewhat later came Wallenberg/Kolmodin's report on the Sultanate's imminent and conclusive collapse:

The Sultan is currently in a position rather like that of the last Byzantine emperors. As then, the sovereign's "region of power" consists of barely more than the capital city, where the rights still available to him are moreover restricted by all sorts of corporations and persons, who themselves admittedly represent the mere shadow of their names. As then, too, the true power lies less in the hands of the finely subdivided hierarchical scale of domestic authorities, for whom His Imperial Majesty still plays the role of a kind of honorary president, than with the "Frankish" naval forces which, however, for their own part, as one seems to notice ever more clearly, are casting uneasy glances toward this same Anatolia, where the Osman dynasty formerly founded its "High Empire" and where Mustafa Kemal is now about to establish the modern Turkish national state.[17]

In another report, Wallenberg/Kolmodin give a lively account of the Sultan's flight in the autumn of 1922:

The flight took place at 7 A.M. this morning, unbeknownst to the palace officials, by means of two English Red Cross automobiles which, from a rear gate of the Yildiz Palace, took the Sultan and his few followers by diverse routes to the Dolma Batché Palace, located just beside the Bosphorus. In a waiting steamer sloop, the escaping Sultan was then transported to His British Majesty's ship *Himalaya*. Whether the ceremonial visits related in the official communiqué actually occurred, I have been unable to ascertain, but it is likely that all possible etiquette was observed by the English so that the fleeing Sultan would for the present preserve all possible prestige as Caliph. The Sultan was accompanied by his son Ertogroul Effendi, a chamberlain Ömar Yaver Pasha, a personal physician, the already mentioned orchestra conductor, two eunuchs, his wardrobe attendant and wig-maker.[18]

Wallenberg acted strongly for the promotion of Swedish business in, and trade relations with, Turkey. He claimed to have "less trouble with the Turks than with the Swedes,"[19] who were suspicious of the new state. Greatly devoted in writing and speech to enlightening Sweden about Turkey's advantages, he wished that a famous Swedish novelist would "through observations of daily life give readers a depiction of how far a people can come on its inherent energy."[20] The person he had in mind was Ludvig Nordström, who in fact came to Constantinople but caught a fever and had to cut his trip short.[21]

---

16 Report No. 91 on the situation in the East during the first quarter of 1921. Constantinople 19/4 1921. UD, vol. HP 566 B. RA.

17 Report No. 152 on the cabinet, Tevfik Pasha's reconstruction. Constantinople 14/6 1921. UD, vol. HP 1149. RA.

18 Report No. 210 on the Sultan's flight. Constantinople 17/11 1922. UD, vol. HP 567. RA.

19 Kaj Falkman, *Turkiet/Gränsfursten,* Stockholm, 1999, p. 208.

20 Gustaf Wallenberg to the cabinet minister Mia-Leche Löfgren. Constantinople 12/12 1927, UD, HP 3C94, Riksarkivet.

Hjalmar Branting wrote a letter of thanks to Wallenberg for a quarterly report:[22]

> With deep interest I have studied the clear and informative presentation in your latest quarterly report on the Eastern situation and the significance which the development can be considered to have for our own country's interests. Thus I do not want to neglect to express my acknowledgement of the way you have thereby fulfilled the informational task that rests with you.[23]

A couple of weeks later, Wallenberg answered with a wish to extend his warm thanks

> for the recognition accorded my efforts to try shedding light on what happens from this important vantage point, but not without that the account of the decisive events during the Anatolian campaign's last phase, which the report contained, was entirely due to Dr Kolmodin whose eminent knowledge and great proficiency in the Turkish language were essential for describing these interesting war movements, since nothing about them has appeared here in the foreign press on the spot.[24]

Kolmodin's working conditions nonetheless became increasingly arduous, and in 1923 he wrote home:

> There are drawbacks in being alone with Wallenberg and a pair of typewriting girls, when one has so much to deal with as this legation under the presently confused transitional circumstances. I have indeed had experience of it previously, but still every time it recurs is a test of strength. Especially, to be sure, when one has allowed, like myself, the legation chief to acquire the habit of entrusting one with far too much that somebody else would do by himself.[25]

In several reports, Wallenberg/Kolmodin write of the Russian "pressure policy." This meant the pressure on the Baltic Sea and Sweden which had been exercised by Russia ever since the days of Peter the Great from his capital city of St. Petersburg. The Russian revolution and the capital's move to Moscow were in this respect a relief from Sweden's standpoint, but they presupposed that Russia gained free access to the world's oceans through the straits of the Bosphorus and Dardanelles. A report on the Treaty of Lausanne's significance for Sweden was written to the Foreign Ministry on 30 September 1923.

At the beginning of this long report, Wallenberg/Kolmodin recall some history: how the Black Sea was a Turkish lake during the first ten sultans, and a

---

21 Ludvig Nordström (1882-1942), a novelist and journalist with populist, as well as global leanings, published his impressions from Turkey in *Världs-Sverge* (Sweden of the world), Stockholm, 1928. This book deals with the "political economy" of Swedish export, which the author comments, now also has reached the Orient. He describes a trip to Anatolia with the purpose of inspecting the ongoing railway constructions and Swedish NOHAB locomotives, which is guided by Kolmodin, about whom he has been told (British diplomat born in India) that "there is no greater authority on questions related to the Near East than him" (p. 8). Nordström's sweeping, and obviously prejudiced generalizations about "European intellectualism and Oriental sexualism" (p. 202) supposedly have to be put down on his own, and not his hosts' account.

22 Report No. 206 on the situation at the third quarter change. Constantinople 26/10 1922. UD, vol. HP 567. RA.

23 Falkman, *Turkiet/Gränsfursten*, p. 55.

24 Wallenberg to Branting. Constantinople 9/12 1922. UD, vol. HP 567. RA.

25 Johannes Kolmodin to his mother. Constantinople 7/5 1923. UUB, T3 1:19.

decline of power occurred during the 18th century, when Russia commenced a struggle with them for access to the ocean through the Black Sea and the straits. England opposed this and, during World War I, Lord Curzon pursued a policy that aimed to contain Russia by dominating and closing the straits. Already after the armistice in 1919 he sent troops to Constantinople, but these worried the other Allies, who also sent troops – which led to a joint formal occupation of the city on 16 March 1920.

> It cannot be doubted that this disappointed the English politician [Lord Curzon], but he still did not give up hope of an opportunity to gain what had been intended. England placed itself, as before, wholly on the Greek side, and the French could tell a good deal about the different kinds of help that Greece obtained from the English. Had England succeeded, directly or indirectly, in taking over Constantinople or achieving complete control of the straits, this would of course have enabled her to apply such an apparatus of suffocation to Russia that the latter country would forever have been in England's power.[26]

The French realized the dangers "since their eyes were opened," and "the question of a French–Russian alliance must arise in a few years." But France was interested in an alliance with a strong Russia; a weak and progress-paralyzed Russia would have been insignificant. Through her apparatus, England would thus be able to attain two objectives: getting Russia's future into her hands, and decreasing the power of France.

After the Turkish victory at Afion Kara Hissar, where the Greek invasion forces were destroyed, the Eastern problem acquired a different appearance. Russia and Turkey now had a common interest in preventing any great power, primarily England, from gaining control of the straits. This led to a *rapprochement* between Ankara and Moscow. As in previous reports, the Swedes recalled tendencies toward "formation and consolidation of a Eurasian bloc: Russia, Turkey, the Caucasian republics, Bukhara, Persia and Afghanistan –

> a phenomenon which had surely given Lord Curzon many sleepless nights and which must have been the most influential cause of Turkey's successes at the Lausanne conference. The victory at Afion Kara Hissar evidently threw Lord Curzon off-balance for a time. He discarded the mask and ordered (in September 1922) the fortification of Kilid-bahr, on the European side of the Dardanelles at the narrowest point. I had an opportunity to follow closely what happened and I reported on it. Through the commander of a salvage steamer stationed at Chanak, I received weekly messages on how the fortification work was proceeding. Before the end of December a new Gibraltar had arisen: 39 cannon of serious calibre were mounted in modern cement placements; 30,000 English troops had been summoned, and there were stores for more than two years. It should be noted that this substantial fortress was built by the English alone, without any help whatever from the French or Italians. The aim was of course, at least originally, to apply the intended apparatus of suffocation with purely English goals and English energy, if the joint occupation of Constantinople had to cease."[27]

But the Treaty of Lausanne removed the threat to the straits' freedom, and two results were achieved for the Eastern policy: Russia's access to the world oceans

---

26 Report No. 166 to Foreign Minister Hederstierna. Constantinople 30/9 1923. UD, HP vol. 567, RA.
27 Ibid.

was ensured, and the traditional hostility between Turkey and Russia was exchanged for a common interest, namely "that no great power shall be able to arrogate dominance over the straits."

> Our position in foreign policy has thus undergone an important change through the Treaty of Lausanne. The danger which we have always taken into account has become less imminent than in a long time, and indeed I believe that the above-mentioned Turkish–Russian common interests will become permanent and develop into a solid background for applying the Straits Convention; hence, the change that Sweden's position in foreign policy has undergone possesses a significance scarcely secondary to that of the Treaty of Roskilde.[*] Considering also the barrier which Finland and the border states constitute, one should be able to look to the future without too much anxiety. Russia, since the World War, through the capital city's move southward and the present location of her productive capacity entirely in the south, has acquired a greater interest than ever before in seeing that development takes place by way of the exit gained there to the world's oceans. Thus too, our legation in Constantinople has acquired an importance which it certainly never had before.
>
> The Diplomatic Committee stated in 1919 that it must be regarded as only a question of time as to when the legation in Constantinople should be withdrawn. The answer to this lies in the situation described above, which has arisen due to the Treaty of Lausanne and which makes it a main political interest for Sweden, here in Constantinople, always to remind Turks as well as Russians and Frenchmen that no great power is ever to seize Constantinople either directly or indirectly so that the Dardanelles route for Russia becomes cut off from the world oceans. Were that to occur, the Russian pressure policy would become manifest.[28]

The paragraph with information about the fortifications at Chanak, in the long report above, was apparently written by Wallenberg, and probably it was also he who served as the witness. The rest was beyond doubt written by Kolmodin. Why else would Wallenberg have made the "correction" by hand? And why should he have made it at all?

At the conferences in Lausanne, Kolmodin participated in person as "expert assistant" to Sweden's representative Adlercreutz, but also devoted himself to conversations with the Turkish delegates (naturally in Turkish). He had previously written to the Foreign Ministry and requested the title of dragoman or first secretary, in agreement with the conditions at other foreign legations in Constantinople. The reason was that his connections with Turkish authorities were becoming difficult. He wrote that "the question may seem trivial, but *for the Turks it is not.*"[29] The Foreign Ministry consulted Wallenberg, who proposed in reply that "Dr. Kolmodin might still serve as dragoman, but be given in addition the title of legation secretary."[30] Kolmodin, who had been dragoman since 1920, thus at last became legation secretary – and although only *"pro tempore,"* this slightly improved his economy.

Wallenberg was now often sick, or absent on travels to promote trade and business relations with Turkey in Sweden and the rest of Europe. Consequently,

---

[*] The reference to the Treaty of Roskilde is in the typewritten report, and is deleted and changed in Wallenberg's handwriting to the Treaty of Brömsebro.

28 Ibid.

29 Johannes Kolmodin to UD, Stockholm. Uppsala 13/2 1923. KUD.

30 Wallenberg to UD, Constantinople 27/4 1923. LUB, Jarring's excerpts, not catalogued.

Kolmodin received more appointments as *chargé d'affaires* and could sign the reports by himself. Some further financial benefits ensued.

One gets an impression that Kolmodin expressed himself rather more simply and freely when he was able to sign by himself without risking objections from Wallenberg. In 1924 the revolution had finished, the sultanate been abolished and the republic proclaimed, with Mustafa Kemal as president of the National Assembly. The Sultan had fled, the Caliphate was no more, but Kolmodin was chargé d'affaires and could write with his own approval:

> In Turkey during the parliamentary pause, the government has on the whole shown somewhat greater initiative than one generally thought it capable of, just as it certainly has demonstrated particular appreciation of avoiding the attentions of the honourable national assembly.

This report also includes, among other things, comments on the Mosul conference and its conclusion, as well as a swing at England:

> ...need to listen to "the simian chattering of the deputies" (as the local English newspaper "Orient News" likes to express itself, with the characteristically British contempt for other peoples' parliamentary institutions)...[31]

The collaboration with Wallenberg was not always ideal:

> [...] it is really wonderful on the Marmara Isles at this time of year. However, I was called in here by a telephone message from the Envoyé early in the morning today; an important cipher had come from U.D. The situation is not very clear in itself, and is still even less clear for them in Stockholm; besides, Wallenberg also confuses it with his difficulty in clearly understanding the messages that he gets from here and there. Unfortunately he is quite dull in the head, but does not want to admit it and let me assist in the talks he conducts. When things become messy afterwards, I have to try and set them right.[32]

His view of Soviet policy and its practitioners is conveyed by Kolmodin (with his own signature) in a report to Foreign Minister Östen Undén:

> Several times I have had occasion to observe the sincere sympathy with which Soviet delegates regard the Turkish republic's president, whenever he undertakes one of his energetic and temperamental attacks on the course of events. "At any rate, there's a true revolutionary who stops at nothing," is the continual refrain in their utterances; and Mr. Potemkin [the Soviet general consul in Constantinople], after a visit to Ankara the other day, explained to me in a voice shaking with emotion how the circle of "new men," who grew up and are growing up around Mustafa Kemal, reminds him of the Soviet group around "Master" Lenin during the first organizational experiments' convulsive working period. This sympathy, which is certainly based less upon agreement of opinions and programmes than on analogous difficulties and consequently similar methods of government, is also undoubtedly mutual; the Soviet example has doubtless played a rather large role since the beginning in the Ankara environment, and the role has grown with time in a way, as the leader's attention and interest have been occupied by the work of interior transformation since peace was restored."[33]

---

31 Political quarterly report No. 158. Constantinople 25/8 1924. UD, HP vol. 567. RA.

32 Johannes Kolmodin to his mother. Constantinople 27/4 1924. UUB, T3 1:19.

33 Report No. 196 to Foreign Minister Undén. Constantinople 3/11 1924. UD, vol. HP 567. RA.

Kolmodin begins to think about his situation in Constantinople:

...What evidently obstructs a possible promotion for me is rightly and primarily that I am just hard to dispense with in the post I have now. That has become much clearer than previously during the past three months, since the Turks have again become sole masters here; and unfortunately Wallenberg grasps it all too well – that is, he would move heaven and earth, *I am afraid*, to prevent a longer leave of absence, or service at home, for me, as this would deprive him of the twig he is sitting on.[34]

Hostility towards England was something Wallenberg and Kolmodin had in common, but only Wallenberg was pro-German. In another report to Undén, the two comment on colonialism:

In considering the subject of Turkey and the great powers, one cannot at all avoid remarking the growing importance that has attached to the colonial problem in this context since nationalism replaced pan-Islamism as the ideal basis of the Turkish state. It surely does no harm for Europeans to realize as soon as possible, especially in quarters which are fortunate enough to have no finger in the pie, that one has to do here with a massive development of dogma, which actually regards as a "crime," and a cause for international infamy, any claim in the form of a colony, mandate, or the like, to take into custody a people of foreign race and religion against its will. England has long been in the very lowest circle of the condemned, as "the recognized enemy of world peace," to whom all "strivings for freedom" must self-evidently be opposed; her burden of sin is so great that the struggle against her can sometimes even justify consorting or indeed collaborating with the other, lesser "criminals." But neither is the latter's condemnation forgotten on such occasions. Italian policy in particular is the object of very deep mistrust for this reason...[35]

In 1924 Johannes Kolmodin married a friend from youth, Eva Forsslöf. There was no honeymoon trip, but the couple moved into the consulate building's upper storey in January 1925. His capacity for work was unchanged, and reports still flowed from his pen. A warm admirer of Mustafa Kemal and his reformation and renovation of Turkey, Kolmodin reports on the leader's decisiveness concerning control over the religious institutions, when writing to the Prime Minister and temporary Foreign Minister, Sandler:

Mr Prime Minister,
    The Turkish reformation à la Gustav Vasa has taken a further step towards its realization through the decisions on the 2nd, by the council of ministers under the national president's chairmanship, which are herewith attached in the French translation by the Anatolian telegraph agency. The decisions refer, as Your Excellency will find, to two different areas: abolishing the dervish congregations and other cloister-like foundations, and normalizing the clothing of civil and religious functionaries.
    Notably in the former respect, the parallel with the Swedish Reformation is obvious. Here too, the reform has been carried out in two stages. The stipulation in the law of 3 March 1924 (on dissolving the ministry for canon law and pious foundations), that the pious foundations' income would thereafter go to the Finance Ministry and the government would see to their sustenance, corresponds most closely to the point in the Västerås agreement that authorized the Crown to take over the monasteries' surplus income; and just as this eventually meant in practice the closure of the monasteries, the same consequence has now been drawn here, only much

---

34 Johannes Kolmodin to his parents. Constantinople 11/1 1924. UUB, T3 1:19.

35 Political quarterly report No. 135. Constantinople 16/8 1925. UD, vol. HP 567. RA.

more rapidly than in Gustav Vasa's Sweden. In both cases, this result was also occasioned by almost reactionary revolts, which the victorious representatives of the modern age assumed, rightly or wrongly, to possess a principal base in the congregations.

As usual with all important decisions, the president has been active in person. During a trip he took in the last days of August to Kastamuni, Inebolu and other places in northern Anatolia, he had already announced the imminent and sensational measures in speeches to the population, which of course were reported and remarked throughout the country. When returning to Ankara on the 1st, he was received by Ismet Pasha and the other cabinet ministers, wearing blameless cylinders. And the dancing dervishes in Pera – the Royal Legation's old neighbours and friends ever since the days when Gerhard Johan Baltzar von Heidenstam was Swedish minister to the High Ottoman Porte, and the great mystical poet so esteemed by him, Sheik Ghalib, was their prior – have danced yesterday for the last time, as far as a human can judge.

Naturally the present Turkish regime's character of enlightened despotism has been further indicated by these events. However, the single-minded and ruthless men of the minority, who set their minds – to quote a saying they love – upon "moving the border between Europe and Asia to Turkey's eastern frontier," now indisputably have all the Turkish state's existing tools of power in their hand.[36]

As a linguist, Kolmodin was conspicuously engaged in the issue of the transition to Roman script. Reporting about it on 20 August 1928 to Foreign Minister J. E. Löfgren, he begins by telling that the Arabic script was replaced by the Roman for the entire Turkish language area in the Soviet Union at a congress in Baku, attended also by Turkish delegates from Ankara.

...That the hesitation – and the resistance – had been greater in Turkey than in the sister republics in Russia is, moreover, nothing to wonder at. Also in Baku, there was certainly an awareness that the intended step was extremely radical; and as proof I can mention that the Azerbaijan republic's president, Agam Ali-oglu, when conversing with Menzel, the German Turkologist, who attended the congress in question as a "hospes," commented on the matter in terms of the following apparent anticlimax: "We Turks are prepared to make any sacrifice at all for the sake of progress. We have offered Allah, we have offered the Holy Koran; and we're also going to offer the holiest thing we've got: the Arabic alphabet."

And yet – how much more strongly than in the comparatively untraditional northern Turkish lands it must be felt, this break with the past that is made with the ultimate "sacrifice," here in Turkey whose rich national literature has had a continuous heritage for over 700 years, and whose unbroken administrative tradition began nearly 500 years ago! To be sure, the old literature and to some extent the old government documents are written in an artificial language, so different from normal contemporary Turkish prose that only a few of the literate Turks can read it today without a dictionary. Besides, the number of illiterates, partly due to the difficulty of learning the Arabic script, which tends to make reading itself a virtual science, still amount to some 80 % of Turkey's population. In these circumstances, one can indubitably find good reasons for undertaking the script reform just now, when a new literary style has begun to break through, and before the republic's efforts at mass education have time to eradicate illiteracy – that is, *if* the undertaking is to occur. But probably there is no trouble in understanding that the hesitations have not only come from the so-called Old Turkish side, and that even the country's leading modern humanists [...] have been among the last to give up resistance.

---

36 Report No. 148 to Prime Minister and *pro tempore* Foreign Minister R. Sandler. Constantinople 5/9 1925. UD, HP vol. 567. RA.

In the president's surroundings, though, according to what I have now and then been able to ascertain during the past three years, a firm belief has long existed in the suitability of nonetheless taking that bold step, which not without reason is seen as the start of Turkey's emergence from the half-coloured Eastern environment and its inclusion in the "white" Western world. Within the government, this standpoint has been represented not chiefly by the Minister of Education, Nedjati, who belongs to the doubters, but by the Foreign Minister, Dr. Tewfik Rouschdy – for whom it was a great triumph when, in the spring, an investigative committee appointed in the Ministry of Education, where the question was being buried, got dissolved on the Gazi's personal initiative and replaced by a mixed commission of parliamentarians, philologists and literati, with the assignment of proposing a Turkish alphabet of Roman type as soon as possible. But in its decisive stage, the question did not actually arise until this July, since the head of state, during his summer residence here in Constantinople, came into contact with one of the reform's most eager supporters among the younger Turkish university graduates, Senior Lecturer Ibrahim Nedjmi (a disciple of Professor Giese, the prominent German Turkologist in Breslau), who first made clear to him that it was really rather easy to express the Turkish language satisfactorily with Roman script, and led him to make the script reform in earnest – "the Turkish language's liberation from the Arabic strait-jacket," as it is now customarily called – into his personal "hobby."

Since then, as always in such cases, it has advanced quickly: and the new alphabet which thus appeared (through discussions in the official committee as well as between this and a kind of superior instance, comprising the head of state himself with assistance from the above-mentioned Nedjmi), is hardly likely to change much more, although the official sanction by the National Assembly cannot be expected before early November. The situation is fairly similar to what happened three years ago, when the famous "hat reform" was likewise carried out in practice with the president's consent, before the formal sovereign [the National Assembly] had a chance to express itself. Through his example and his personal propaganda – which take diverse forms, sometimes serious ones, as when he ordered a few days ago that all acts presented for his signature must be written in Roman script, and sometimes more humorous, as when he subjects all the visiting ministers and deputies to his specialty of making little interrogations – Mustafa Kemal has already resolved the matter.

After describing the new letters and making some remarks on them, Kolmodin ends with a "hope that the Turks will find in their new alphabet a useful instrument for the ever closer spiritual and material cooperation with Europe that they seek."[37] Some days later, Kolmodin met with the Turkish Foreign Minister, Dr. Tewfik Rouschdy Bey, who dwelt primarily upon the main question of the moment: the introduction of the Roman script.

He recalled how once, already in 1925, he had spoken with me about it and I had told him that, *if* it was to be done, it should be done soon, and now he wanted to know whether I thought it had succeeded, regarding both the system as a whole and the details. Of the comments I offered during the conversation, he said that he wanted to forward them, the same evening, to Mustafa Kemal, who had informed him that the latter's private adviser on the alphabet question, Ibrahim Nedjmi, had reportedly benefited by discussing it with me.[38]

---

37 Report No. 117 on Turkey's transition to Roman script. Constantinople 20/8 1928. UD, HP vol. 568. RA

38 *Confidential* report on conversation with the Turkish Foreign Minister. Constantinople 23/8 1928. UD, HP vol. 568. RA.

At times, however, Kolmodin does not easily understand how the new reforms are to fit into the Turkish context, such as the regulation about the clothing of civil servants, which he sent to the Foreign Ministry with the following remarks:

>...In one respect the regulation indicates a rather remarkable step further along the road taken towards the modernization of social forms on a European pattern. Islamic principles have not previously recognized any mourning garb, and its use by Christian peoples has been regarded – and presumably still is, in pietistic Islamic quarters – rather as a sign of some inferiority in the Christian religion, which does not give believers the same joyous assurance of going straight to Paradise that is provided by Islam. Only a short time ago, it would thus certainly still have been quite inconceivable for a Turkish ceremonial regulation to contain specifications of special clothing at funerals.[39]

In 1930 Kolmodin reports on an undeniably sensational event: the formation of an opposition party, authorized by the head of state and "dictator" himself. After much reasoning about this, Kolmodin sums up its main significance:

>...that the great leading personage had now considered the time to be ripe for moving the Turkish people up, as it were, to a higher class in the school – with full political "maturity" in the Western sense as the goal – where he himself, by right of genius, served as the rector.[40]

In the wake of many years' hard work without any proper promotion, Kolmodin began to grow tired of the legation duties and to think about the future. Wishing to devote himself to science again, he asked Sven Hedin and Nathan Söderblom to find out whether a professorship was available in Scandinavia or the Baltic area. None was, but Professor Monroe invited him to become a professor of Oriental ancient history at Columbia University in New York. Before taking such a post, however, Kolmodin wanted to write treatises and complete the works he had at hand. He calculated that half a year in Uppsala would be needed, and made an agreement on the time until 1934 with his new employer since 1931, Emperor Haile Selassie. But these plans were not to be realized, for already in 1933 Johannes Kolmodin died in Addis Ababa.

The Foreign Ministry's treatment of Kolmodin is a deplorable story. As has been noted, he became a dragoman in 1920 and a temporary legation secretary in 1923. Only in 1928, after eleven years of service, was he finally made First Secretary of the legation. He did not become a legation counsellor until he left Constantinople for Addis Ababa, and then with "unattached" status. On the other hand, there he acquired the leading post in Abyssinia, as the personal political adviser to the Emperor.

The parts of reports that have been presented above are no more than glimpses of a very comprehensive body of material dealing with Turkey's modern history, seen through diplomatic eyes. Yet the 1920s can be termed the "golden age" for Sweden's oldest legation. Two essentially distinct personalities – the minister and our last, most illustrious dragoman – were responsible, each in his way, for the respect and honour which the legation earned in Europe and the East.

---

39 Report No. 180 on civil servants' clothing. Constantinople 17/10 1925. UD, HP vol. 567. RA.

40 Report No. 162 to Foreign Minister Ramel on the new phase in the Turkish constitutional development. Constantinople 21/8 1930. UD, HP vol. 569. RA.

Excerpts from the Diplomatic Reports[*]

ELISABETH ÖZDALGA

In this section, a minor selection of the diplomatic reports mainly composed by Johannes Kolmodin during his stay in Constantinople are presented.[1] The reader should keep in mind that this kind of reports are written as events unfold, when the outcome of the conflicts and encounters described is by no means given. However, the limitations of "on-the-spot" or short-term reporting is compensated for by Kolmodin's determination to present in-depth analyses and by his style of writing, both of which offered opportunities for him to demonstrate his broad historical knowledge and unusual sensitivity to political issues. The result of this sensitivity to long-term perspectives was his ability to visualise future outcomes. To this should be added his realism and truthfulness. Taken together, these characteristics have ensured the importance of the reports as historical source material and bestow a topical value on his commentaries of world events.

The first quoted report (18 January 1921) is rendered in full. It was written about five months after the Treaty of Sèvres had been signed by the sultan's government (10 August 1920). With this treaty, the Ottomans reached the nadir of degradation, since it amounted to nothing less than the break-up of the empire into a number of smaller states and foreign spheres of interest. By the time the treaty was signed, however, the superiority in power relations it expressed had already been challenged on the ground. After the peace conference in Versailles in January 1919, Greece had, with the encouragement of Britain, occupied Smyrna (15 May 1919). As an immediate response to this intrusion, Turkish forces under the leadership of Mustafa Kemal (Atatürk), but without the consent of the sultan's government in Istanbul, had started a resistance movement against the colonial powers (Declaration of Independence in Amasya on 21 June 1919). When this Swedish diplomatic report was written, the War of Independence was already in full swing. Just the week before the report was sent off, from 6 to 10 January 1921, Turkish troops had succeeded checking the Greek advance at the so-called First Battle of İnönü. The fact that the national independence movement in Anatolia was to be taken seriously was also borne out by the sultan's administration's difficulties in paying salaries to its civil servants, while the "Anatolian salaries" were being paid regularly.

At this time, Britain had started to have second thoughts about its backing of the Greek invasion of Smyrna and western Anatolia. The report tells of a division within the local British High Commission between an imperialistic view, aimed at suppressing Turkey at any price, and a liberal view, which was seeking ways to reach mutual understanding. The report hardly conceals its contentment that none of the strategies seems, for the time being, to be successful. The other Allies, France and especially Italy, are described as less intransigent.

---

[*] Selected diplomatic reports translated by Jon van Leuven

[1] Kolmodin arrived in Constantinople in 1917 and left in 1931, but, as Carl Gustaf Kolmodin has pointed out in the previous chapter, his contributions to the diplomatic reporting was between 1920 and 1929.

The report also tells of the effect of developments in the Caucasus, where the Whites under Colonel Wrangel suffered losses against the Reds, and large numbers of Russians, troops and civilians, have escaped to Constantinople.

The reaction on the part of the Christian population in Anatolia to the peace agreements and the evolving War of Independence is also touched upon. The report contains interesting observations on the kinds of national or religious identities dominating Anatolia at this time. As reflected in the report, it was by no means a given that the Orthodox population would sympathise with the invading Greek forces, nor, for that matter with the ecumenical patriarchate in Constantinople. The second report quoted (9 May 1921), also rendered in full, deals exclusively with the question of the Christian minorities in Anatolia and their relationship to the patriarchate in Constantinople. At the time the report was written, it did not stand to reason that the "Greeks" living in Anatolia looked upon the Greek army as a liberator.

The third quotation is an excerpt from a longer report. It was written in the middle of the summer of 1921 (25 June) and reflects some of the internal conflicts within the nationalist leadership, headquartered in Ankara since 27 December 1919. The first Grand National Assembly had met in Ankara on 23 April 1920. The report warns against an oversimplified reading of the different groups within the National Assembly. The split is not between moderate "Kemalists" and a group of adventurers trying to reinvigorate the ideas of Enver Pasha – the leader of the Committee of Union and Progress who, at the end of the First World War, tried to conquer Central Asia. What was at stake was something more tactical, since there was wide consensus in the National Assembly on the goal of defending Turkey's independence within its national borders.

The fourth quote is an excerpt from a report written on 15 November 1921. It reflects a feeling of resentment at the arrogance of the conquering colonial powers, and glorifies the energy set in motion by the sound striving for national liberation. The importance of a strong leader in the struggle for national independence is also underlined. The odds on victory for the Turkish forces have been strengthened and in Constantinople there is talk of "the Anatolian miracle."

The fifth quotation is from 4 March 1924, the day after the abolition of the caliphate. The War of Independence is over, the sultanate has been abolished, the republic instituted, and Mustafa Kemal has been elected president. This is a period of deep reform. Secularism is one of the characteristic traits of this reform movement. According to the report, the abolition of the caliphate was not as essential as one may think. The reason for this is that the Turkish leaders themselves were mistaken about its character. Thinking along European-Christian lines, they believed, when abolishing the sultanate, that it would be possible to "distinguish between the caliphate and the sultanate." According to the report, they did not realise then, but had since done so, that the caliphate had always been "purely secular by its nature."

In the sixth excerpt, the question of how Mustafa Kemal dealt with the problem of recruiting new administrative cadres is discussed. In connection with this issue, the attitude towards the opposition is also touched upon, as is the increasingly authoritarian tendency in Mustafa Kemal's leadership. As the new regime settles down, with the help of rather authoritarian means, the enthusiasm apparent in the previous reports for the Turkish national leaders flags. This is illustrated in the reports of the executions following upon the Sheikh Said revolt in eastern Anatolia during the spring of 1925. These events are reflected in the report of 1 July 1925, which is rendered in full.

The eighth quotation is an excerpt from a report dated 16 August 1925. During the Sheikh Said revolt the Law for Maintenance of Public Order, which gave the government extraordinary powers, had been issued (4 March 1925). In the process of enforcing it, various opposition groups were suppressed and many executions carried out. An opposition party – the Progressive Republican Party – had been permitted in November 1924, but had already been shut down by the following summer, June 1925. Against the backdrop of these developments the report discusses the character of the regime, and compares it, although not unfavourably, to the "terror" of the Bolshevik regime.

The treatment of the opposition is further commented on in the ninth report (19 August 1926), which is rendered in full. The next, tenth quotation, is an excerpt from a report dated 28 August 1926. Both reports deal with the independence courts and the prosecution of the opposition. There are keen observations on domestic affairs and inter/intra-party strife, but Kolmodin, who alone prepared and signed these last two reports, has lost much of his enthusiasm. It seems he is getting tired both of his work at the embassy and of his reporting on the developments in daily politics in Turkey. Still, in the last excerpt selected (22 October 1927), his old aversion to the imperialistic powers shines through. He seems to be proud of the fact that Atatürk in his long speech – *Nutuk* – in which he gave his own account of the independence war, the revolution, and the first years of modernising and secularising reforms, tells of how, even in the desperate situation of 1919-20, he had turned down the offer of an American mandate. This heroic struggle for national independence expressed values Kolmodin understood very well.

I - 18.1.1921

The present political situation, seen from Constantinople's horizon, does not appear devoted to bringing the Oriental question nearer its solution. Those basic ideas on which a new order of things must be founded concerning the Turkish power are probably not as easy, either, to make a lasting reality as to formulate in monographic, well-elaborated paragraphs. The reason for this must be sought first and foremost in the fact that the treaty dictated at Sèvres, through its excessive sternness, has overshot the goal and underestimated both Turkey's stamina and the difficulty of uniting the victorious powers' interests in a joint trusteeship. The antagonism between the Allied parties in the Turkish game becomes ever more perceptible and is naturally most obvious here at the actual point of friction.

England's play with the Greek cards, so as to secure for its own sake its domination of the Straits and its influence in Asia Minor, will assuredly be continued regardless of the defeat of Venizelos, provided that the Greek people under their restored king prove to be an equally good trump to deal out. Whether Greece under King Constantine's sceptre can really be gathered into the show of force which is required in order to perform the role assigned her by the Treaty of Sèvres, however, can be doubted on good grounds and is particularly disputable after the events of recent days. As we know, the Greek army in Asia Minor celebrated its New Year with a great offensive, which was meant not only to convince the coming Paris Conference of Greece's firm intention to carry out her deposed Prime Minister's policy, but also to prove that she was fully capable of her mandate task. The offensive initially brought the Greek troops without much difficulty into possession of Biledjik, and forward to the immediate vicinity of Yeni-Chehir with the possibility of controlling the railroad to Ankara. There it was instantly thrown back by a strong Turkish counterattack, forcing the Greek army to return with extreme losses to its old positions. The triumphant bulletins from Athens were changed after a few days into the explanation that the whole advance was planned from the beginning only for reconnaissance purposes, and that the previous positions had been regained with rich booty once this goal was reached. Yet the serious situation is best demonstrated by the English being compelled to detach a substantial force of troops, reportedly numbering 10,000 men, who were now shipped over to support the Greeks' threatened Broussa front from Isnid [Iznik]. A request for help from the French was presumably also made, but been refused.

Even if one wants to believe the Greek army could subjugate ("pacify") Anatolia, or could only in the long run defend the country's borders staked out by the Treaty of Sèvres – which in itself must be termed a strategic master-stroke – one can nonetheless confidently assume that the internal Greek fragmentation and party opposition will paralyse the country's power, and render rather illusory the benefit England can draw from its new vassal state. Here in Constantinople, the high seat of Hellenism and the focus of Greek great-power dreams, the unexpected news of Venizelos' fall released such violent bitterness within the large Greek colony that people were prepared to revolt and, quite seriously, discussed the question of grabbing from Old Greece the recently acquired northern regions of Thrace etc., the islands and Smyrna. While the feelings have now somewhat calmed down since the political declarations from Athens, the unrest is still strong, and not least manifest among the occupation troops in Thrace and Smyrna. The government has also in significant degree found it necessary to make use of discharges, transfers or personnel changes among the politicising and revolution-minded officers. These preventive measures have even extended to Constantinople, and led to the changing of military delegations and the recall of several Greek officers in residence here. Nor has it been designed to pacify the mood that the head of the Greek Church, the local Ecumenical Patriarch, has taken a stance against King Constantine.

Adding to this the weak economic status of Greece, which requires large subsidies to keep her outward reputation in force, we should not be surprised if England has begun to wonder whether it is holding the right cards in the Turkish game. The previous contempt for Mustafa Kemal and his "bandits" has also weakened considerably, and it is indicative that the communiqués of the Anatolian "high commissioner" are now published in the English press organ here, while the Turkish newspapers are allowed by the censor to speak of "our brave army," which has shown itself worthy of its old traditions. One must clearly be ready to switch saddles in case Greece fails to pass the test, but then one has nobody else to send forth with military might so as to suppress the new Turkish power in Anatolia. If this situation arises, and assuming that England at least for the present is unable to pursue a real war of its own against Anatolia, the English policy until now will have run into a blind alley, which cannot be escaped without consequences. On the other hand, the time lost by the Entente, with negotiations and half-measures for restoring order among the Anatolian insurgents, has been well used and there is now a freshly organised Turkish realm to be reckoned with – which has made itself independent of the Sultan and the occupied capital city, manages its internal affairs through its own parliament and administrative organs, signs treaties with foreign powers, and possesses an army whose efficiency at least on the strategic defensive cannot be faulted. The economic conditions in regard to Anatolian Turkey appear – at any rate in comparison with the impoverished government in Constantinople – to be in a relatively favourable state because of access to the country's rich natural resources, and partly due to the supply of gold from Moscow, which has indisputably occurred and has enabled the government in Ankara to cover most of the currency in circulation. While the Turkish civil servants here in Constantinople have for months awaited the payment of their wages, it is reported that the Anatolian salaries are paid in proper order and that the requisitions from farmers have been partly payable in gold.

No agreement as to the best way of resolving the Anatolian question exists at least within the local British High Commission, where two distinct lines of opinion have faced each other for some time. The one is intransigent and represents the imperialistic view of suppressing Turkey at any price; the other is more liberal, recognising Turkey's importance for the Oriental state of equilibrium, and seeking paths of mutual understanding. The former alignment, which has tried to reach its goal through the Greeks' repeated offensives supported by the English, through attempts to bring about revolts against Mustafa Kemal and to bribe his leading men, or through the efforts – doomed from the outset – at having the Sultan himself organise the civil war with "faithful" government troops recruited here, has hitherto enjoyed no more success than the latter alignment, which strives for a solution by negotiation and, most recently, hoped to find it through the Turkish government commission sent to Ankara under the Interior Minister, Izzet Pasha.

This commission left Constantinople at the beginning of December and, after nearly two months' absence, has still not delivered itself of any sign of life, except a telegram to the Supreme Porte that it had arrived happily in Ankara. I have had the fact confirmed by the Turkish Foreign Minister as well as the Italian and French High Commissioners; the latter, for his part, vigorously complained of having tried through several channels to get in telegraphic contact with Ankara, yet received no answer. The telegrams must have reached there, he thought, but to correspond by telegraph one also needed somebody who answered on the other side. The long silence is presumably in part an effect of the customary Turkish delaying policy, here especially motivated by a desire to wait for the Paris conference's announcements at the end of the present month; but it can also probably be connected with negotiations going on between Ankara and Moscow, whose outcome is bound to affect the situation and the willingness to negotiate with Constantinople. As time has passed, the hopes that were possibly entertained in the Entente camp, of a peaceful agreement on the basis of the dispatched government commission's negotiations, have had to be given up increasingly – and the question now is whether the commission intends to return at all, or whether it aims to stay in Ankara where it was given a notably warm reception.

The waiting for results has evidently become too long for the English, and the intransigent alignment's advocates have regained their influence. Thus the Greek offensive, naturally with England's approval and aid, has been started to convince Mustafa Kemal that the time for negotiations is over, and that the hopes for some profit from Venizelos's defeat could be set aside. The same tactic was used to influence Damad Ferid Pasha and the Turkish delegation's wish for peace at the negotiations in Paris during the spring of 1920. Then, too, a Greek-English offensive was launched in Asia Minor, with the consequence that the delegation went home and that the Turkish divan found itself compelled, albeit through less representative hands, to sign the treaty. Whether the most recently staged offensive, with its obviously small success, will have a corresponding impact on Izzet Pasha's delegation in Ankara or on Mustafa Kemal's desire for peace is more than doubtful.

In comparison with the English political leadership, the role that may be played by the other Allies here at the scene of war is of secondary character – or perhaps rather of supportive nature, willingly or not. The French policy, as it appears at closer range here, basically stands in sharp opposition to the English, primarily in that unlike the latter it does not put the main emphasis on Mustafa Kemal's fighting, but on warding off the Bolshevik threat. Their economic, and not least cultural, interests to protect in Turkey as well as Syria and Cilicia are too great for the French to look calmly on the present Russian concentrations against both Rumania and the Caucasus, and they are quite aware that the storm which is evidently approaching England from the Moslem world will also fall upon French interests. There are also the old and, despite the war, uneradicated sympathies which the French people still feel for Turkey, and which led the old Turkophile Pierre Loti in his book last year, *La morte de notre chère France en Orient*, to publish a large collection of letters from compatriots residing here, sharply condemning France's Oriental policy both in relation to Turkey and for the inability to assert French interests strongly enough against England. This book contains especially disrespectful statements about the French High Commissioner office's leadership hitherto, and it is symptomatic of the divergence prevailing even within the French administration that the book's sales were not hindered by the headquarters and military censor. Neither is it any secret that the understanding between the French headquarters and High Commissioner office has left much else to be desired, ever since the time when General Franchet d'Esperey departed from Constantinople in connection with the occupation by the English, of which he was reputedly not even informed. The conflict of interests, here as also within the English leadership, tends to mean that it is the military element which represents a view more liberal and sympathetic toward Turkey, while the foremost diplomacy, certainly without much satisfaction on the French side, must hold the official front that is shared with England. Among the French headquarters' officers there is also a lively perception that England's support on the issues dearest to the French, namely disarmament of Germany and the reparations, had to be bought at the cost of French interests in the Orient. This is probably the most immediate reason why their cooperation with the diplomatic leadership has not been the best, and why the relations with their English comrades in arms, when not totally lacking, are limited to maintaining correct politeness. One can even hear, from more outspoken circles in the French headquarters, such heretical comments as that, once the war is over, France must reach an understanding with Germany as soon as possible in order to protect their interests with the requisite energy against Anglo-Saxon hegemony. It can be assumed that the divergences between the military and diplomatic leaderships are at least one of the reasons for the change occurring now in January, when France's High Commissioner M. Defrance has been transferred to the ambassador's post in Madrid and will be replaced here by General Pellé, the Czech army's organiser, who took a prominent stance during the war and was previously the French military attaché in Berlin, at which time I had the opportunity to get to know him in 1911. Whereas France has thus considered the situation to demand that the diplomatic leadership be likewise placed in military hands, England has gone the opposite way in that its former High Commissioner, Admiral de Robeck, was replaced during December by a diplomat, the previous minister in Warsaw, Sir Horace Rumbold.

While the English policy has utilised and still evidently reckons with the Greek army to guard its interests against Mustafa Kemal, the French had supposed that the Wrangel army in South Russia could be counted on to guard its own interests against the Soviet Union. Since the game was lost through the Crimean evacuation, France has taken upon herself, as we know, the heavy humanitarian task of protecting both the Wrangel troops of around 80,000 men and the 100,000-odd Russian civilian refugees who followed them here to Constantinople. The practical difficulties and political risks that inevitably result have, of course, not been lacking. By taking in all these generally quite impoverished refugees during the present period of extremely high prices and prevailing overpopulation, a new element of social unrest has been created, and the already sufficiently marked conglomeration of conflicting interests has been further refined. Still more worrying, though, is that this new Russian population in Constantinople can count on support from an armed Russian force if necessary, which is at least partly based in the capital city's immediate neighbourhood. The illusion of being able to maintain under arms and reorganise the Wrangel army under French command for future assignments has already proved deceptive, and the risk of having these troops too close has also led the French now in January to evacuate the Russian camp at Tchataldja and transfer the troops there to the island of Lemnos – a measure which, however, could not be conducted without mutiny among the Russian soldiers and a bloody clash with several casualties on both sides. The evacuation of Crimea has obviously brought not only "whites" but also a great number of "red" elements, strengthening the Bolshevik propaganda that has long been produced here. In terms of the fulfilment of Czar Peter's testament there is otherwise less significance nowadays in the colour, and more in the value of having a settled and prepared population of Russians in Constantinople. Including previous migrations during the war, this Russian population must amount to at least 200,000. At a recent talk with the chief of the Allied gendarmerie in Constantinople, General Harrington, this subject came up and he also expressed fear of unrest due to the Russians, and his misgivings about the Russian troops not having been immediately disarmed.

If, then, both the English and the French Oriental policies have lately incurred some miscalculations, this has been less true of the Italian, which as we know has played more or less openly from the start with the Turkish cards, and has found a natural link to the Turkish interests in a common effort to oppose Greece's growing power. While these Italian sympathies for Turkey have not, with respect to the united Allied front and to dependence especially on England, been able to take any official expression, they are all the more noticeable in private social life. Within the Italian High Commissioner's office and associated circles, there must consequently be a hearty desire for the success of Turkish nationalism and, in contrast to England, nothing against negotiating with Mustafa Kemal, any more than Italy in contrast to France is against negotiating with the Soviet Union if the desired peace can thus be attained. Italy's benevolent stance toward Turkey has been marked not least through the change that likewise occurred in the Italian leadership during the

Elisabeth Özdalga   151

autumn, when the former High Commissioner, Maissa, was transferred as governor to Rhodes and replaced, after some time of interregnum, by Italy's latest ambassador in Turkey, Marquis Garroni, who is well known for his Turkish sympathies. On my first visit to him at the beginning of this month, he also gave a fairly exhaustive account of his view on the current situation. Firstly he deplored the policy which had led to the present difficulties, and particularly the mistake which in his opinion had been committed by bringing the Wrangel army here to Turkey. Regarding the Turkish government commission that was sent out, he had reason to suppose that it would waste no haste in returning, and seemed to believe that internal negotiations between Turkish authorities could not easily lead to the result desired by the Allies. Concerning Greece, he wished her well but was personally convinced that the Greeks had been given more than they could digest, thereby creating a situation which would have new complications. He ended by stressing that he never missed an opportunity to show his colleagues the futility of the means by which they have hitherto tried to resolve the Turkish question.

A final impression of the general state of affairs, as it looks from Constantinople's horizon in mid-January, is that all the above-outlined conflicts of interest in the game of Turkey can be remedied only through compromises and concessions with due attention to the recently altered circumstances, which appear to warrant more regard for the Turkish realm's conditions of life. The French Prime Minister's programme statements also justify a hope for at least temporary remedy by that route. In any case, neither the English nor the French are thinking of leaving Constantinople, to judge by the reconnaissance going on now to make further room for the troop camps planned here.

Signed: E. Lind av Hageby

II - 9.5.1921

I have mentioned, in my latest report on the situation at the beginning of the new quarter, that lately even the Orthodox in Anatolia, like the Gregorian ("Armenian") Christians already earlier, have shown tendencies of starting to organise themselves on their own, independently of the Greek Patriarchate here which is under influences that are foreign or at any rate against the Turkish state. According to the most recent information received, this seems to involve something still more radical than previously assumed. It probably concerns a popular Church movement, simultaneously at quite separate places – and what is more, while the Gregorians at least until now have preserved Armenian as their cultic language, the Orthodox apparently want to go all the way and replace Greek in the cult with Turkish.

In the end of March, when the Greeks launched their last, so ingloriously unsuccessful offensive, telegrams began to stream into Ankara from the Orthodox priests and congregations around Anatolia. One telegram from the Bishop in Havza (south-west of Samsoun) said: "Since the Ecumenical Patriarchate, exceeding its authority, undertook to try exploiting its spiritual influence for political aims and thereby place us in a suspicious light before our lawful government and our Islamic countrymen, we wish no longer to have anything to do with it." The priesthood and congregation in Kaisari (Caesarea in Cappadocia) telegraphed: "In the establishment of the independent Turkish patriarchate, as we desire, we see the means of putting a stop for the future to the atrocious slander against our patriotism, which the European policy in conjunction with the Ecumenical Patriarchate has attempted to spread." The Orthodox congregation in Gömüsj-Hadji-Köj (west of Amasia) declared: "We 'Greeks' who now live in Anatolia are aware that basically we are nothing other than pure Turks of the Seljuk tribe who long ago adopted Christianity." A telegram with mass signatures from Isparta (north of Adalia) stated among other things: "We are all, including our priests, Turks and Turks alone, and as such could not feel the slightest solidarity with the Patriarchate in Constantinople." Throughout, all these so-called Greeks maintained that they were incapable of any language but Turkish and that they therefore wished to use this mother tongue of theirs in the liturgy. A dispatch from Tosia (in the *vilayet* of Kastamouni) appealed especially for rapidity in dealing with the issue due to this aspect of essence for the nation's unity.

The "great national assembly," already in the beginning of April, appointed a committee to work out proposals for regulating the planned Turkish-Orthodox church's juridical status. Everything indicates that both the assembly itself and its government fully realise the meaning and value of the fact that one – and perhaps the most important – of these spiritual corporations, which for so long have tended to call themselves and develop themselves into "nations" (the Orthodox church in Turkey), has thus split apart on the difference of nationality and, for the most part, consciously rejected the Greek claims to "liberate" them.

It might be expected, too, that Canterbury's intimate friendship with Fanar will cool somewhat after what has happened. Christianity's future and status in Turkey, which is being seriously jeopardised by the Ecumenical Patriarchate, is without doubt in no small measure dependent on the happy accomplishment of the initiated Anatolian schism (largely reminiscent of the earlier Bulgarian one, with its still current contrast between "patriarchalists" and "exarchists"). And the future of Christianity should actually interest an English archbishop more than those of Greece – even if the latter's case is represented by a particularly venerable institution from the viewpoint of church history.

Signed: Gustaf Wallenberg

III - 25.6.1921

Anatolia. Although what has been related by a certain segment of the press here and in Europe, about intense struggles in the Ankara parliament between moderates and extremists, should on the whole be regarded as tendentious exaggeration, it is only plausible that every sort of clash of opinion has occurred and will occur there, despite the unity in principle about the national demands which was once more strongly demonstrated during the national government's reconstruction in the middle of May. One must very definitely consider it a stereotyped simplification of the situation when the issue is thus presented, as if the actual "Kemalists" were the moderate followers of "a westward orientation" and the extremists – with their more eastwardly directed programme – were really Enver's men rather than Mustafa Kemal's, inspired by zeal to prepare the return of this Unionist leader who has been banned by the Entente, and therefore inclined towards a war to the utmost against the West on the Bolsheviks' side. Such is clearly not the case: on the contrary, both groups in the national assembly are undoubtedly "Kemalists" in the sense that they see Turkey's independence within its national borders as the goal, and that they are not prone to risk this goal for pan-Islamic or pan-Turanistic chimaeras à la Enver. The main difference between them is surely just the one well known from public debates in the European combatant countries – that the moderates are primarily anxious not to neglect any opportunity to make a decent end of the war, while the extremists chiefly worry about the will to win being weakened through peace debates and peace resolutions at the wrong time. Mustafa Kemal himself, certain anyhow of being able to count on the former if things came to a choice between him and Enver, has shrewdly taken the chairmanship of the majority group in the assembly, which has united around the programme of putting defeatism at the front, and thereby apparently managed rather safely to isolate the inopportune Enveristic agitation.

Besides, the danger – if we are justified in speaking of any real one – probably was and is located at, not behind, the front. Even for a personally strong man who does not shrink from responsibility, it is already no easy matter to achieve incontestable authority over old professional comrades, some of whom are also senior in the ranks. And Mustafa Kemal is perhaps not entirely innocent of having allowed himself, with the overestimation of parliamentary life that often emerges in soldiers turned politicians, to become so absorbed in it that he has lost a degree of desirable contact with the army and its commanders. The associated risk, however, must have been largely neutralised through his being able to reckon, ever since the work of reorganisation began, with a supporter who is by all accounts absolutely reliable and free from political aspirations: Ismet Pasha, the victor in both battles at In-Önü in January and April, who most recently as Chief of the General Staff has gathered in his hand the supreme command of the whole western front, from Izmid in the north to Denizli in the south. At the same time, when the very ambitious and self-assured Refet Pasha, hitherto the supreme commander of the southern part of the front, who might be suspected of not being completely immune to potential Enveristic invitations, has been transferred to the honourable post of commander for the coastal defence (which is doubtless considered in need of a shake-up after the Greek raid in the Black Sea a couple of weeks ago), it is likely that the intention was not only to unite the battle front for a possible final struggle, but to counteract in good time the tendency, presumably strongest in his division, towards personal orientation around a popular and competent, yet somewhat capricious, general.

In any event, the strikingly sharp invective against Enver and his strivings to gain way in Anatolia, which could be read in the semi-official Ankara newspaper Hakimijet-i-millie ("People's Rule") more or less simultaneously with this reorganisation of the supreme command, need not be taken to mean that Mustafa Kemal has really feared so much from that direction. Within such Entente circles here, which have previously endeavoured to see things as they probably are, and criticised the recurrent fables of shallow Greek optimism about an incipient dissolution of the Turkish nationalist camp, one is at least more inclined to assume that the main purpose of this demonstration (like others previously in the same style) has been to let the Anatolian national leader personally stand as the indispensable guarantor against Enver and the Unionists in the eyes of the Entente powers, whose own interests should then be served by not economising on their compliance towards him.

Signed: Gustaf Wallenberg

IV - 15.11.1921

The by now scarcely relevant Treaty of Sèvres admittedly did not represent a universal human ideal, any more than did Greek imperialism (the Venizelan and the Constantinian) or the rather openly conceded British interests and efforts which once unleashed it and set certain limits for it. Indeed, not even any Christian or European ideal was expressed therein, as the Crusade concept ought nowadays to be rightly considered a typical example of an obsolete idea. But since this idea's renewed appearance as a determining factor was presumably also the most characteristic manifestation of the sanguine, unrealistic belief in being able to arrange the world as one pleases simply because one has conquered, its decline is at any rate the most palpable proof that real life outweighs theories. Unexpected even for many of the most thoughtful Turks themselves, Turkey's regeneration – "the Anatolian miracle," as the phenomenon is now called from the viewpoint of Istanbul – is nonetheless fundamentally just a new instance of how the deep inner coherence that unconsciously grows within a people, during centuries of more or less willingly borne collective exertions and sufferings under seemingly overpowering external pressure, possesses an utterly incalculable potential energy which, at least if the great personality of a leader is at hand, can assert itself against and above all those scattered projects whose promoters usually feel entitled to condemn what they find unknown or strange, in the name of their perhaps still fairly narrow cultural ideals.

Signed: Gustaf Wallenberg

V - 4.3.1924

"The Caliph is deposed. The caliphate, as a part of the very concept of the state or republic, has been abolished." This probably constitutes less a concession to adherents of the cited theory than a somewhat veiled admission of having been mistaken when, nearly a year and a half ago, it was believed on the basis of a European-Christian rather than Oriental-Islamic outlook that one could "distinguish between the caliphate and the sultanate," since the former's mission too, as was stressed already then in the report on the matter from this embassy, has always undoubtedly been purely secular by its nature. In view of the justification asserted in the law text itself, the abolition now emerges as, so to speak, the consequence of this newly gained insight.

Signed: Gustaf Wallenberg

VI - 3.11.1924

"Essentially, there have never been, nor are there, any reactionaries in Turkey," declared Mustafa Kemal. "What existed was a certain hesitance, a certain unease in the mind; but the new prospect that opened up to all eyes after the republic's proclamation, and after the liquidation it made necessary of the remaining superfluous institutions (the caliphate etc.), restored inner calm to even the doubtful and disturbed. Since then, only one further possibility can be considered, namely that some ordinary politicians, some simple careerist types, would endeavour to revive that hesitance and those loose fantasies with the aim of thereby creating a position for himself. I assure you, I guarantee with my entire being that as soon as such persons, in whatever form and manner and with whichever means they may have, begin to make their presence perceptible, they would not escape becoming objects of the Turkish nation's merciless persecution."

The national president has thus unmistakably laid down how he views the situation. He sees it in very simplified contours, as is natural for these strongly will-endowed personalities who carry out radical revolutions in history. That he is rather unjust to his old friends Adnan and Reuf, there is no doubt; but this does not mean he has not, perhaps in his intuitive way, seen quite correctly when he assumes that their and their sympathisers' demands for allowing the more highly competent to lead, if these were fulfilled now, could only lead to letting the traditions from "l'ancien régime" blow in through every gap and crack in the republic's half-completed new edifice. Better, then, to put up with the "incompetence" shown by so many pioneers, until they have time to be brought up by experience! Besides, they have the advantage of being, as a rule, easier to discipline and less prone to the temptation of having their own opinions on programme issues!

Several times I have had occasion to observe the sincere sympathy with which Soviet delegates regard the Turkish republic's president, whenever he undertakes one of his energetic and temperamental attacks on the course of events. "At any rate, there's a true revolutionary who stops at nothing," is the continual refrain in their utterances; and Mr. Potemkin [the Soviet general consul in Constantinople], after a visit to Ankara the other day, explained to me in a voice shaking with emotion how the circle of "new men," who grew up and are growing up around Mustafa Kemal, reminds him of the Soviet group around "Master" Lenin during the first organizational experiments' convulsive working period. This sympathy, which is certainly based less upon agreement of opinions and programmes than on analogous difficulties and consequently similar methods of government, is also undoubtedly mutual; the Soviet example has doubtless played a rather large role since the beginning in the Ankara environment, and the role has grown with time in a way, as the leader's attention and interest have been occupied by the work of interior transformation since peace was restored.

There was also a suggestion of this in his promised great speech before the national assembly, which commenced on Saturday afternoon but, being an official act of state, naturally did not contain any real polemics.

Taken in its context as indicated above, the president's performance certainly implies that he is still confident of having the army wholly in his hand. Perhaps he feels even more secure than previously in this respect after the opposition generals' changeover in the senate, where they too have at this stage probably begun to get an idea of what limited opportunities it has for asserting its fictitious power against the emperor's actual power. "The prospects for a reconstruction of the ministry have been diminished," it is said significantly this morning in a private telegram to the unionist newspaper "Tanine."

Signed: Johannes Kolmodin

VII - 1.7.1925

On 28 June the "independence court" in Diyar-Bekir at last announced the expected sentence of death upon the rebel leader Sheik Sa'id and his associates, numbering 47 persons in total. The sentence was carried out immediately. Any appeal against the independence court's judgment was, of course, precluded from the outset, and moreover the republic's authorities had clearly made up their minds to crush, once and for all, the Kurdish clan system as represented by its chiefs – with what success, the future will reveal.

156   *Elisabeth Özdalga*

In any event, the comparatively long time taken by the trial appears to have its explanation in the special secondary aim of discrediting the legal opposition and the opposition press, which – according to what I have already emphasized on a previous occasion – was evidently the main theme for the judging parliamentary commission during the interrogations. Sheik Sa'id himself, who oddly enough seems to have gotten the notion that his services in this respect might be thanked with exemption from the death penalty, has thereby displayed greater compliance than anyone else – which, to be sure, must have been enhanced by the fact that, once he started on this path, he was presumably better prepared than his completely illiterate comrades to furnish more or less weighty testimony of the kind desired.

The trial records, although subjected to military censorship before they could be published in the press, allow the conclusion that the public prosecutor, in order to keep the worthy Sheik in this favourable disposition until the end, saved for the final arguments the most damaging proofs against him personally (such as a letter he wrote, some weeks before the rebellion began, to one of the other sheiks, showing plainly that it was all "premeditated"). Further, these records are of extreme interest as they demonstrate that both Sheik Sa'id and the other defendants, however easily handled in general, consistently and firmly denied having entertained any nationally Kurdish aims, or been in touch with foreign powers for such purposes – in spite of the judges' obvious efforts, scarcely well-advised from the Turkish standpoint, to make them admit even this. On the contrary, the reason for all the unrest, according to the captured rebel chiefs' own statements, has been the republic's dubious neglect of Islamic canonical law – nothing else.

Whatever opinion one may have of Sheik Sa'id's performance during the trial, it has not been concealed by the authorised newspaper accounts that he went to his death with great natural dignity. When one of the attending journalists, who gained access to his prison cell before the departure for the place of execution, requested him to write a line of farewell in a notebook, he set down after a moment's thought an Arabic *hadis* (traditional prophetic utterance) to the effect that "death on the gallows is no shame, when one meets it for Allah's and religion's sake." The commander at the execution place, Mursel Pasha, asked him: "Now tell me honestly and sincerely, who do you consider to be Turkey's worst enemy?" and he declared outright: "England, of course." One of the court members present therefore enquired: "Don't you understand that Turkey is actually, even now, the defender of Islam?" To this he merely replied: "If Allah wills it, so shall it be." Those were his last words.

That the above-mentioned military censor has released such information as is repeated here may be wondered at; and perhaps there is particular reason to regard its allowing England to be pointed out in the way which has happened as a proof that it has hardly been mature enough for its task. But even though this is clearly not the only blunder committed by the republic's authorities on the occasion, the fact remains that it does not decrease the interest of the declaration by Sheik Sa'id, whose genuineness seems at any rate to be indubitable.

Signed: Gustaf Wallenberg

VIII - 16.8.1925

Overshadowing everything in Turkey's domestic politics during the half-year has been the revolt in Kurdistan, which – like its subsidiary phenomena of revolutionary conspiracies or signs of them elsewhere in the country – can be said to have characterised the indispensable aftermath of last year's great decision on secularisation.

It can hardly be disputed that this feud (Dackefejd)[2] within the Turkish republic has on the whole borne out the view which, as there are evidently grounds to assume, has constantly been represented by the national president himself, and whose content in brief is that the course of reform, so resolutely initiated, actually does not correspond to the real majority's will and therefore still needs to be defended with claws and teeth, as long as one does not want to give it up. This "Jacobinism" was what broke through with Fethi Bey's retirement and Ismet Pasha's return to power in the beginning of March; and under the prevailing circumstances it is only quite natural that the "Girondists" of varying hue – all those friends of reform, not rare during the Turkish revolution either, who overestimate the conquering force of ideas in themselves and underestimate the power of traditions among the people – have increasingly come to a deadlock during the subsequent struggle and that their organisation, the so-called progressivist republican party, could at last be dissolved by the government in early June, seemingly without drawing any attention or further involvement by anybody.

Despite the superficial resemblances one can find with a little good will between the current domestic political situation in Turkey and that in Russia – and although it is also doubtless the case that the Soviet Union's official representatives here have long hoped for, and done what they could to emphasize, the need even here for a suitable dose of terror, through which they presumably expect from their own standpoint a further strengthening of the ties between Angora and Moscow – there is every reason to beware of gratuitous and hasty analogies. The functioning Turkish independence courts have certainly taken tough measures, but at least their administration of justice contrasts with that of the Russian Cheka under public control and, unlike it, they have no executive authority independent of and competing with the normal executive state organ, but are required to rely entirely on the latter's assistance. In this respect the Russian revolution is clearly not a model for the Turkish, but both the Turks and Russians have separately imitated the French, whose special cultivation of the classical revolutionary doctrine is far from having inspired emulation.

The issues connected with the application and development of the peculiar republican "diarchy" (the theoretical assembly's power and the practical presidential power) have been temporarily set aside rather completely, as is natural in the given situation. With the extraordinary powers acquired by the president's government through the law passed for two years on the restoration of order, there is apparently nothing for the national assembly to do but act, like the rump Parliament under Cromwell, as a sort of legalisation apparatus, satisfying itself with at least saving the principle of rule by assembly until more normal situations, at the risk of otherwise putting even this in jeopardy like its above-mentioned West European model.

I have it from the very highest places that Mustafa Kemal, at a closed meeting in the republican people's party just before the assembly began its holidays at the

---

2 "Dackefejd," after a revolt by Swedish peasants in 1542 led by Nils Dacke, against the centralising reforms under the autocratic King Gustav Vasa I.

end of April, openly declared that if the country should one day send a group of "reactionary" deputies to the national assembly, he would not let these deputies get off the train in Ankara. The people's will, explained the president, ought to have free rein within municipal politics, but in national politics the condition for respecting it was that it agreed with "our better insight."

Signed: Gustaf Wallenberg

IX - 19.8.1926.

The trial going on at present before the independence court in Ankara against the survivors of the former central committee of "Union and Progress," as well as some persons close to them, was announced almost as a kind of corollary of the assassination trial in Smyrna; and the prosecutor's theory also appears to be that the defendants' political activity during recent years had logically led to the assassination attempt, even if they were not aware of it. But besides the fact that he definitely could not get a conviction from any regular Turkish court merely by "proving" this, it is clear from the published trial records that the theory in question has in several cases been only an excuse for obtaining opportunities to make embarrassing inquiries about their previous life to certain objectionable persons, in order to undermine their moral reputation and that of the former Unionist party. The interrogations have thus been characterised largely by a tedious recitation of relationships and circumstances which must be called totally irrelevant, both to the assassination and to the issue, initially combined with it, of the use of the former Unionist party's funds; and one has to remind oneself continually that the independence court is primarily an organisation of political struggle – although unlike the Russian Cheka it works publicly and therefore also with public means – if one is not to get the impression pretty often that it has utterly lost the thread and no longer knows where it is going.

The trial's aspect of a political (and only to a very minor degree juridical) action is reflected also in its effects within the "spheres" at Ankara that are now beginning to emerge. In Smyrna, Ismet Pasha had reached his actual goal, which was apparently to see that the popular generals Kiazim Kara-Bekir, Ali Fuad, Reefet and others were placed "out of the case," so that their passing of judgment would not put too much pressure on the officer corps' loyalty; but it seems that, to ensure this result, he had not stopped short of fomenting the tendency to turn it all against the Unionists, towards whom he must not have felt personally that he had any reason to show indulgence. On this point, he surely differs from several of his colleagues in the government, who on various grounds did not like this turn of the screw, and the situation at present is the virtual paradox that the Prime Minister actually has no one entirely on his side but his erstwhile antagonist Redjeb, the Minister of War, who now as always is an advocate of severe methods.

As is usual with all such antagonism in the government, this new conflict also comes closest to a fight for the president himself. How it may end is something one can only guess for the time being. The present regime has undoubtedly been strengthened by the reconciliation that Ismet brought about between Mustafa Kemal and Kiazim Kara-Bekir with colleagues, which was demonstrated during recent weeks by all manner of small attentions from both sides. But this arrangement can either be employed as an argument for the view that they should take the chance to make a thorough end of the civil opposition (as Ismet plainly desires),

The real distinction, however, is not between science and the humanities, but between descriptive scholarship and creative scholarship, between discovering and inventing, between proving the existence of something, although unknown, and creating something that did not exist before – a new thought, a new idea, a new theory.

This "creativist" view of scholarship has certainly not gone unchallenged. Although she is principally attracted by such an approach, the British Orientalist Professor Ann Lambton has also expressed her hesitations concerning my thoughts,[4] referring to them in the following way:

> He [Professor Toll] considers that the intrinsic and ultimate purpose of oriental studies in all their variety – as of all studies in the humanities [in all studies, not least in science, Ch T] – is to contribute to human culture. Scholarship for him is a creative art and the scholar an artist. In the light of this perception, he suggests that what the orientalist contributes is his picture of Islam and Islamic civilization, a picture based on substantial fact but created out of his imagination. He sees the orientalist as an explorer driven by intellectual curiosity, striving to find out what was unknown before he made it known, an imaginative artist, creating what nobody had created before him in order to obtain prestige, fame and worldly immortality.
>
> This is a somewhat idiosyncratic view. An imaginative understanding, however desirable, will tend towards uncertainty unless it is controlled by precise learning. The freedom of exploration must also be circumscribed by the reality of the past. The orientalist ought, no doubt, to be an artist, but more importantly, he must be governed by the techniques of his particular craft. He needs an imaginative and sympathetic understanding, but he must also be taught to be critical and with this, I have no doubt, Professor Toll would agree. Those engaged in oriental studies, as all engaged in intellectual investigations, seek the truth within the confines of their particular province, and the quality of their work is to be judged on purely intellectual grounds.[5]

Thus far Professor Lambton. In the following discussion, I will not be as magisterial as the title of this chapter might indicate. I am only going to try, by means of some examples from my own province, Semitic philology, to arrive at a view of the possible goal of our work as scholars.[6]

My previous contention was that what is badly or poorly understood could be a more inspiring avenue for further research than fully fledged solutions, since the former forces you to try better to understand. I would like to illustrate this by an example. In Hosea 4:10 in the Old Testament we read: "They (the people of Israel) eat without being satisfied, they fornicate without ...," and there follows a form of the Hebrew verb *paras,* which H.S. Nyberg and H.W. Wolf and the usual Bible translations render as "to multiply itself," i.e., "they eat without being satisfied, they fornicate without multiplying themselves." But this is hardly correct: you eat in order to be satisfied, but you do not fornicate in order to multiply yourself, and the verb *paras* does not mean "to multiply itself" but "to penetrate"

---

4 See Christopher Toll: "The Purpose of Islamic Studies," in K. Ferdinand and M. Mozaffari eds: *Islam: State and Society,* London: Curzon, 1988, pp. 13-25, 196-8.

5 Ann Lambton: "Introduction," in K. Ferdinand and M. Mozaffari eds: *Islam: State and Society,* pp. 7 f.

6 The ideas I am going to use as examples do not represent any actual or important currents in Semitic philology, they are but my attempts at a solution of problems that I more or less accidentally have come across. And my ideas do not represent any actual currents within the philosophy or theory of science, which is not my province, but are only a contribution to a discussion in which we all participate.

(e.g., through a wall). In this translation, the passage does not seem to be correctly understood, and that forces you to try harder to understand it. The next step would be to imagine that the verb having the meaning "to penetrate" could, in this context, be used in its sexual sense. If you cannot penetrate, if you are impotent, the fornication is a failure, in the same way as the eating is a failure when you are never satisfied. A support for this rendering is the Greek translation kateuqunvsin, meaning "to straighten," which could be another expression for potency, and in any case has nothing to do with multiplying itself.

Thus, from the original meaning "to penetrate," the verb in a sexual sense means "to be potent," and then again, without the sexual sense, it expresses "power" in general and God's power especially, and in a negative sense "violence" – all significations to be found in the Old Testament.

I invented this theory[7] because I thought that a word in the Hosea text was incorrectly understood. Therefore, I do not consider it a bad thing when the rendering of a theory turns out to be less convincing, because it is exactly such cases that generate new efforts.

Now, two questions arise: why did I want to present a new rendering and to support it with a new theory? And how do I know that my rendering is better than the previous one and that my theory is more convincing?

The answer to the first question could be – as we have seen – that, as a scholar, I look for truth. Less high-toned, one could say that a scholar tends to be curious: if it is not in this way, it ought to be in another way – which one?

This points to an affinity with art, because as the Swedish painter and critic Otto Carlsund has said: "The childish curiosity of the artist is the motive force in his creative work."[8] One way to satisfy one's curiosity is to ask other people, but if there are no others prepared to answer, or you are not satisfied with their answers, you will have to find the answer yourself – you are face to face with a challenge. A scholar is thus not only curious, but he is also prepared to respond to a challenge rather than to make himself comfortable.

This is an example of the importance of free will. We are, every day all our life, faced with different choices, but principally, it is always the same choice: between making the effort and making ourselves comfortable; to choose to do what is difficult or what is easier or even what is easiest, namely, not to do anything at all. The reason why we prefer to make an effort, to choose the difficult, is that this is what causes the most joy. The joy of what we have done seems to be proportionate to the effort we have made, irrespective of what we have done. The reading of a book causes us more joy the more the interest, engagement and knowledge we have invested in it. It is the same with our feelings: they cause us more joy the stronger they are.

The effort to create something new causes us the same joy as that of the artist. There may be in this joy a certain amount of vanity – it is me who has made this effort, it is me who has created this theory that I find better than those of my predecessors and colleagues, it is my name that is mentioned when this theory is quoted. Still, it is often overlooked that it is more flattering when a theory is quoted as an established fact without its author being mentioned, than the other way around.

---

7 Christopher Toll, "Die Wurzel PRS im Hebräischen," *Orientalia Suecana* 21/1972, pp. 73-86.

8 *Festskrift till Gösta Berg*, Lund 1993.

If, instead of out of joy, you are forced on by the passion of truth and you look upon your theory as truth, other theories have to be untrue. Then you have a moral view of scholarship, which explains the vehement polemics arising when scholars defend their truths or attack the untruth of other scholars.

But how do I know that my theory is better and more convincing – that is the second question to be discussed in this chapter. That the verb *paras* can be used to signify "violence" has been explained in another way by another scholar, who would not have brought forward his theory had he not considered it as true.[9] According to him, the verb means "to divide" and is used for the division of land between families: the bigger the family, the bigger its share. Thus, the root would signify the size of the family, of its possessions, its growing and spreading, and the noun would have the meaning "landowner," from which the meaning "assaulter" and "to commit violence" would be derived. Apart from the fact that the verb actually means "to penetrate" and not "to divide," and that there is, as far as I know, no instance found for the meaning "landowner," a development from "landowner" to "assaulter" seems more to illustrate the manner of speaking of the twentieth century than an ancient language. The theory seems to be influenced by the conceptions of contemporary society. Perhaps this theory could be said to present a socially subjective truth?

I should like to add another example of two "truths." My starting point is again my theory that *paras*, originally meaning "to penetrate" in a sexual sense, has got the meaning "to be potent" and then "to be powerful" in general. Such a development is not without parallels. The Hebrew verb *naqab* means "to pierce," and the feminine passive participle *neqeba* with the meaning "woman" shows the sexual meaning, and when the masculine passive participle means "chieftain" the original meaning is undoubtedly "possessor of power." Also the negative sense, corresponding to the "violence" of *paras*, is found in the expression *naqab æt-hashshæm*, literally "to pierce the Name," i.e., "to blaspheme."

It is an old observation that Semitic roots beginning with the consonants PR-, as in *paras,* have a common primary sense "to penetrate" or "to split." This also applies to roots beginning with the phonetically related BR-. It would thus be interesting to see whether my theory could solve the problems related to the root of the Hebrew words *bæræk* "knee," *beraka* "blessing," and *bereka* "pond."[10] Usually, "blessing" has been considered as related to genuflection, but then one is obviously taken in by the word "to bless" – and still more the Latin "benedire"– being understood as a verb of utterance. But the Hebrew verb signifies a transmission of power and does not presuppose any particular bodily attitude on the part of the one who is filled with power. The noun *beraka* means "benefactio" rather than "benedictio," and there are no examples of the receiver of a blessing being on his knees.

It is thus difficult to perceive a connection between "blessing" and "knee," not to mention "pond." But "knee" is not the only meaning of *bæræk* – sometimes it has the meaning "penis." The word for "knee" is then considered as a euphemism for "penis," but one should be reluctant to presuppose euphemisms – the old

---

9 J.J. Glück, "The Verb PRS in the Bible and in the Qumran Literature," *Revue de Qumran* 5, 1964-65, pp. 123-7.

10 See my "Ausdrücke für 'Kraft' im Alten Testament mit besonderer Rücksicht auf die Wurzel BRK," *Zeitschrift für die alttestamentliche Wissenschaft* 94, 1982, pp. 111-23.

Semites were not particularly prudish – and, besides, "knee" can hardly be looked upon as a good metaphor for "penis." We can see that the original meaning preserved in the word for "pond," something pierced, the sexual meaning we find in the word for "penis" – homonymous with the word for "knee" from another root – and the development from "potency" to "power" in general is illustrated by the word for "blessing."

Against this theory, Professor F. Rundgren in Uppsala has proposed another, which again considers a connection with the word for "knee."[11] He maintains that the father placed his son on his knees when he blessed him, and he mentions the old Nordic word "knäsätta." Since there is no evidence that a blessing was transmitted in this way, and since the power conferred by the blessing is of divine rather than of paternal origin, and since "knäsätta" means "to legitimise" or "to adopt" and not "to bless," this theory does not seem convincing to me. But interesting in this context is the personal background of the author of the theory. It is seldom that this is as evident in a scholarly paper as is the case here. Rundgren's theory is published in a memorial publication for the late Professor Björn Collinder, and from the introduction to Rundgren's paper we learn that Rundgren lost his father in his young years and had seen in Collinder a second father. It seems evident to me that this theory of the father placing his son on his knees was influenced by these personal circumstances. This would leave us with an individually subjective truth.

Rundgren is also a proponent of truth as the goal of scholarship, but this truth is for him also a means to make man free and to lessen the suffering in the world. Rundgren does not differentiate between scholarship and life and looks upon scholarship as a way of life.[12]

If the truth is conditioned by our personal circumstances, particular to ourselves, it could be original, but if it is dependent on the society in which we live, it is predictable and could be replaced by another conventional "truth." That means that new original truths can exist side by side – they are complementary to one another – while new conventional "truths" replace the old ones.

Popper's thesis that a truth functions only as long as it has not been falsified and replaced by a new functional truth is then valid for descriptive scholarship and for conventional truths. For creative scholarship, we can adopt the words of Lessing that a final truth would check all discussion, or, as the Tunisian scholar Hichem Djaït has said, "L'idée de perfection bloque tout processus de perfectionnement."[13] Thus one could say that all kinds of theories are contributions to a constantly continued discussion.

My contention is that there may also be a third kind of truth, different from both the only eternal one and the functional temporary one, namely, the unique aesthetic one.

The study of the word *beraka* ("blessing") and phonetically and semantically related words might have a certain importance for the understanding of the text

11 F. Rundgren, "Das Wort für 'segnen' im Althebräischen," *Linguistica et philologica, Gedenkschrift für Björn Collinder (1894-1983),* hrsg. v. O. Gschwantler et al., Wien 1984, pp. 391-6.

12 F. Rundgren, "Vetenskapen som livsform," *Kungl. Vitterhets Historie och Antikvitets Akademiens Årsbok* 1972, pp. 149-56.

13 G.E. Lessing, *Nathan der Weise,* 1779; cf., H. Arendt, "On Humanity in Dark Times: Thoughts about Lessing," in her *Men in DarkTtimes,* London: Pelican, 1973; H. Djaït, *L'Europe et l'Islam,* Paris: Seuil, 1978 p. 79.

of the Old Testament. One could think, however, that, given the study over so many generations and centuries, the text of the Old Testament would be fairly well known, and that there is not much to add. Still, the Old Testament is the object of research at universities all over the world. The Canadian novelist and university teacher Robertson Davies has said, "We tend to think of human knowledge as progressive; because we know more and more, our parents and grandparents are back numbers. But a contrary theory is possible – that we simply recognize different things at different times and in different ways."

Does that mean that we are not getting closer to the truth of the Old Testament in every generation, but that in every generation we are approaching the truth of the Old Testament from different directions and view it in different ways? It is often said that a biography tells more about the author than about the object. But the purpose is probably not for art and scholarship to express the personality of the authors, i.e., to reflect their agony, as art has been misused since the beginning of the Age of Romanticism in which we still live.

Still, it might be that the study of the Old Testament – as of any subject – is of value not because of what it tells us of its subject matter, but because research, like art, has an intrinsic value: that one scholar's subjectivity is not corrected by that of another, but that they are complementary to each other; that this is what makes scholarship so rich; that scholarly studies in their own right are contributions to our culture in the same way as paintings, poems and musical works are.

When studying the Old Testament, the ambition is to get back to an original text, such as one imagines it was recited for the first time. But does such a text exist? Cannot a text even from the beginning have been recited now in this way, now in that? We know that writers such as August Strindberg wrote and rewrote their works, and nobody would maintain that only the first version of their texts represents the true text. And why should a forgotten first version be truer than one that has been preserved and influential for generations. By the original text something new was created, but this also happened with every change in the text. And what is even truer: what someone originally wanted to say or what the readers actually understood?

That is why Tor Andrae wrote not only about Muhammad but about "die Person Muhammeds in Lehre und Glauben seiner Gemeinde,"[14] and why the Gospel shows not Jesus but Jesus as seen by the first Christian community. Tradition and reception provide a picture that is no less true than a reconstructed original.

Throughout the history of the Catholic Church, generations of painters have striven to present to us a picture of the Virgin Mary. They have certainly all striven to create what was for them and their patrons her true picture. But is there a true picture of her? Would an older picture be truer than a more recent one? Is not the artistic quality determinative of its value rather than any truth about its object? And is not every artist and every scholar in every generation able to contribute his picture and his version, all of them of value notwithstanding different starting-points and different results – nay because of their different results, which enrich our culture.

If we had only one true picture of the Virgin Mary, if we had only one uncontroversial interpretation of the Old Testament, if all scholarly works concerned with the text of the Old Testament that did not contain the truth had never been

---

14 Tor Andrae, *Die Person Muhammeds in Lehre und Glauben seiner Gemeinde,* (Dissertation, Uppsala) Stockholm: Norstedt, 1917.

written, would our culture not have been poorer in spite of our having had the truth? There are maybe many truths which do not exclude one another. I can adhere to one of the many theories about the Semitic verb or have my own theory of the Aramaic ideograms in Pahlavi, and still see with equanimity that other scholars adhere to other theories.

Now, my theory about the ideograms has been accepted,[15] my theory about the roots PR- and BR- has not, but that does not prevent me from being quite happy that I have been able to think it out. H.S. Nyberg saw in the texts of the Old Testament a Canaanite god 'Al, who was never accepted by Old Testament scholars, but Nyberg nevertheless used to say, "My 'Al is a first-rate god, indeed."

I also wonder whether truth is always very interesting. The theory that Jesus never existed demands, both to be maintained or to be refuted, a mass of learning and acumen in argumentation, and you can take part in or follow such a discussion with much enthusiasm. But if it were an established fact that Jesus had never lived (it would of course be a feat to establish this), this truth would be much less interesting than what we could call the aesthetic truth about Jesus in the Gospel, which would then possibly be still more ardently discussed.

About truth all ought to agree, but does not that make truth rather trivial, like beauty when all agree about it. Beauty is in the eye of the beholder, and maybe truth is also?

In history, truth would be a chronological report on everything that has happened, both small and great. But that is not how we understand history. History is a choice of what is essential and meaningful. And it is the historian who chooses what is essential and meaningful. If everybody made the same choice and saw the same meaning, we would not need even one smart historian.

The same applies to the individual. What is the true picture of a man or woman? The photograph, showing only a given moment; a painting in which the artist has united a great number of impressions that he has received during the sittings; or the picture I have made during maybe many years of acquaintance? What is the truth about a human life? That is what the individual himself decides, looking upon his own life, positively or negatively according to a certain viewpoint, distributing lights and shades, deciding what is important and what is unimportant. The same life could be viewed in many different ways, and who decides which is the true way?

Of Marivaux, who wrote the first modern novel "La vie de Marianne" (1731), it has been said: "The author does not view the world as from an outlook tower. A reader who wants an overview will despair – there is none. Life has no shape, it consist of millions, milliards of moments, which constantly are shaken around, changing pattern and look." That is why writers, artists and scholars are needed to help us by creating survey views and meanings.

To arrange and to create survey views, to bring together and to separate is also the aim of scholarship, according to Stig Strömholm, former vice-chancellor of Uppsala University and president of the Swedish Academy of Literature, History

---

15 Christopher Toll, "Die aramäischen Ideogramme im Mittelpersischen," *Zeitschrift der Deutschen Morgenländischen Gesellschaft,* Supplement VIII: XXIV, Stuttgart: W. Diem and A. Falaturi, 1990, pp. 24-45. Reviewed by P. Gignoux in *Abstracta Iranica* 14, 1991 no. 153: "Cette excellente étude montre de manière convaincante comment les idéogrammes araméens en moyen-perse et pehlevi des livre ... furent fabriqués par des scribes bilingues et lettrés."

and Antiquities. He means that this demands more discipline and rationality, precision and certainty than art, the aim of which is to afford experience. Strömholm also maintains that the efforts within the humanities to present the humanities as more improvised, free and independent than science, in order to match the popularity of art and literature, are misdirected. Lastly, Strömholm points out the utility of the humanities, which make it easier to find one's bearings in life, supplementing science and technology by studying those who maintain them, and provide us with knowledge about our acts by showing their causes and effects, conditions and consequences.

In my view, however, art and literature demand the same discipline and rationality, precision and certainty. Science presents the same experience as art, what is now often called "flow."[16] But rather than competing with art and literature, the humanities have tried to compete with science in order to appear exact and useful.

Semitic philology – or any scholarship – and its utility are outside the scope of this chapter. In my view, utility is also outside the scope of science and art. The utility of science and of the humanities is often obvious but always secondary. As human beings we are, of course, dependent on utility for our survival – this we have in common with animals, and so far utility is primary.[17] But what distinguishes us from animals and makes us human is free will and thus the ability to create – what is beyond mere survival, that is what we call culture. And the aim of culture is not to be true or useful but to bring forth joy, *la joie de vivre*. The greater the challenge, and the greater the enthusiasm, intensity and perseverance of the artists, the writers, and the scholars, the greater the joy.

Do we strive after an eternal unattainable truth? Are we satisfied with a truth, which according to Popper is temporary, lasting only as long as the theory has not been falsified? Or are we, if we have the will and the courage, striving in life, art and scholarship for what is original, bold, simple and beautiful? And when we say, this is true, or at least one more step towards truth, do we actually mean this is beautiful, this fascinates us, delights us, enriches us? Do we strive after an aesthetic truth? Is it so that scholarship, in order to be an art, has to go from the description with its data, which could be true or false, to the creation with its theories, which, as in art, generally can be judged only from an aesthetic point of view.

This question can be approached from different angles. A German colleague has said (and I find his words worth being quoted in this context):

Als Philologen und Historiker führen wir den Gespräch mit den Menschen der Vergangenheit, besonders mit den großen einzelnen, um die Gegenwart und uns selbst besser zu verstehen und Maßstäbe für die Gestaltung der Zukunft zu gewinnen. In dieser Weise alle drei Zeiten mit einander verbindend suchen wir die Tiefe des geschichtlichen Lebens umfassend zu ergründen. Dieses lebendige Gespräch über Zeiten hinweg, das von jeder Generation erneuert werden muß, gibt den Geisteswissenschaften ihren bleibenden Sinn und bewahrt sie davor, sich unter einem wachsenden Berg folgenlosen Richtigkeiten selbst zu begraben ... Wahr und echt ist in Religion und Kunst [and I wish to add, in scholarship, Ch T] was mir neue Erfahrungen erschließt, mir einen Zuwachs an Sein und Sinn bringt.[18]

---

16 Csikszentmihalyi, M., *Flow:the Psychology of Optimal Experience,* Harper Perennial, London, 1990.

17 Christopher Toll, "The Purpose of Islamic Studies," p. 22.

18 K. Beyer, "Das syrische Perlenlied," *Zeitschrift der Deutschen Morgenländischen Gesellschaft,* 140, 1990:234-59, p. 250.

That we are engaged in a discourse with people of the past can hardly be said generally. When I study[19] the development of the meaning of a Semitic root, or from the starting point that words for "people," e.g., the Hebrew word *goy,* often tend to mean "foreigners," "the others," I also interpret the Aramaic word *nâsh* as "the others" and the expression *bar nâsh,* "Son of Man," as Jesus called himself, as "the foreigner" who has nowhere to put his head, or "another," as in Swedish and Danish a modest expression for "I," I am hardly engaged in a discourse with the wise men of the past. The discourse is rather with past and present colleagues who in the expression "Son of Man" wanted to see an eschatological title alluding to Daniel 7:13, where there is, however, no "son of man" but someone looking like a human; or who saw the expression as dissimulated from *bannas* meaning "vassal" and then "landowner," "master," "man"; or in the Aramaic *bar* did not see the Aramaic word for "son" but the preposition "outside" – "the one outside humanity."

The artist, with whom I compare the scholar, also has another discourse, with the buyer, the patron. A few generations ago, almost all art was created in the cooperation of artist and patron. The patron who wanted to have the work of the artist in his home and who paid for it made demands upon the artist, challenging the artist to do his utmost. But who is the patron of the scholar, for whom do we work, who is challenging us, forcing us to do our best? It is seldom those who pay us, except in certain cases where members of the medical or technological profession are asked to create something new.

Another question, which I can only hint at, is, what price are we willing to pay for our creative work? That it demands efforts I have already mentioned – all creative work does. It could also demand poverty or at least debts and an uncertain income, also for one's family. It can even expose oneself and one's family to persecution. When will the price be too high?

I look in this discussion upon scholarship as an art. I do not see it as a way of life, not even one way of many. To be a scholar is accidental – scholarship is only one among many kinds of artistic expression from which one can choose. It is also possible to create something new and original and fascinating and delightful in other fields, e.g., in commerce, and in bygone times one talked about the art of politics and the art of war.

I do not see truth as a goal or scholarship as a means to diminish suffering or to enhance freedom – it could do that too, but that is secondary. I do not apply a moral view to scholarship, only to its methods, that you do not fake your data upon which you build your theory. But the theory itself can be judged only from an aesthetic point of view.

For scholarly results – my own and those of others – I use the same criteria as for any work of art: a painting, a musical work, a philosophical idea, a building. Does it delight, stimulate, enthuse? Then the artist has succeeded. What produces this delight is the originality, the simplicity, the harmony, but also the order, the method, the clarity, and, further, that it suits my conception of things, increases my understanding and enthusiasm and calls forth my inherent joy, my *joie de vivre.* And when I enjoyed the work of others, it is because I wanted to do it myself, if I had the idea, if I had found the right expression, if it had been in my power. I think

---

19 Christopher Toll, "Zur Bedeutung des aramäischen Ausdruckes *bar nâs," Orientalia Suecana* 33-35, 1984-86 (*Festschrift* F. Rundgren), pp.421-8.

that what Somerset Maugham said about a work of art applies also to a scholarly work: "The only meaning a picture has is the meaning it has for you."[20]

When all scholarly ideas and theories, as all other works of art, are added together to make up the sum of our intellectual culture, they have all somehow contributed to a higher truth, as in the words of M.D. Hooker: "... there is sometimes merit in very diverse views; each may convey part of the truth, distorted when taken on its own, but playing its own part in the total pattern."[21]

To sum up, I look upon scholarship as discovering truth in facts that have until then been unknown, and inventing it in theories which did not exist before – not eternal truths, not functional temporary truths, but what I like to call aesthetic truths that are different for different epochs and different authors – delighting author and beholder alike, and together making up our culture, the aim of which is to increase the joy in the world.

---

20 Somerset Maugham, *The Summing Up,* 1938.

21 M.D. Hooker, "Is the Son of Man Problem Really Insoluble?" *Text and Iinterpretation (Festschrift* M. Black), Cambridge: Cambridge University Press, 1979, pp. 155-68.

Biographical notes

Ahnlund, Knut (b. 1923). Professor of history of literature, author, literary critic, and member of the Swedish Academy (1983).

Ahnlund, Nils (1889–1957). Professor of history at Stockholm University (1927-55), member of the Swedish Academy (1941), father of Knut Ahnlund.

Alin, Oscar (1846-1900). Professor of political science at Uppsala University (1882-89). Influential conservative politician and member of parliament (First Chamber, 1889). Opposed to the dissolution of the union with Norway. Rector of Uppsala University in 1899, one year before his death.

Anckarsvärd, Per Gustaf August Cosswa (1865–1953). Diplomat, envoy in Constantinople (1906-18), Sofia (1914), Warsaw (1920-31).

Andersson, Ivar (1891-1980). Editor-in-chief of different Swedish newspapers, a.o. the Stockholm daily *Svenska Dagbladet* from 1940.

Atatürk, Mustafa Kemal (1881-1938). Turkish army officer, leader of the national independence movement (1919-22), reformist, and president of Turkey (1923-38). He maintained that Turkey should remain neutral at the outbreak of the First World War, but was also vigilant against any Russian advances. He was given command of the 19th division of Thrace in 1915 and it is generally accepted that the Turkish success at Gallipoli in 1915 was largely inspired by his courage and clear-sightedness.

Bennedich, Carl (1880–1939). Lieutenant on the general staff at the time of the "courtyard speech" on 6 February 1914, a speech made by the King Gustaf V in front of a crowd of 30,000 demonstrators arising from a constitutional crisis between the king and the liberal government under Prime Minister Karl Staaf. Bennedich was a leading authority of his day on Charles XII as field commander. He was promoted to colonel in 1932.

Björnståhl, Jacob Jonas (1731-79). Swedish Orientalist who studied in Uppsala, where he attended Carl von Linnaeus's lectures. He travelled widely in Europe and the Ottoman Empire (1767-79) and died in Salonika. His books on travel were published posthumously by Carl Chrisoffer Gjörwell (1-6, 1780-1785).

Boëthius, Axel (1889-1969). Archaeologist, professor of classical antiquity at Gothenburg University (1934-55), rector of the same university (1946-51). Director of the Swedish Institute in Rome (1926-35, 1952-53 and 1955-57) and leader of the excavations of Mycenae. Main work: *Roman Architecture from its Classical to its Imperial Phase* (1941). Volunteer officer in Finland, 1918.

Boëthius, Bertil (1885-1974). Professor of economy and forestry, archivist, director of Stockholm City Archives (1930-44), director-general of the National Archives (1944-50). Main editor of *Swedish Biographical Encyclopedia* (1918-31). His historical interests were concentrated on Swedish foreign policy, especially during the 17th century.

Boström, Christopher Jacob (1797-1866). Influential conservative philosopher of the idealist school. Professor of moral philosophy at Uppsala University (1842-63).

Böök, Fredrik (1883-1961). Literary historian, literary critic, and author. For a short period, professor of the history of literature at Lund University (1920-24). Member of the Swedish Academy (1922). One of the most versatile, powerful, and controversial literary critics of all epochs in Sweden, whose editions of great Swedish poets and monographs on Erik Johan Stagnelius (1793-1823), Esaias Tegnér (1843-1928), Victoria Benedictsson (1850-88), etc. are still read and quoted. As a Germanophile, he had some sympathy for the Nazis, but never supported their anti-Semitism, which he condemned.

Brandes, Georg (1842-1927). Influential Nietzsche-influenced Danish literary historian, lecturer, and critic of Jewish origin. Ph.D. in 1870. Travelled extensively in Europe, where he became personally acquainted with Hippolyte Taine, Ernest Renan, and John Stuart Mill.

Branting, Hjalmar (1860–1925). Social democratic leader, prime minister in the first Social Democratic government in 1920 and in several later governments during the 1920s. One of Sweden's most important political figures of the 20th century. Branting strongly promoted Sweden's entry into the League of Nations, in which he supported the interests of small countries. Awarded a shared Nobel Peace Prize in 1921.

Chamberlain, Houston Stuart (1855-1927). British-born political philosopher whose theories of the racial superiority of the Aryan race in European culture influenced the development of National Socialism. His anti-Semitism was further developed and utilised by other thinkers.

Ebert, Friedrich (1871-1925). German social democratic statesman and the first president (1919-25) of the German Republic.

Elvander, Nils (f. 1928). Political scientist and professor of political science at Uppsala University (1979). Among his greater works are *Harald Hjärne och konservatismen* (1961) and *Intresseorganisationerna i dagens Sverige* (1966).

Eneman, Michael (1776-1814). Clergyman and Orientalist in Uppsala. Eager to travel to the Orient, he called on Charles XII at Bender to get permission and support for that purpose. H his requests were agreed to on the condition that he serve two years as clergyman at the Swedish legation in Constantinople. After further travels to Smyrna, Alexandria, Sinai, and many other places, he was appointed professor of Oriental languages at Uppsala University. Shortly after his arrival in Uppsala, he died of pulmonary tuberculosis. His comprehensive memoranda in Latin were translated into Swedish and published in 1889 by K.U. Nylander.

Engberg, Arthur (1888-1944). Journalist, active public debater and member of the Social Democratic Party. Member of parliament (Second Chamber 1918-41, First Chamber 1941-44) and minister of education (1932-39). As a student of philosophy in Uppsala, he was active in the social democratic student association, Laboremus.

Engelbrektsson, Engelbrekt (d.1436). a mine owner of the petty nobility who led a popular rebellion in 1434 against King Erich of Pomerania, who strove to weld the Scandinavian kingdoms into a centralised absolute monarchy.

Enver Pasha (1881-1922). Leading member of the Committee of Union and Progress, and participant in the 1908 revolution in Turkey. General in the Ottoman army and war minister after 1913. Sought Ottoman participation in the First World War. At the end of the war, tried to organise a worldwide Muslim revolutionary movement with Soviet support. Later became a convinced pan-Turkist. Died in a battle against the Red Army.

Geijer, Erik Gustaf (1783-1847). Liberal historian, philosopher, author, composer, and professor of history at Uppsala University from 1817. Geijer was one of the most important public figures in 19th century Swedish intellectual history.

Hageby, Erik August Lind af (1874-1949). Colonel and diplomat. Envoy at the Swedish legation in Constantinople, 1918-20.

Hanner, Knut (1888–1973). Swedish physician at the Haile Selassie Hospital, as well as Swedish consul in Addis Ababa, 1929-36. The emperor's representative for the recruitment of Johannes Kolmodin.

Haralds, Hjalmar (1876-1931). Literary figure active in Gothenburg.

Hedin, Sven (1865-1952). World-famous explorer, with three great expeditions to Central Asia (1893-97, 1899-1902, 1905-09) behind him, including the discovery of trans-Himalaya [??] and the sources of the Indus and Brahmaputra. Hedin was a deeply conservative and fervent anti-democrat, who strove for greater royal power and had good contacts with King Gustaf V and Queen Victoria. Member of the Swedish Academy (1913).

Heidenstam, Verner von (1859-1940). Conservative literary personality, poet, and novelist, member of the Swedish Academy (1912), Noble Prize winner (1916). Controversy with August Strindberg ("Strindbergsfejden"), 1910.

Herlitz, Nils (1888-1978). Historian, disciple of Harald Hjärne, whose magnum opus *Carl XII: the Upheaval in Europe 1697-1703* (1902) he followed up, covering the period 1703-06. Herlitz was professor of political science (1927-35) and law (1927-55) at Stockholm University, and conservative member of parliament (First Chamber 1933-55).

Hindenburg, Paul von (1847-1934). German Field Marshal, considered his country's greatest hero of the First World War.

Hjärne, Erland (1887-1969). Professor of history at Uppsala University (1930-52). Son of Harald Hjärne, whose collected works he edited.

Hjärne, Harald (1848–1922). Professor of history at Uppsala University (1885-1913). Politically active, first as a liberal, but from the turn of the century as a conservative. Member of parliament (Second Chamber 1902-08, First Chamber 1912-18). Member of the Swedish Academy (1903). Admired by the conservative student association, Heimdal, even though he did not share all its opinions.

Inönü, Ismet Pasha (1884-1973). Member of the Committee for Union and Progress. Served as chief of staff under Mustafa Kemal Pasha on the eastern front in 1916. Worked for the nationalist movement. Appointed commander of the western front in 1921. Led the Turkish delegation at the peace negotiations in Lausanne. Prime minister in 1923-24, 1925-27. President after Atatürk died in 1938 (1938-50). Prominent politician in the postwar period and leader of the Republican People's Party until 1972.

Iwarson, J. (1887-1947). Pastor for the Swedish Evangelical Mission in Eritrea 1897-1909, 1910-20, 1923-35. Author of *På färdevägar i Ostafrika* (Travelling in East Africa, Stockholm: 1935), in which he describes his journeys with Adolf and Johannes Kolmodin in Ethiopia and Eritrea in 1908-10.

Karabekir, Kazim Pasha (1882-1948). Purely military career. Joined the Committee of Union and Progress in 1907. Appointed commander of the Ninth Army in eastern Anatolia in March 1919. His troops formed the backbone of the national independence movement. Defeated the Armenians in 1920. Critical of Mustafa Kemal's monopolisation of power. Founded the opposition Progressive Republican Party in 1924. Arrested and tried in connection with the Izmir conspiracy in 1926, but freed. Reentered the National Assembly only after Atatürk's death in 1938.

Key, Ellen (1849-1926). Liberal feminist, educationist, lecturer, and author.

Kjellberg, Lennart (1857-1936). Archaeologist, especially known for excavations in Larisa, western Anatolia. Professor at Uppsala University, 1918-22.

Kjellén, Rudolf (1864-1922). Political scientist and professor at Gothenburg University (1901-16), later at Uppsala. Ultraconservative nationalist. Member of parliament (Second Chamber 1905–08, First Chamber 1911-17). Led the young rightists in Gothenburg, taught the doctrine of states as geographical organisms ("geopolitik") and became one of the forerunners of the Nazi ideology.

Kolmodin, Adolf (1855-1928). Father of Johannes Kolmodin, theologian, ordained in 1880. Director of the SEM theological institute in Johannelund (1893-1903). Professor of exegetics at Uppsala University (1909-20). Principal of Fjellstedt School (for prospective clergymen) 1920-28. Editor of *Svensk Missionstidning* (1913-28). Married to Nelly von Post in 1882. The couple had seven sons – Johannes being the oldest – and one daughter.

Lidforss, Bengt (1868-1923). Professor of botany in Uppsala in 1910, later in Lund; polemical journalist, influential socialist; defended anti-church, anti-religious, and anti-Semitic ideas.

Lidman, Sven (1882-1960). Poet, novelist, political activist, and editor of the nationalistic *Svensk Lösen*, 1916-19. Underwent a religious conversion in 1917 and joined the Pentecostal movement in 1921, in which he worked as a newspaper editor and leading preacher. In 1948, expelled from the movement after a conflict with its leadership. Wrote several autobiographical books during the 1950s.

Liebknecht, Karl (1871-1919). German communist of the Spartacist movement.

Lindman, Arvid (1862-1936). Naval officer (1882-92), rear-admiral (1907), industrial leader, and rightist politician, usually called "the admiral." Prime minister (1906-11, 1928-30) and foreign minister (1917). Known as a skilful and inspiring party leader; a pragmatic but not unscrupulous mediator. Stood up for the principles of democracy and strongly rejected Nazism and fascism.

Littmann, Enno (1875-1958). Appointed professor of Semitic languages in Strasbourg (1906), Göttingen (1914), Bonn (1916), and Tübingen (1921-51).

Lorents, Yngve (1887-1978). Editor of the Swedish encyclopaedia, *Nordisk Familjebok*.

Ludendorff, Erich (1865-1937). German officer, promoted to general (1916), important strategist and military leader during the First World War.

Lönnrot, Elias (1802-84). Researcher of Finnish folk poetry and language. District medical officer (1833-53), professor of Finnish language and literature at Helsinki University (1853-63). Editor of the Finnish national epic *Kalevala,* based on collections of folk poems, reproduced as lyrical narratives.

Max, Prince of Baden (1867-1929). Seen as regent of the German empire. Announced the abdication of the Kaiser on 9 November 1918, when the German republic was declared, formed its first cabinet, and handed over power to the socialists.

Medhen, Twoldo (1866-1930). Studied at Johannelund (1883-87). Ordained minister by Adolf Kolmodin. Later became one of the leaders of the Eritrean church and took part in the translation of the New Testament both into Tigré and Tigrinya.

Mohn, Paul (1898-1959). Swedish diplomat and mediator in the Middle East, Afghanistan, Iran, Turkistan. His language skills and talent for negotiation led to international work during the Second World War and the postwar era. The Constantinople period (1917-18) is treated in his memoirs *Krumelur i tidens marginal* (Curlicue in the Margin of Time, Stockholm: 1961).

Molin, Adrian (1880-1942). Conservative politician, journalist, and founder of the magazines *Det nya Sverige* and *Hem i Sverige*. Active in the movement against emigration and founder of the "own-your-own-home association." Showed some Nazi leanings during the 1930s.

Nansen, Fridtjof (1861-1930). Norwegian explorer, oceanographer, and diplomat. Took part in a polar expedition, 1893-96. Active in the exchange of prisoners of war 1920-22. Awarded the Nobel Peace Prize in 1922.

Nordström, Ludvig (1882-1942). Author and reformer from Norrland (northern parts of Sweden), who worked for, among other things, a cleaner Sweden. Published his impressions of a shorter journey to Turkey in *Världs-Sverge* (Stockholm: 1928).

Norström, Vitalis (1856-1916): Nietzsche- and Bergson-influenced philosopher, professor at Gothenburg University (1893), member of the Swedish Academy (1907). Active in the cultural/public debate.

Nyberg, Henrik Samuel (1889-1974). Professor of Semitic languages with competence in Iranian languages at Uppsala University (1931-56). Member of the Swedish Academy (1948).

Palme, Olof (1884–1918). Historian in Uppsala, leading representative of the conservative Uppsala student association, Heimdal. Activist, who paid the ultimate price in the battle for Finland's liberation and fell at the head of the Swedish Brigade outside Tammerfors in April 1918. Uncle of the Swedish Prime Minister Olof Palme (1927-86).

Reutersköld, Carl Axel (1870-1944). Conservative jurist, professor of administrative law. Personal friend of his teacher Oscar Alin. One of the thirteen founders of the student association Heimdal in 1891. Started out as conservative, but later joined Bondepartiet (The Farmers' Party). Member of parliament for that party in 1919 (First Chamber). Defended the 1809 constitution and supported Rudolf Kjellén in his opposition to the dissolution of the union with Norway in 1905.

Rosenius, Carl Olof (1816-1868). Prominent leader within the Swedish revivalist movement and one of the most important founders of Evangeliska Fosterlandsstiftelsen (The Swedish Evangelical Mission, SEM). Editor of *Pietisten* (1842-68).

Rückert, Friedrich (1788-1866). German poet and translator of Oriental lyrics.

Scheidemann, Philip (1865-1939). Prominent majority socialist leader, state secretary in Max von Baden's cabinet in October 1918, member of Friedrich Ebert's provisional government, and the first chancellor of the Weimar Republic in 1919.

Söderblom, Nathan (1866-1931). Professor of theology (1901-14), ecumenical pioneer in Sweden and world-wide. Sweden's archbishop (1914–31). Member of the Swedish Academy (1921). Awarded the Nobel Peace Prize in 1930

Staaf, Karl (1860-1915). Liberal politician, prime minister (1905-06 and 1911-14), member of parliament (Second Chamber 1896-1915). Worked for universal suffrage and parliamentarianism. King Gustaf V's "courtyard speech" in February 1914 led to his government's resignation. Single-minded and uncompromising, he contributed to the radicalisation of politics and democratisation of society.

Strindberg, August (1849-1912). One of Sweden's most renowned and prolific authors and social critics. Uncompleted academic studies in Uppsala, worked for some time as a freelance journalist, librarian at the Royal Library in Stockholm in 1847. Well-known dramas *Fadern* (1887), *Fröken Julie* (1888), *Ett drömspel* (1902).

Uggla, Arvid (1883-1964). Chief librarian of Uppsala University Library. Specialist on the works and times of the botanist, Carl von Linnaeus.

Ullin, Hilda (1863-1952). Secretary of the Swedish Embassy in Istanbul and photographer, working for the famous photographer, G. Berggren.

Wallenberg, Gustaf Oscar (1863-1937). Sweden's first ambassador to Tokyo and Peking (1906-18). Ambassador to Constantinople (1920-30). Stayed in Turkey after retirement and died during a temporary visit to Sweden.

Venizelos, Eleutherios (1864-1936). Greek statesman (liberal). Prime minister several times between 1910-33. Repeated conflicts with Constantine I and George II. Venizelos's policies during the Balkan Wars and the First World War contributed to the territorial expansion of his country, but the war against Turkey 1919-23 ended in failure.

Wirsén, Einar af (1875-1945). Officer, serving during the Balkan Wars of 1912-13. Military attaché at the Swedish legation in Constantinople (1915-20). Chairman of the League of Nations' commission for resolving the Mosul question (1924-25). Swedish ambassador in Berlin (1925) and Rome (1937-40).

Wilson, Woodrow (1856-1924). President (Democrat) of the United States (1913-21). Rector at Princeton University (1902-10). Proclaimed U.S. neutrality in the First World War, but declared war on Germany in 1916. In January 1918, he proclaimed the "Fourteen Points," which he regarded as an essential basis for a just and lasting peace. Wilson played a leading part at the Peace Conference in Paris, 1918.

Vougt, Allan (1895-1953). Publisher and politician (social democrat). Chief editor of the social-democratic daily *Arbetet* (1924-44). Member of parliament (Second Chamber 1929-48, First Chamber 1950-53). Served as minister of defence and provincial governor after the end of the Second World War.

Wrangel, Pjotr (1878-1928). Russian officer, baron. Took part in the Russo-Japanese war 1904-05. Led a cavalry unit during the First World War. After the 1917 revolution he joined Denikin's White army in Crimea, and succeeded Denikin in April 1920. After being defeated by the Red army in November the same year, he escaped abroad, continuing his struggle against the Bolsheviks. Died in exile in Brussels.

Zetterstéen, Karl Villhelm (1866-1953). Philologist, professor of Oriental languages at Lund University (1895-1904), and Semitic languages at Uppsala University (1904-31). Eminent teacher. Co-founder of *Le Monde Oriental* (1909) and its chief editor 1922-28. Well-known for his translation of the Koran (1917).

Sources: *Nationalencyklopedin* (Höganäs: 1989); *Svenskt Biografiskt Lexikon* (Stockholm: 1997); Erik J. Zürcher: *Turkey. A Modern History*, (London: I.B. Tauris, 1993).